METAL TOYS

An All-Color Guide to the Art of Collecting International Playthings

METAL TOYS

An All-Color Guide to the Art of Collecting International Playthings

by Gordon Gardiner and Alistair Morris

a Salamander book
Published by Salamander Books Limited
LONDON

A Salamander Book · Acknowledgements

Published by
Salamander Books
129-137 York Way
London N7 9LG
United Kingdom

© Salamander Books Ltd., 1984

Distributed by Random House Value Publishing, Inc.
40 Engelhard Avenue
Avenel, New Jersey 07001

A CIP catalog record for this book is available from
the Library of Congress.

ISBN 0 517 14124 8

In the preparation of this book we received the most
generous assistance and advice from toy collectors and
museum directors and staff. Without the help of the
individuals and organizations listed below, this record of
the metal toys of the 19th and 20th centuries could not
have been assembled.

Special thanks both for making available toys from
their collections and giving us facilities for photography
are due to:
Allen Levy, The London Toy & Model Museum,
October House, 23 Craven Hill, London W.2.;
Joe Lyndhurst, Warnham War Museum, West Sussex;
Shaun Magee Pedal Car Collection,
Bishop's Waltham, Hampshire;
Ron McCrindell, London.

Editor: Richard O'Neill   **Designer:** Barry Savage
Photography:
Terry Dilliway, © Salamander Books Ltd.
Filmset: Modern Text Typesetting Ltd.
Color reproduction:
Tempus Litho Ltd., Rodney Howe Ltd.
Printed by: Henri Proost et Cie, Belgium

Our thanks for the loan of toys for photography are
given also to:
Geoffrey Baker,
Liss, Hampshire
Dendy B. Easton/Dendy P. Easton,
Sussex
Louise Gardiner/Gavin Gardiner,
Bognor Regis, Sussex
David Griffiths/Roydon Griffiths,
Sussex
Michael Heydon,
Horsham, Sussex
Richard Lonsdale,
Barnham, Sussex
Peter Moore,
Motor Book Postal Auctions, West Chiltington, Sussex
Vera Oliver/Tony Oliver,
Eaton Wick, Berkshire
Danny O'Neill,
Christ's Hospital, Sussex
Peter Pawson,
Findon, Sussex

David Pressland,
Dulwich, London
Andrew Rose,
Liss, Hampshire
Alan Wickham,
"Trains", Bognor Regis, Sussex
Clive Willoughby,
Pagham, Sussex

For further help in the preparation of this book,
we thank also:

Maureen Cartwright
Bob Daws
Hazel Gardiner
Bernard Fitzsimons
Richard Hunt
Jessica Johnson
Yvonne Lyndhurst
Justine Michaels
James Opie

Contents

Foreword

I began to collect tinplate toys about thirty years ago, and the first items I acquired were Gauge "0" railroad models. I had loved toy trains since I was a boy, in the 1920s, when I was the proud possessor of a simple Hornby 0-4-0 locomotive and tender and two four-wheeled coaches, together with the smallest of the steam-powered locomotives made by the British firm of Bowman. After the War, I began to collect railroad items, beginning, as I have said, with Gauge "0" models. But this enthusiasm just for Gauge "0" lasted only until I saw my first Gauge "1" item: a tinplate coach displayed in the window of what was then the shop of the famous Bassett-Lowke company, at 112, High Holborn, London. I was very much taken by the sheer size of this gorgeously-lithographed coach, as compared to Gauge "0", and so I bought my first Gauge "1" model, a composite bogie coach in L.S.W.R. (London and South Western Railway) livery, made by Carette of Nuremburg for Bassett-Lowke, at a "sale price" of £2 10s. 0d (£2.50, $3.55). It would cost rather more than that today!

It was some years before I managed to acquire the matching full-compartment (five passenger compartments and two lavatories) coach which set the pattern for the Carette/Bassett-Lowke series, later maintained by Bing/Bassett-Lowke. However, from the purchase of the first coach I was firmly hooked on Gauge "1" (although still very interested in Gauge "0") and, by combing junk shops, street markets, and jumble sales, and by monitoring neighborhood newspapers and specialist magazines, I gradually built up a comprehensive collection of the items listed in Bassett-Lowke's catalogs. This was, of course, before the days of the "swap-meets" that now form such an important part of the collector's world.

I suppose that it was my admiration for the fine railroad models produced by the great German triumvirate—Carette, Bing, and Marklin—that led me on to begin acquiring the fine tinplate automobiles bearing their trademarks, along with those of other famous makers like Distler, Fischer, Günthermann, and Lehmann of Germany, and CIJ, Jep, and Citroën of France. And this, in turn, led on to my greatest pleasure: the collecting of tinplate boats.

Tinplate boats (a selection from my collection is shown on *pages 126-133*) are to my mind the most attractive of all metal toys. They are also, unfortunately for the would-be collector, about the rarest. The larger and finer examples appear to have been made in very small numbers: the splendid battleship HMS *Terrible* (shown at *Inset, pages 124-125*), the "number one" item in my collection, and now on loan to the London Toy & Model Museum, bears beneath its superstructure the maker's number "7", probably indicating that this model by Marklin was limited to a small, individually-numbered, run. Even when production was not so limited, boats seem to have sold in much smaller numbers than locomotives or automobiles, both because they were comparatively expensive and because they were "summer", rather than all-the-year-round, toys.

There is, however, a reverse side to this picture. In the case of both boats and railroad items, many fine models have survived in good condition simply because they were, in the first place, very expensive toys, bought for the children of the well-to-do and generally played with under the supervision of a governess or "nanny". Certainly, it seems that the more expensive a toy originally was, the more care was taken of it. This is well illustrated in the case of railroad models: items in Gauge "0", which were manufactured in larger quantities and sold more cheaply, are now rarer than similar items in Gauge "1", which were more expensive and were made in smaller numbers.

Discussion of rarity and comparative prices leads us inevitably to consideration of the prices that the present-day collector must be prepared to pay for his toys. I was lucky in that I began to collect, in the case of boats at any rate, at a time when there was no great interest in that category, so that I was able to acquire specimens that I certainly could not afford today, when fine boats by makers like Marklin may fetch

five-figure prices at auction in the UK and USA. In the earlier post-War years, collectors' interest centered mainly on railroad items, and even in that category prices remained reasonable until around the mid-1960s.

In 1966, however, the famous international auction house of Christie's began to hold specialized toy sales and this example was soon followed by other major auction houses. Interest in toys of all kinds grew rapidly; more and more collectors began to seek fine toys; and the "price explosion" was detonated. The question of value is a vexed one. I know that there are some who collect for value or investment, speculatively or as a possible hedge against inflation—but I would not say that they are true collectors. Of course, it's nice to know that your collection is an appreciating asset, and there is nothing to be said against acquiring items in the hope that they may be sold at a profit in order to finance the purchase of some long-desired toy for your collection. But my advice to all collectors is: by all means buy the best examples you can afford, build the most attractive and valuable collection you can, but don't collect simply for value or you will never gain true pleasure from your collection.

For a new collector at the present time, however, "the best examples you can afford" may fall into a rather limited category so far as good-quality tinplate toys are concerned. (You will find in this book plenty of useful advice on collecting toys of other kinds, such as diecast vehicles or hollow-cast soldiers, but I am limiting my remarks to my own speciality.) Today, the presence of a Bing, Carette, or especially a Marklin trademark on a tinplate toy is a sure guarantee of a very high price—and as the prices of toys by the most famous makers rise, collectors increasingly turn to the work of lesser makers, forcing up those prices.

My advice to the new collector who hopes to acquire tinplate toys would be to look for Japanese-made items of the 1950s and 1960s, of which a good selection is shown in this book, notably on *pages 70-75, 82-83,* and *138-139.* Predominantly automotive toys, usually battery- or friction-powered, these are often most attractive, and may still be found at prices the average collector can afford. I only hope that this

suggestion won't lead to another price explosion! In the case of earlier tinplate toys, it is worth noting that it may prove less expensive to buy from a specialist dealer rather than at auctions: at auctions, bidders sometimes get carried away with enthusiasm and prices can soar.

Turning from the practical side of collecting to the philosophical, I suppose that I must make some answer to the inevitable question: "Why do you collect toys?" It must be admitted that one is, in some measure, trying to recapture one's childhood. In my own case, for example, my collection now includes the Hornby "Blue Train" that I longed for when a boy—and a simple Bowman steam locomotive identical with the one I then possessed.

I try never to forget that toys were meant for children—and that toys were meant to be played with. I know that some collectors maintain their toys as static exhibits in glass cases, but I try to keep all my collection in working order. Most of my railroad models are regularly run and my boats are fairly often on the water, sometimes in the regattas held on the boating lakes of London's parks. My larger boats have even been ventured in the sea (in a dead calm, I hasten to add) off the Devon coast. This may sound a bit risky—imagine watching a Marklin battleship like HMS *Terrible* disappearing majestically over the horizon—but the greater danger is from the spirit-fired boilers of steam-powered locomotives and boats: one really needs asbestos fingers, and I have more than once severely singed my mustache!

In fact, the shortest, simplest, and only answer to the question "Why collect?" is that I collect toys because I love them. I hope that this is the answer that would be given by most of my fellow-collectors, all over the world—and I hope that this book will help to show you why we collect toys, and why we love them.

Ron McCrindell

Ron McCrindell, London, England

Introduction

Gordon Gardiner and Alistair Morris

It is, without doubt, impossible to produce a book on any subject that will please all of its readers all of the time. However, in the case of this book we feel that we have one great advantage over most authors. For our subject is "Toys", and, however diverse the characters of humankind may be in their years of maturity, they all have one thing in common: they once were children. And the one thing that all children, excepting only those in the most unfortunate circumstances, have in common is, they all play with toys.

Most readers of this book will have at least a few memories of a time when a model locomotive, a toy farm, a box of soldiers, even so small an object as a diecast automobile, opened up for them the way to a world of magic and imagination. It would be possible, although is is not within our remit here to do so, to speculate at length on the psychological drives that lie behind the fact that mature men and women may derive great pleasure from the playthings of childhood. We address ourselves here to collectors, and to those who would like to be collectors, of toys, whose pleasure must be presumed to lie in the satisfaction of the mature urge for gathering and classifying "collectibles", judged as such on aesthetic grounds, rather than in attempting to recapture the days of their own childhoods; but we note also that, beyond the many thousands of toy collectors all over the world, there must be an innumerable number of adults who have preserved some childhood favorite as a reminder of happiness past.

HISTORY IN PLAYTHINGS

Such "escapism" (an unfairly maligned motive, we feel) aside, there are many more practical reasons for collecting and studying toys. For the social historian, the toys of a past time throw an illuminating light on the society in which they were produced. Look, for example, at the British-made metal soldiers on *pages 156-173*. The firm of Britains Ltd, London, began to produce these hollow-cast figures in the 1890s, the heyday of the British Empire, and their immense popularity worldwide reflects an attitude to the military virtues that is now far less widespread. Note particularly the earlier types of boxes in which these figures were packed for sale *(pages 174-175)*: they bear not only the names, and sometimes the badges, of famous British regiments, but also their battle honors.

Even for the non-collector, the appeal of toys extends beyond what they represent to what they are in themselves. The ingenious mechanisms of many of the "novelty" toys shown on *pages 18-25*, for example, will fascinate the mechanically-minded. The styles of packaging and decoration of toys—from the *art nouveau* motifs on the boxes of soldiers shown on *pages 174-175*, through the *art deco* printed designs on many tin toys of the 1930s, to the "realistic" color finishes of modern, Japanese-made, toy automobiles *(pages 70-75* and *82-83)*—provide a history in miniature of popular taste in design during the period covered by this book.

SCOPE OF THE BOOK

This book is not, however, a history of toys. It is aimed at the collector, and in particular at the novice or would-be collector, and is intended to present an overall survey of the kind of material that may come his or her way. The period covered is roughly that of the last 120 years: an age of increasing production, and then of mass-production, leading to a number and variety of toys —and their consequent availability to the modern collector—that did not previously exist. In the period covered by this book, markets expanded greatly,

Above: *These two toys have been selected to give an indication of scale on certain spreads. The early hollow-cast infantryman by Britains is to the standard 2·125in (54mm) scale, and measures 56mm to the top of his helmet spike. The Jaguar XK120, Dinky Toy No 157, was introduced in 1954 and withdrawn from the range in 1962; later examples were finished in a two-tone paint scheme. The auto is 3·82in (97mm) long, and both toys are shown here actual size.*

Left: *October 1942, and 20 cases of toys, many from abroad, are sorted ready for despatch to children in British hospitals as gifts from toy manufacturer Mr. Stephen Colman, of Barnsbury, North London.*

and the inventiveness and enterprise of toy makers expanded to match them.

Only *metal* toys are included—but these, of course, constitute in any case by far the largest category of toy and, for obvious reasons, the one that embraces the greatest number of surviving examples. The criteria on which items were selected for inclusion in this book were, basically, their probable availability to the "average" collector in Europe and the United States—although some very rare and valuable examples are shown, particularly among the toy ships *(pages 120-133)*, simply because it was felt that such magnificent specimens of the toymaker's art could not be omitted; and their condition. We have excluded items in very poor condition and we have tried to show all the toys as nearly as possible in their original condition: where restoration has been carried out, or where parts are missing, this has generally been noted in the captions.

PLAY-WEAR

Inevitably, the condition in which toys of the past are found today will be variable (see the detailed notes on the terms used by collectors and dealers to describe condition, *page 13*). The collector should never forget that toys were made for children—and there can be few of us who will not remember some disaster to one of our childhood playthings: a toy forgotten in the garden and left at the mercy of the elements; the metal soldiers who lost heads or arms in an over-enthusiastic "carpet battle"; the over-winding that put out of commission the mechanism of a clockwork automobile or locomotive. Add to these misfortunes the generally robust nature of children's play, and the fact that in many families toys will have been "handed on" from older to younger siblings, even from generation to generation, and it is hardly suprising that many of the items that now come the collector's way are in the state that dealers politely describe as "play-worn"!

Nor is play the only hazard that the metal toy must face: the brightest enameled or lithographed finish will fade with time, unless the toy is most carefully preserved, and rust will invade and even consume tinplate toys stored in damp conditions. "Metal fatigue" is an insidious enemy of diecast toys. It is caused by an unstable alloy (ie, its constituents having different shrinkage and expansion rates) in the toy's composition. If the toy is kept, as many are, in an uncontrolled temperature, the constituents "fight" and will eventually cause disintegration: the first symptoms being a slight expansion of the metal, followed by the development of cracks and/or blisters in the article's finish and fabric.

It is for these reasons that the "classic" metal toys—such as "novelties" like those shown on *pages 18-23*, early railroad items *(pages 30-35)*, the earlier tinplate automobiles *(pages 66-69)*, and many toy boats *(pages 124-133)*—are now in short supply and, if in good condition, expensive.

BEGINNING A COLLECTION

The novice collector must begin by making a number of decisions. First, he must decide which aspect of the world of toys interests him (or her; the use of the male pronoun throughout this book, for brevity only, should not be allowed to obscure the fact that there are very many female collectors). In taking this decision, he will inevitably be led to face a second: what kind of toys can he afford to collect? He must consider the likely availability of the material that interests him, and what opportunities he may have to seek out and purchase specimens. And, of course, he must consider what space he has available for the display and/or storage of his collection as it grows.

There are probably quite a few toy collectors who now regret that they did not, when starting out, face up to these decisions. It is all too easy to rush out in the first flush of enthusiasm and spend too much money on attractive but unrelated items: unrelated, that is, in being so disparate that they will later present insuperable problems in deciding the direction in which the collection is to be developed. Or, in the desire to accumulate material quickly, the new collector may buy items in such poor condition that they will never lend themselves to the attractive visual display that provides a great part of the satisfaction to be gained from a well-ordered collection. Even if the early purchases are of well-related, "quality" items, in fine condition, the collector may find that he has committed himself to a field of specialization in which, because of rarity or expense, new acquisitions are likely to be so rare that the joy of "capturing" a specimen is too infrequent to sustain the initial enthusiasm that led him to it.

This advice, given from experience, may seem a little intimidating. But the would-be collector should not be deterred. For, and again speaking from experience, we can say that the assembly of a well-balanced collection of properly-related items, attractively displayed, and supported by the genuine collector's real understanding of his subject, gives a pleasure that goes far beyond the power of our words to describe.

FINDING A THEME

This book is arranged in such a way as to assist the novice collector in finding a theme, in deciding what kind of toy he will collect. The possible areas of specialization are, however, far greater in number than a mere listing of our section headings would suggest. Within the "Railroad Toys" *(pages 26-61)* category, for example, the collector may decide to specialize in items of one particular "gauge" only; in items by one particular maker; or in items by makers of one particular nationality — and these, in themselves, are areas large enough to permit of further division. In the case of "Automotive Toys" *(pages 62-121),* the collector may choose to collect one category of vehicle—private automobiles, commercial vehicles, racing cars, motorcycles, fire engines, etc—or, perhaps, vehicles representing one famous marque only, such as Ford, Mercedes, or Jaguar. In this context, it is worth noting that although collectors

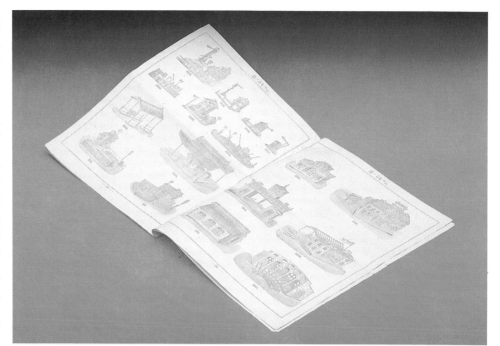

of tinplate vehicles and collectors of diecast vehicles generally form two quite distinct camps, the collector of a single marque may feel it quite acceptable to "cross the line" and to obtain examples made in either form.

It would be possible to continue here at some length with suggestions regarding possible areas of specialization. However, the reader is directed to the shorter introductions to the various sections, where possible areas of specialization within each of the fields discussed are generally noted.

SEEING AND BUYING

The novice collector should take every opportunity of increasing his understanding of the subject, both within and beyond his own area of specialization, by examining toys. As a result of the general interest, in recent years, in the artifacts of the more immediate past, most major museums in Europe and the

USA now have on display some toys of the past century, and in some cities there are excellent museums devoted to playthings alone. In the United Kingdom, there are particularly fine collections at the Bethnal Green Museum of Childhood, London; the London Toy & Model Museum (who most kindly made available a large number of fine specimens for photography for this book); and the Museum of Childhood, Edinburgh, Scotland. Visit such museums whenever possible, remembering that the items on display will be sometimes changed (few museums have the space to display their entire collections at one time), and that special loan exhibitions may well be mounted from time to time.

As interest in toys and toy collecting has increased, so has the number of specialist dealers, few of whom will object to the novice—who may, after all, be tomorrow's "big spender"— browsing among their stock. Antique

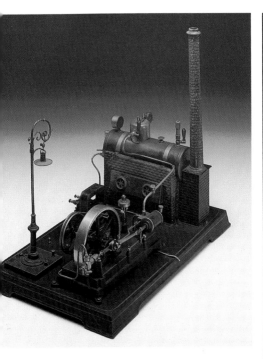

Above: *Good example of a stationary steam engine, produced by Doll in Germany, c1914. The engine drives a generator to power the electric light.*

Above left: *Pages 30 and 31 of a Marklin catalog, showing some of the buildings and other accessories available to match this famous manufacturer's Gauge "II" (54mm, 2·125in) model railroads.*

Left: *Late-pattern box for the CIJ P2 Alfa Romeo (see pages 76-77), which was produced from the mid-1920s to the mid-1930s. The earlier pattern of box had a separate lift-off lid.*

Above right: *Two examples of the many tourist souvenirs produced by Japanese manufacturers since the 1960s: these portray San Francisco cable cars, and were purchased from current stock in 1982.*

Right: *At the old Crystal Palace auto racing track at Crystal Palace, South London, young pedal car drivers line up for the Royal Automobile Club's Junior Grand Prix held in June 1965.*

shops, junk shops, flea markets, and garage sales are, of course, a hunting ground for collectors of all persuasions, but the toy collector may do best at the "auto-jumbles" now regularly organized by automobile enthusiasts. Automotive toys, from diecast models to "kiddie cars", often turn up at these meetings, since many "car buffs", although not toy collectors, often collect models of their favorite marques, and non-automotive toys may also be found.

Note, however, that at auto-jumbles, "boot sales", and similar venues where amateur dealers predominate, there is a chance that, although bargains may be found, the prices asked may be higher than those that would be encountered with a professional dealer. Inexperienced vendors, perhaps from imperfect understanding of "price guides", as mentioned below, are sometimes inclined to believe that all "old" toys are not only collectable but also valuable.

SWAP-MEETS AND AUCTIONS

More expert judgment of the true worth of toys is likely to be encountered at "swap-meets", a fairly recent development in the collectors' world and one which increasingly features among the activities of collectors in Europe and, especially, in the USA. As the name suggests, swap-meets are gatherings at which collectors may sell or exchange toys, and the novice can learn a great deal simply by attending such a meeting, whether or not he intends doing business. Membership of a collectors' society, whether on a local or an international level, or a subscription to one of the many journals that now cater for collectors in all fields will usually ensure knowledge of the venues of swap-meets that may be of interest.

The more experienced collector will probably sooner or later think of buying or selling at auction. The major inter-

national auction houses, such as Sotheby's, Christies, and Phillips, now regularly mount special toy sales, and the collector should not fear that these famous names always indicate high prices. Remember also that auction houses are always ready to give advice on their buying and selling procedures.

The collector who intends to buy at auction should be sure to attend the "view": the time appointed before the sale when the forthcoming lots may be examined. Even if he does not intend to buy, the view may give him the opportunity to see and handle rare items. Generally speaking, items are bought at auction "as seen", but also "as cataloged"; if an item purchased proves to be not as described in the catalog, a refund may be obtained.

Remember, too, that many auction houses now levy a "buyer's premium" of some 10 per cent — to which, in the UK, Value Added Tax (VAT) must be added.

Rare or unusual toys are probably better sold at auction than elsewhere, since with the more speculative items this may be the only way of establishing their true value on the open market. Most major auction houses will accept for sale "lots" (ie, single toys or collections) with a minimum value of around £50.00 (around $75.00). A reserve price (ie, a price below which the lot shall not be sold) is agreed between the vendor and the auctioneer, and the lot is cataloged and put up for sale. The reserve price must be realistic, for if the lot does not reach its reserve, a "not sold commission" may be payable by the vendor. Note, also, that a successful sale will entail payment to the auction house by the vendor of a commission of around 10-15 per cent. (Conditions as described in the above paragraphs will, of course, vary somewhat between auction houses.)

VALUE OF TOYS

What is a toy worth? The answer is the product of an equation involving four major factors. These are, not necessarily in order of importance: condition; rarity; desirability; availability. Every collector must work out the equation in terms of his own particular speciality; only a very broad guide to values can be given here.

At the top end of the market come the "classic" tinplate toys, which may sell at auction for many thousands of pounds. For example, a tinplate battleship by Marklin, Germany, dating from the early years of this century and not unlike the example shown at *Inset, pages 124-125,* was sold by Sotheby's, New York, for $21,000 (£14,800) in 1980; a fine tinplate automobile by Carette, Germany, dating from c1910,

sold for £6,000 ($8,500) at a sale held by Sotheby's, London, in 1983. At the lower end of the market, diecast cars made in the 1950s by Dinky Toys, Great Britain, although now highly collectable, may still be bought for around £5 ($7) or less, while single toy soldiers may be bought for £1-£2 ($1.40-$2.80). Soldiers in sets (especially boxed sets; for remember always that the presence of the original packaging may increase the value of a toy by 50 per cent, or by very much more in some cases) are, of course, expensive—but the true collector, not concerned with investment potential, may build up an attractive collection of single soldiers quite cheaply.

Although "investment" is a word avoided by most true collectors, it would be foolish to deny that most of us derive pleasure from the thought that we have acquired an item that will maintain or increase its value and that may be turned into cash—perhaps to allow for the purchase of an even more desirable item—should the need arise. Generally speaking, most popular collectors' items have increased in value, some spectacularly, in recent years; even during the recent recession, toy prices held up very well.

It is partly true to say that a toy's value is no more and no less than the price that the collector who desires it is prepared to pay. However, many

As a general rule, toys should not be cleaned (and see below under "Restoration"). Dusting with a soft cloth should be all that is necessary. However, die-cast items, and the exterior surfaces of tinplate toys, may if absolutely necessary be gently washed with mild soap and warm water, again using a soft cloth. Avoid the use of abrasives—and remember that the toy must be very carefully dried afterwards.

CONDITION

Although, as we have said, the collector should always endeavor to obtain toys in the best possible condition, it is inevitable that there will be occasions when a much-desired specimen is only available in "play-worn" condition. As a guide to potential buyers, the toys offered for sale by auction houses and reputable dealers may be graded in terms similar to those that follow.

Mint:

As new, in its original box (if a boxed item) and with the box itself in good condition. If the box or packaging is not in fine original condition, the description "Factory Fresh" is sometimes applied, rather than "Mint".

Very Good:

The toy shows slight wear, possibly with some damage or fading of its finish, but with all its parts complete and undamaged. It may or may not be in the original box or packaging.

Good:

A sound example of the toy, but with noticeable wear from handling and use and without box or packaging.

Play-Worn:

As the term implies, a toy which has seen considerable use: it may have damaged or missing parts and may even have been repainted. Unless it is a rare or much-desired specimen, the collector will do well to consider carefully the price asked before deciding to buy a toy in this condition, and should ask himself whether it will be possible for him to re-sell it, having acquired a better example, at a later date.

RESTORATION

If the collector does decide to acquire a "play-worn" example of a rare toy, he may wish to restore it as nearly as possible to its original condition: indeed, there are collectors whose main interest lies in restoration and who will purchase play-worn toys simply for this purpose. However, the average collector, unless he has great and well-founded confidence in his own ability, is best advised to entrust such work to a professional restorer. The process will not be cheap but, properly carried out, it will enhance

"classic" toys and items by well known makers have a fairly well-established market price. The novice collector will do well to study the prices asked by major dealers, and the records of prices reached at auction, before buying "quality" items. But it is worth noting, also, that certain kinds of toy may at certain times be "unfashionable"—and it is then that bargains may be obtained. The only way to establish these speculative areas is by watching the market.

PRESERVATION AND DISPLAY

Attics, where temperatures may fluctuate considerably, and basements, where dampness is always a possibility, are not to be recommended for the storage or display of a toy collection. Living rooms, where temperatures are usually fairly constant, are much to be preferred—and, in any case, the true collector will wish to have his treasures where they can be readily viewed by himself and others.

By far the best units for storage and display are glazed cabinets: they allow the toys to be in full view, while at the same time protecting them from accidental damage and preventing them from gathering dust. If such cabinets are not available, open shelving is the second-best choice, preferably of the adjustable type in order to allow for the most pleasing arrangements of larger and smaller items.

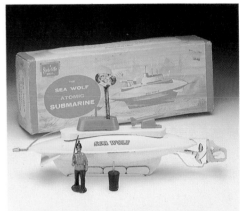

both the appeal and the value of the toy (although not, of course, to the level of the value of a fine unrestored example); amateur restoration will generally add little to the appearance and will detract from the value.

Restoration, whether amateur or professional, should not be lightly embarked upon. If the collector envisages selling the toy at some time in the future, it may be better left unrestored, since some collectors will always prefer an unrestored item, however play-worn, to one not in original condition.

If the collector is offered a toy that has been restored, he should base his judgment on the fidelity of the restoration to the original. As a rough guide, it may be said that in the case of rare toys, restoration—depending always on the amount of restoration and the quality of the work—may reduce value by some 10-20 per cent. In the case of less important toys, restoration may halve the value, or worse.

PRICE GUIDES

With the increasing interest in toy collecting, a large number of reference books—some of them highly specialized and dealing with the output of one toymaker only—have been forthcoming from publishers all over the world. A list of recommended reference works, including many titles suitable for the novice collector, is given on *pages 200-201*.

Special mention must be made of the various "price guides" that the collector may encounter. These can be most useful—we ourselves have produced two works of this kind—but a word of caution is necessary. The information

given in price guides must always be interpreted in terms of current market conditions. Remember, also, that the prices quoted generally refer to toys in, at least, "very good" condition, and that the prices are usually based on auction records. Prices at auction may vary widely in accordance with a number of imponderables: the venue, the presence or absence of major dealers and collectors, the "mood" of the bidding, and so on.

For three important reasons, this book is not a price guide. First, it is intended for an international readership, and prices will vary from country to country in accordance with the availability of material. Second, price guides "date" fairly quickly, and it is hoped that this work of color reference may be of use to collectors for some years to come. Third, this book is intended to be an introduction to the pleasure that can be derived from collecting toys, not as a guide to collecting for investment.

RARITY SCALE

We have, however, attempted throughout this book to give, wherever it is meaningful or possible to do so, an indication of the comparative rarity of the toys illustrated on the photographic spreads. Every item on every spread is individually captioned, and at the end of most captions the reader will find a classification of the toy's rarity in comparison with other toys of its kind; ie, a set of soldiers may be classified as "rare" in comparison with other soldiers: it will not, of course, be of the same degree of rarity (and of value implied thereby) as a tinplate automobile by Carette or a Marklin battleship.

The classification system we have used is as follows:

Rare:

A toy seldom encountered, even by collectors who are in regular contact with international auction houses and specialist dealers. This may include toys produced in limited numbers (because of the expense of production and high selling price; because sales were limited; or because the production life was cut short by war or some other reason), and may also indicate toys with a low survival rate, such as early toy aircraft, which were very fragile, and model submarines, which were most subject to accidental loss.

Scarce:

A toy infrequently encountered, but often to be found at major auctions, through specialist dealers, and sometimes at swap-meets. The fact that a toy

CAPTION STYLE

Where we have quoted, in the captions, the original retail prices of toys, taken from contemporary catalogs, these are expressed in British pre-decimal currency—"Pounds, Shillings, Pence"; as in "£2 7s 6d"—with the equivalents in British decimal currency and in US currency at the approximate rate of exchange prevailing early in 1984 in parentheses; eg, "£2 7s 6d (£2.37½, $3.37)", or "2s 9d (14p, 20c)".

Readers outside the USA should note that in the case of automotive toys, US terms are used throughout. For the guidance of readers unfamiliar with these, we append a brief glossary:

US Usage	Non-US Usage
Fender	Wing
Gasoline	Petrol
Gear Shift	Gear Lever
Hood	Bonnet
License Plate	Number Plate
Monkey Wrench	Spanner
Sedan	Saloon
Station Wagon	Estate Car/ Shooting Brake
Top	Roof
Trailer or Camper	Caravan
Trailer Truck	Articulated Lorry
Trunk	Boot
Windshield	Windscreen

is "scarce" does not necessarily imply a high value: it indicates that the toy is eagerly sought after by collectors and that demand exceeds supply.

Limited:

A toy that will not be frequently encountered, but one which is more likely to be found by the average collector than a toy classified as "scarce". In this category, for example, we place such famous and fairly valuable toys as the Alfa Romeo P2 Racing Cars made by CIJ, France, shown on *pages 76-77*.

Common:

A toy that most dealers will have in stock or that will be readily available, supply exceeding demand. Again, however, the fact that a toy is classified as "common" (sometimes with the modifiers "fairly" or "very") does not necessarily mean that it is of low value. Condition is of the greatest importance when consider-

ing toys in this category: there is little point in buying a "common" item in poor condition, since a further search may well be rewarded by the acquisition of a superior example.

Unclassified:

A toy to which we have assigned no classification may generally be understood to rank on our scale somewhere between "limited" and "common". In the case of diecast vehicles, for example, supply roughly equals demand among collectors and we have singled out for classification as "limited" only those which we know to be in shorter supply; and as "common", only those that we know to be available in large numbers. Elsewhere, some items are unclassified because they fall into areas where collectors' interest is, as yet, somewhat limited, and where there exist insufficient criteria to allow for the establishment of a classification.

PLAYTIME

Ron McCrindell, who has contributed the "Foreword" to this book and who most kindly allowed us to photograph many toy boats *(pages 126-133)* from his magnificent collection, is one of the most respected figures among European toy collectors. In concluding our introduction to the art of toy collecting, we believe that we can give no better advice than to quote his very wise words to us: "Never forget that toys were made for children—and toys are meant to be played with!"

It is a poor collector, or at any rate one who denies himself the full pleasure to be gained from his collection, who does not sometimes take his toys from their display cases for "play": for demonstration to an audience of fellow enthusiasts or, better still, children.

Mechanical Novelties

A "novelty toy" is one that exerts its appeal not so much by its attractive appearance, or by its fidelity to the "real" human or animal figure or object which it represents, as by the ingenuity of its mechanism: its prime function is to amuse by mechanical action rather than to amaze by its realism.

The category is, perhaps, the most interesting of all for the toy collector, for many novelty toys have undergone little change in basic design since the turn of the century. For example, the clockwork Beetle shown at (15), *pages 22-23*, is a Japanese-made version of a novelty toy first marketed by the German firm of Lehmann in *c*1900—and although the example shown dates from the 1930s, similar examples might be found dating from any decade of the 20th century. Similarly, such simple novelty toys as clockwork mice, see (22), *pages 22-23*, or spinning tops, see (16), *pages 20-21*, may be found in examples made by makers of many

nationalities and dating from any time during the past eighty or more years.

US-MADE NOVELTIES

Among the earliest-dated novelty toys shown on *pages 18-25* are examples of the work of US toymakers of the later 19th century. Indeed, American makers were about the first in the field with mechanical toys (mainly clockwork-, steam-, or gravity-driven); such names as Stevens and Brown and Edward Ives had come into prominence by around the 1850s-1860s. Surviving examples of early mechanical toys in tinplate by American makers are now scarce and expensive, but novelties made of cast iron—a favorite material of US makers— have, for obvious reasons, a higher survival rate. Among the American- made novelties shown here are a cast- iron "Uncle Sam" Money Bank, at (14), *pages 22-23*—an example of a very popular and attractive genre, in which some collectors specialize—and a rather

unusual (since the majority of cast-iron toys are unpowered) clockwork-driven Sulky Racer, shown at (5), *pages 22-23*. The latter, dating from a time when sulky racing was a mass-appeal sport in the USA, makes manifest another att- ractive aspect of novelties (shared to a certain extent by other toys): the way in which they reflect the popular taste of the times in which they were produced.

Another notable US-made novelty, shown at (8), *pages 18-19*, although of a much later date, is the "Doughboy Tank" made by Louis Marx. The Marx company was one of the world's leading makers of tinplate novelties in the years before and after World War II. In the 1930s, it was a pioneer in the production of "space" or "science-fiction" toys—al- though the example shown of a 1930s- vintage tinplate Rocket Ship, at (13), *pages 20-21*, is of Japanese manufacture. At that time, many Japanese-made toys were copies of Western originals (like the Lehmann Beetle, mentioned

Above: *"Mr Turnip", a diecast, painted string puppet based on a character from a 1950s BBC television series. This example was sold by Selfridges store in London. Height: 7in (17·8cm).*

Left: *Lehmann's "Drunken Sailor", an early 20th century tinplate toy, dances a jig when wound up at the back. The Lighthouse toy has a clockwork boat and a battery-powered light.*

above), but in recent years, with plastics dominating Western production, Japanese makers have established a near-monopoly in tinplate production.

FRENCH & GERMAN MAKERS

Perhaps the two most famous names in the production of novelty toys in the 20th century are those of Fernand Martin (Bonnet et Cie, after World War I) of Paris, France, and Ernst Paul Lehmann of Brandenburg, Germany. (The Lehmann manufactory was carried on under its founder's name at Nuremburg, West Germany, following World War II.) Martin's output was very large in the later 19th and early 20th centuries, and the company specialized in toys that rather resembled the "automata", or animated dolls, of the 18th and 19th centuries. Its products, now mainly scarce and expensive, are typified by tinplate human figures, often with removable fabric clothing, that perform everyday actions: street musicians,

porters with baggage trolleys, butchers chopping meat, and similar subjects.

The products of Lehmann are probably of greater importance to the average collector, since they are more frequently found, the firm being long in production, and are generally more varied in type (although study of Lehmann toys will show that the firm often designed several different models around the same clockwork mechanism). A good selection of Lehmann novelties is shown on the following pages: on *pages 18-19*, for example, note the early "MAN DA RIN", a classic tinplate novelty, at (1), "Adam" the Porter at (3), the automotive-style "Naughty Nephew" at (4), and one version of the very popular "Bucking Broncho" genre at (8).

Many novelty toys of the earlier period are hand-enameled and bear no maker's mark, making attribution very difficult. Thus, of the Fireman of *c*1900, shown at (5), *pages 18-19,* we can say only that it is in the style of F. Martin, and for such "classics" as the Pool Player (1) and the Tightrope Walker (2), *pages 20-21,* we can deduce only the maker's probable nationality on stylistic evidence. On toys of later date, makers' marks are more common, enabling us to show examples that are certainly the work of such prominent German makers as Stock, Doll, Hess, Blomer & Schüler, Arnold, and Schuco. Of these, the firm of Schuco (Schreyer and Company), is particularly noted for the ingenuity of mechanism and high standard of finish of its mechanical toys of the 1930s: note the Pig Band, a toy produced by Schuco in a number of variations, shown at (20), *pages 22-23*.

It is worthy of note that, with the exception of such accessories as mills, forges, and workshops to be powered by stationary steam engines, the famous German makers Bing, Carette, and Marklin, who feature so prominently in other sections of this book, were not notably active in the field of mechanical novelty toys. Marklin made only a few novelties, although these were of very high quality, and a Roller-Skating Bear by Bing is shown at (11) on *pages 22-23.*

We have included in our selection of novelty toys steam accessories—such as the Saw Mill by Doll et Cie, Germany, at (2), *pages 18-19*—"penny toys", and "track-operating toys" (as distinct from toy railroads). "Penny toys" are so called because they were made to be sold at that price in Great Britain (or for a few cents in the United States) by street pedlars and in some stores in the years before World War I. The major center of production was Nuremburg, Germany, and the bestknown name associated with these simple tinplate models (which span almost every conceivable type of toy) is that of J. Ph. Meier of Nuremburg: see the "Platform

Train" by Meier at (10) on *pages 20-21,* where a number of other "penny toys" that, like the majority of such toys, bear no maker's mark, are shown. Track-operating toys, in production from *c*1900 to the present day, are shown on *pages 24-25;* note the brief introduction.

COLLECTING NOVELTY TOYS

Although many mechanical novelties are so ingenious and attractive that a fascinating collection may be formed from only a few examples, they are far from being the easiest toys to collect. Unlike some other kinds of toy, that are generally disposed of when there is no longer a child in the family of an age to play with them, novelties are often retained for their sentimental value, or simply because of the amusement they give to adults as well as children, and may not reach the collectors' market until two or three generations after their date of manufacture. For this reason, and because of their scarcity for other reasons outlined below, novelties may be very costly in comparison with toys of equivalent, or even higher, quality in other categories.

As with other toys, the possession of the original box will usually enhance the value—but in the case of novelties, the box is not nearly so important as completeness and working order. Because they are comparatively fragile but at the same time have a high "play value" (ie, they usually receive considerable usage), novelties will often be found not only in "play-worn" condition as regards finish, but also with damaged or missing parts. Such parts may be very difficult to replace, sometimes calling for special manufacture. A faulty or inoperative mechanism will, of course, seriously affect the appeal of a toy in which mechanical action is the main attraction: however, clockwork motors are usually fairly simple and may be reparable by the competent amateur. For some collectors, especially in the field of novelties, restoration of damaged toys is as great a pleasure as the acquisition of perfect specimens. Remember, however, that a damaged toy may have to be disassembled for renovation. In the case of soldered tinplate toys, joints may have to be melted to expose the mechanism, and the finish will inevitably suffer. Tab-and-slot constructed toys may be easier to disassemble, but great care must be taken.

Mechanisms and moving parts may be very lightly lubricated if necessary, but (assuming that full-scale restoration is not needed) no renovation of the finish should be undertaken other than a light wash with mild soap, followed by thorough drying with a soft cloth. Like other toys, novelties are best displayed in glazed cabinets, at an even temperature and away from direct sunlight.

1 Lehmann's "MAN DA RIN" was almost certainly one of the many "Chinese" toys inspired by the Boxer Rebellion of 1900. This toy has the early Lehmann trademark on the front and sides of the sedan chair, and bears the patent date "12 Mai 1903". It is powered by a clockwork mechanism in the lower half of the chair: hidden wheels propel the chair, and the coolies' legs are articulated to give them a realistic gait. The mandarin urges on the leading coolie by tugging on his pigtail. Length: 7·3in (185mm). Limited.

2 A water-driven Saw Mill by the German manufacturer Doll et Cie, dating from before 1920. This toy was intended to be powered by a steam engine, via a driving band on the wheel visible behind the chimney, but the mill wheel could also be hand-operated. Water is pumped into the mill's upper gallery, flowing thence onto the vanes of the water wheel, turning it anticlockwise, and causing the saw to reciprocate via the crank-shaft. Note the hand-enameled finish and the realistic pressed-tin roof and log. Width: 6·7in (17cm); height: 5·7 in (14·5cm). Limited.

3 "Adam" the Porter, by Lehmann; a popular toy with a long production life, this example dating from c1910. Clockwork concealed in the torso drives articulated legs. The detachable trunk bears the patent date "2 Jan 06" on the edge of the lid, with "E·P·L" (for Ernst Paul Lehmann) on the lid itself. The Lehmann trademark is lithographed on the porter's trousers;

his upper body is hand enameled. Length: 8·27in (210mm). Limited.

4 "Naughty Nephew", another novelty from Lehmann's extensive range; this example dating from c1908. When the clockwork-driven vehicle is moving, the sailor-suited Nephew attempts to grab the steering tiller from Uncle—and receives an admonitory slap. The rear of the vehicle bears the Lehmann trademark and the patent date "May 12 1903". Length: 4·92in (125mm). Limited.

5 Dating from c1900, this Fireman is one of a number of popular climbing toys of the period. Clockwork in the hand-enameled torso, wound by the non-removable cast key at the shoulder, operates a crankshaft that drives the legs in a climbing motion; the

fixed arms have hands pegged to fit the sides of a ladder. Height: 7·48in (190mm). Scarce.

6 Clockwork Swimming Seal, a realistic novelty animal by Lehmann, dating from c1920. It is mounted on a tricycle under-carriage: clockwork drives the front wheel, also activating the flippers, and the tail wheel steers a zig-zag course. A bell on the collar was standard. Length: 7in (178mm). Scarce.

7 Another popular Lehmann novelty, the "Bucking Broncho", remained in production for several years; this bears the patent date "19 June 1906". Clockwork in the wheeled base drives it forward and causes the broncho to buck realistically in an attempt to unseat the cowboy, who has pivoted hands.

Note that Lehmann produced a similar toy without clockwork. Length: 6·1in (155mm). Limited.

8 This colorful clockwork-driven tinplate Tank (loosely modeled on the lozenge-shaped British Mark II tank of World War I) was made as the "Doughboy Tank" by the US maker Marx in c1935. As the tank moves along, the marksman slowly appears from his hatch, aims his rifle (as seen), and then quickly disappears. An almost identical toy was produced in Germany in the 1920s: examples bear the legend "Made in Germany", with no manu-

"Penny Toy" Van by G. Fischer, Germany, made before 1920. A cheap tinplate toy with attractive printed detail; note trademark on cab door. Length: 2·36in (60mm).

facturer's name, and are finished in different colors. Length: 9·5in (241mm). Limited.

9 "Paddy's Pride", an amusing novelty of a popular type; this example produced by Stock of Solingen, Germany, in c1920. Note Stock's trademark on the blue ribbon that encircles the prize porker. Clockwork within the "upturned bath" cart drives the rear wheels and causes "Paddy" to urge on the pig, which also has a wheel concealed beneath the blue ribbon. The toy can be set to move in circles. Other makers produced variations on this theme in the first decades of the century; notably Lehmann, whose "Paddy" had no cart, but rode precariously astride his fat pig. Length: 8in (203mm). Limited.

1 Pool Player by an unidentified German maker, c1910. This "classic" tinplate novelty was produced in various styles and sizes by several makers. A clockwork motor beneath the table powers the player's cue via a concealed rod, and also returns balls to play. Length: 11in (279mm). Limited.

2 Tightrope Walker by an unidentified maker, probably French, c1900. This ingenious tinplate balancing toy works by gravity. One end of the tightrope is fixed in a slightly higher position than the other, and the deeply-recessed front wheel of the wheelbarrow is placed on the rope at the upper end. The toy is kept upright by the lead weight —the "balance pole" is for effect only—and as it moves, the figure's

legs "walk" via cranks from the front wheel. Length: 4·92in (125mm). Scarce.

3 Walking Dog by Blomer & Schüler, Nuremburg, West Germany, c1948-50. "Jumbo", the elephant trademark of this maker, is printed on the collar tag of this novelty. Length: 7·48in (190mm).

4 Walking Turkey by Blomer & Schüler, c1948-50. A most colorfully printed tinplate novelty, this clockwork-powered bird raises and spreads its tail as it walks. Length: 5·51in (140mm).

5 "Penny Toy" Automobile by an unidentified maker, probably German, c1910. This simple tinplate automobile is flywheel-driven. The extended spindle of the rear-mounted flywheel rests on the rear wheels: when a cord wound

around the spindle is pulled sharply, the power of the revolving flywheel is transmitted by friction. Length: 3·94in (100mm). Limited.

6 "Penny Toy" Sewing Machine by an unidentified German maker, c1910. In lightweight tinplate this is not a working model. Height: 3·54in (90mm).

7 "Penny Toy" Locomotive by an unidentified German maker, c1910. A pull-along toy with simple lithographed detail. Length: 3·35in (85mm).

8 Monorail Car by an unidentified German maker—it bears a trademark, "HR" within a shield— dating from the 1920s. The streamlined car of lightweight tinplate was probably intended to run on a circular monorail (the track shown is not original), on

a radial arm connected to a clockwork driving mechanism. Length: 6·5in (165mm). Limited.

9 Santa Claus by Arnold, West Germany, 1950s. A clockwork-powered tinplate novelty for the Christmas season. The maker's trademark features prominently on the sack seen in the rear view. Height: 3·75in (95mm).

10 "Penny Toy" Platform Train by J. Ph. Meier, Nuremburg, Germany, c1900. This pull-along tinplate toy with pressed-tin detail and gilt wheels bears the "Dog Cart" trademark of a leading "penny toy" maker. Length: 3·94in (100mm).

11 Hydroplane by an unidentified maker, possibly Japanese, 1950s. This clockwork-powered tinplate "carpet toy" has brightly-printed detail. Length: 5·9in (150mm).

12 Speedboat by J. L. Hess, Nuremburg, Germany, 1920s. A tinplate "carpet toy" typical of a range from this maker in the 1920s; flywheel-powered. Length: 11·81in (300mm).

13 Rocket Ship by an unidentified maker, probably Japanese, 1930s. A fairly early "science fiction" toy; clockwork-powered. The on-off control lever can be seen at the tail, along with the remains of the original "sparking" device. Length: 7·09in (180mm).

14 "Beatrix" Tricycle Automobile by Stock, Solingen, Germany, c1914. A simple clockwork mechanism drives the rear wheel of the tinplate auto via a wire spring. The steering is non-variable, and the radially-spoked wheels, with printed tires, are made of two dished tin

sections. Length: 4·53in (115mm).

15 Scissors Grinder by Arnold, West Germany, c1950. A tinplate novelty with an electric motor that drives the grinding-wheel via a connecting band (missing); a flint on the underside of the scissors produces a shower of sparks. Length: 5·71in (145mm).

16 Spinning Tops by an unidentified maker, possibly Japanese, post-1945. The arm on the rack-and-pinion plunger (left) engages with the projection at the upper side (right, in photograph) of the top to give a long-lasting "spin" when the plunger is "pumped" before removal. Common.

17 "Penny Toy" Pony and Trap by an unidentified Germany maker, c1910, with brightly gilt finish. Length: 4·13in (105mm).

18 "Penny Toy" Horse and Cart by an unidentified German maker, c1910. A lithographed-tinplate horse pulls a pressed-tin cart. Length: 4·33in (110mm).

19 Soldier by an unidentified German maker, c1930. The detail of this clockwork-powered tinplate infantryman features the uniform of a British "Tommy", with equipment of German Army type. Length: 7·28in (185mm).

(Left) Balancing clown, probably by a French maker, c1900; a hand-enameled tinplate toy. (Right) Rolling-Ball Game, probably French, c1900: the counter-weighted bucket takes a ball from the dispenser at the top, returns by gravity to the base, and tips the ball into a tray with numbered apertures.

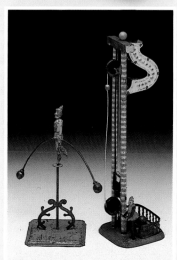

All the toys shown on this spread were photographed at the London Toy & Model Museum.

1 Donald Duck Tricyclist by an unidentified maker, c1950. The composition figure, with cloth trousers, rides a tinplate tricycle. Clockwork drives the rear wheels, causing the figure's legs to move in a realistic pedaling motion. The creations of Walt Disney have long provided a rich area of inspiration for toy manufacturers: Mickey Mouse, Donald Duck, Goofy, and other characters are to be found in many forms. Height: 4in (102mm). Fairly common.

2 Clockwork Mouse by an unidentified maker (possibly Japanese). A modern item — similar toys remain in production — this has a pressed tinplate body and cloth tail. Length: 3·5in (89mm). Fairly common.

3 Hen and Chicken Cart by Hans Eberl, Nuremburg, Germany, c1918. This toy is driven forward by clockwork concealed within the cart (note winder) that also sets the chicken in motion. Length: 8·5in (216mm). Limited.

4 Airplane Novelty by Schuco, Germany, mid-1930s. The "New York-Paris" flyer — the design evidently influenced by the "record" solo flights of the period — is plush-covered and pilots a printed tin monoplane. Length: 4in (102mm).

5 Sulky Racer by an American maker, early 20th century. Racing in light two-wheeled carts known as sulkies was a popular sport in the USA and several US makers produced toys of the kind shown

here. It is cast iron, a traditional material of US toymakers until at last overtaken by tinplate. However, instead of being pull-/push-along, like most cast-iron toys, this incorporates a somewhat bulky clockwork mechanism. American cast-iron toys of this period have been reproduced, often with inferior finish by Continental makers. Length 8·875in (225mm). Scarce.

6 Clockwork Grasshopper by a European maker, dating from the 1940s. Insect novelties were produced both before and after World War II, and this is typical of post-war European production in bearing no maker's mark. Length: 7·125in (181mm). Common.

7 "Zikra" by Lehmann, Germany: a tinplate toy with a long production life beginning c1915. Clockwork in

the cart (note winder) causes the zebra to kick and buck, while the clown driver hauls at the reins. Lehmann produced more than one toy of this type, notably the "Balky Mule". Length: 7·125in (181mm).

8 Cyclist by Günthermann, Nuremburg, Germany, c1900. Clockwork powers the rear wheel in realistic manner by way of a chain drive; the tinplate cyclist pedals a wire bicycle with white rubber tires. Length: 7·5in (190mm). Very scarce.

9 Native and Crocodile; a large, well-detailed version of a popular tinplate novelty which was produced (latterly in smaller sizes only) until the 1950s. Clockwork drives a pair of wheels linked to the crocodile's jaws, which open and close as it travels forward. Length: 15in (381mm). Common.

10 "Zig-Zag" by Lehmann, a tinplate novelty, c1910. An ingenious clockwork mechanism makes the "car" sway and swing while following an erratic course. Length: 5·625in (143mm). Scarce.

11 Roller-Skating Bear by Bing, Germany, c1910. Added charm is given to this clockwork toy by its covering of simulated fur. Note the maker's mark as an ear-tag. Height: 8·5in (216mm). Scarce.

12-13 Traveling Circus by a European maker, c1950. An ambitious tinplate toy: the circus wagon (13), with a detachable folding cage, is drawn by an elephant which "walks" when activated by rods clockwork-driven via a cranked axle beneath the wagon. The simple tinplate animals and clown, on connecting rods (12),

are drawn along behind. Length (elephant and wagon together): 17·5in (445mm).

14 "Uncle Sam" Money Bank; an American cast-iron novelty, c1890, and typical of a very popular genre of the period. A coin placed in "Uncle Sam's" hand is dropped into the "U.S." bag when the figure's right arm is activated by pressure on its beard. Height: 11·25in (286mm). Scarce.

15 Clockwork Beetle by Egaway, Japan, dating from before World War II. Beetles which walked and flapped their wings were popular novelties, and this one is a copy—complete with facsimile trademark—of the famous tinplate beetle made by Lehmann from c1900 to the late 1920s. Length: 3·75in (95mm).

16 "Toonerville Trolley" by H. Fischer, Nuremburg, c1925. This tinplate toy was based on an American strip cartoon (note copyright line above winder); it moves forward, rocking and swaying on its eccentric wheels, stops, and restarts, when the driver cranks his handle. Also to be found in a smaller version, this toy is 5·25in (133mm) long. Scarce.

17 Dancing Bear by a German maker, pre-World War II. When its clockwork is wound, the articulated tinplate figure alternately bends and stands upright. Note ring through nose, and cloth apron. Height: 6·125in (156mm).

18 "Li-La" by Lehmann, c1910. A classic clockwork tinplate toy: the driver steers the horseless carriage on an erratic course, while one

sister pushes open the cab hatch with her parasol and the other belabors the dog, which turns its head. A number of color and wheel variants exist. Length: 5·25in (133mm). Limited.

19 "Tut-Tut" by Lehmann, another classic tinplate novelty, c1910. Beneath the car, a bellows worked by the clockwork motor causes the amusingly oversized driver to sound his trumpet as he careers erratically along. Length: 6·75in (171mm). Limited.

20 Pig Band by Schuco, c1936. When wound, the three musicians of cloth-covered tinplate mime the playing of drum, flute, and fiddle. Schuco produced variations on this theme: a military band is also to be found. Height (single figure): 5·1in (130mm). Common.

The simple mechanical toy that operates on a track evolved only a little later than the train set. But although by no means new, the concept seems to have taken on a new lease of life after World War II. Comparatively unsophisticated and fairly robust "novelties", these toys are generally inexpensively-produced and are presumably aimed at children too young to appreciate a "real" train set. To an older child, the simple operation of these toys would soon become of little interest. From the collector's point of view, however, mechanical mediocrity is often outweighed by pleasing design and attractive printed detail.

1 Rack Railway by Chad Valley, Great Britain, dating from c1950. The clockwork-driven car climbs the pivoted rack section under the power of its motor, a cog-wheel beneath it engaging with slots in the track. Upon reaching the summit, as the section tips forward, the motor cuts out and the car relies upon gravity to descend the second pivoted section, run up and back along the lower section, and return to the foot of the rack to make another clockwork-powered ascent. Overall length of track-base: 42·5in (108cm).

2 "Delhi Local Shuttle" by an Indian maker, dating from c1980. A brightly-colored "tramcar" toy with a wealth of printed detail—and note the manufacturer's trademark and name, in an Asian script, on the side of the station to the left in the photograph. The clockwork-powered tramcar pursues the "there and back again" course usual with these toys on its alternating (cross-over) tracks. Length: 25·6in (65cm). Common.

3 "Carpet Toy" Locomotive by INGAP, Padua, Italy, dating from c1950. The simple clockwork-powered locomotive, numbered "552", is something of an intruder on this spread, since it is a "floor toy"—of a kind popular since the 19th century—and is not intended to run on a track. Its tinplate side on which a 2-6-0 wheel configuration is printed conceals, in fact, four wheels only. Length: 6·5in (16·5cm).

4 "Condor" Signal Train by an unidentified German maker, dating from the 1950s. The clockwork-powered locomotive, numbered "20 512" and with printed detail showing a 2-8-4 wheel configuration, operates the signals by tripping track-mounted levers. Length: 28·5in (72·5cm).

5 Liner and Lighthouse by Arnold, West Germany, dating from the 1950s—a variation on the land-based themes of the other novelties shown on this spread. The liner is mounted on a pivoted mechanism that causes it to "pitch" quite convincingly as it moves between the lighthouse and the harbor building, the latter concealing a clockwork motor. Note that here—as in the toys shown at (6), (8), (9), and (10)—it is the powered track that operates the non-powered vehicle. Length: 14·8in (37·5cm).

6 Turntable Train by Arnold, West

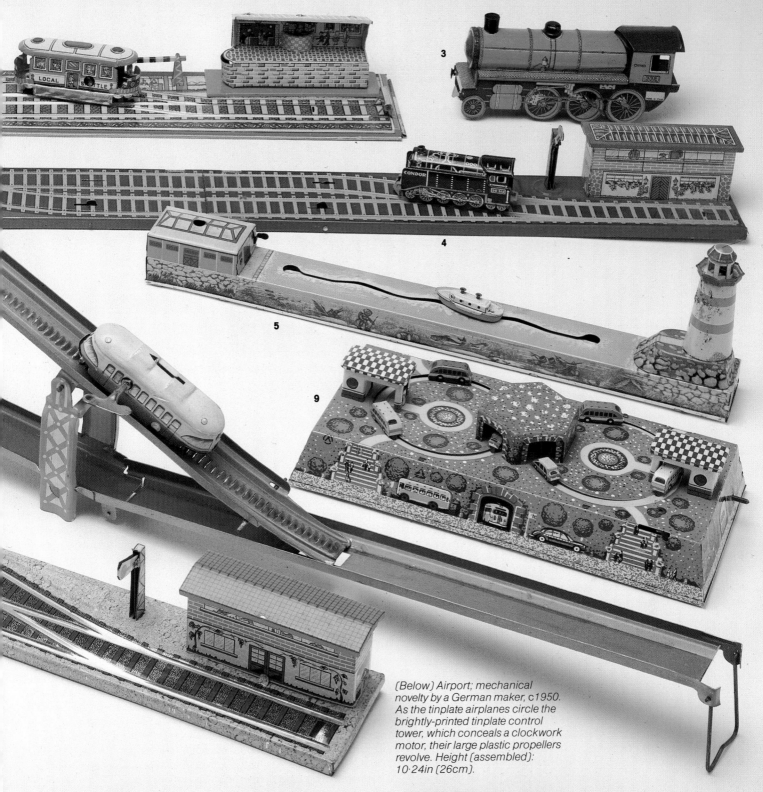

(Below) Airport; mechanical novelty by a German maker, c1950. As the tinplate airplanes circle the brightly-printed tinplate control tower, which conceals a clockwork motor, their large plastic propellers revolve. Height (assembled): 10·24in (26cm).

Germany, dating from c1948-50. The locomotive, turning on the turntables at either end of the track, pulls or pushes its coach between engine shed and station (the latter concealing the toy's clockwork motor). Note the attractively-printed detail of road transport beneath an embankment—as on the very similar French-made toy at (8)—along the side of the base. Length: 14·8in (37·5cm).

7 "Flèche d'Or" Rail Car by an unidentified French maker, dating from the 1950s. The removable key for the clockwork-powered rail car is shown here in place for winding. As in (4), the car trips the signals as it travels between the stations. Length: 30in (76cm).

8 Turntable Train by an unidentified French maker, dating from the

mid-1950s. Operation is similar to that described at (6) and, again, it is the clockwork-powered track, engaging on the underside of the locomotive, that drives the toy. Note the winding shaft in the station roof. Length: 14·8in (37·5cm).

9 Highway Toy by an unidentified Soviet Russian maker, dating from the 1970s; see the earlier, German-made version of this toy shown at (10). Two buses and an automobile are fixed on each of the two separate circular tracks, running beneath a raised central tunnel. The tracks are powered by a clockwork motor in the base of the brightly-printed toy; note the winding shaft on the right in the photograph. Length of base: 9·55in (24·25cm). Common.

10 Highway Toy by a West German maker (possibly "Technofix", Gebrüder Einfalt; a maker particularly noted for the production of toys of this kind in the post-World War II period), dating from c1950. In design and operation it closely resembles the later Soviet-made toy shown at (9), but in this example only two automobiles are moved by each of the two circular tracks. Length of base: 8·96in (22·75cm).

11 "Carpet Toy" Rail Car by an unidentified Japanese maker, probably dating from the 1930s. Like (3), this vehicle is not intended to run on a track. The clockwork-powered car, of futuristic shape, has wheels fixed at an angle so that it will run a circular course. Length: 3·54in (9cm).

Railroad Toys

It was steam that powered the Industrial Revolution and paved the way for the "brave new world" of the 19th century. It is, therefore, hardly suprising that the earliest locomotives (the first passenger-carrying lines, somewhat postdating industrial application of steam, were opened in Europe and the USA in the late 1820s-early 1830s) were very soon an important subject of the toymakers' art.

FLOOR TRAINS

Toy locomotives, sometimes with coaches or trucks, of the unpowered pull- or push-along type appeared in the nurseries of Europe and the USA before the 1840s. The earliest examples were often of wood and were "one-off" toys, made to order by local craftsmen. Early "floor trains", or "carpet toys"—see the examples on *pages 30-31*—were not intended to run on rails. Nor were the first simple live-steam models which, by the early 1860s, began to appear in very small numbers from makers who were interested in testing out the market for toys of this kind.

In the United States, the early commercial railroad toys were often constructed of cast-iron (US toymakers being noted for their work in this material), whereas French and German makers generally favored soldered tinplate. A notable early type of commercially-produced toy was the "platform train"—see (2-4) and (5), *pages 30-31*—which consisted of a simple representation of a locomotive and its rolling stock, all mounted on the same wheeled base or on a succession of such bases. A further, very popular, type of early railroad toy, although one outside the scope of this book, was the large wooden locomotive capable of carrying a child, which was pulled by a playmate or, perhaps, "scooted" along.

EARLY POWERED LOCOMOTIVES

The earliest powered toy locomotives were driven by simple steam engines with oscillating cylinders; ie, the cylinder, into which steam was forced from the boiler, was pivoted on a block fixed to the locomotive's chassis, and thus remained always in line with the connecting rod as the wheel, driven by the rod, turned. Such locomotives, of which early examples exist by such famous makers as Plank of Nuremburg, Germany, are often known as "piddlers" or "dribblers", since their oscillating cylinders tended to deposit a trail of moisture in their wake. Examples are shown on *pages 32-33*.

One alternative to steam-power in this early period was "spring-power", having little to do with clockwork proper. The best-known example is the mechanism called "Hall's Patent"—see (1), *pages 30-31*—in which a coil-spring inside the locomotive's boiler space is wound by a handle mounted on one wheel and transmits power to the axle.

There were also flywheel-driven models, of which a fairly late example is shown at (10), *pages 30-31*. Here, the locomotive's boiler space houses a flywheel, its spindle protruding through oval slots to rest on the tops of the locomotive's driving wheels. A sharp tug on a cord wrapped around the shaft of the flywheel sets it spinning, and the momentum of the heavy wheel is transmitted to the driving wheels via the spindle. This was, obviously, not a mechanically-efficient system. It was suited only to lighter-weight models and never became particularly popular; consequently production was limited, and flywheel-powered locomotives are now comparatively rare.

HAND-MADE MODELS

It should be noted that at around the same time as the models described above appeared on the market, around the late 1860s-early-1870s, it was possible in the United Kingdom (although the custom does not appear to have been popular elsewhere) to buy rough-cast parts, boilers, cylinders, etc, from which a toy locomotive could be assembled by a competent amateur.

Hand-made "one-off" models of that kind—which bear no maker's name and, of course, cannot be traced through any catalog—may be encountered by the collector. They may generally be distinguished from professionally-made "demonstration" models (which were

made for the prospective customers of railroad constructors and are, of course, not toys) by their comparatively unsophisticated finish and coarse (ie, inconsistent) scales.

ON THE RAILS

Some of the steam-driven "piddlers" and "dribblers" were built to run on rails, and by the 1880s enterprising toymakers were producing steam-powered (and some clockwork-powered) locomotives that could be purchased complete with simple rail layouts; usually a circular track. Thus appeared the "train set" as the 20th century would know it.

The clockwork-powered locomotive, having a more complex mechanism and being more subject to mechanical failure if not carefully handled, than steam, took some time to find favor. By c1900, however, clockwork had gained, at least, parity with steam, and by this time makers such as Marklin of Goppingen, Germany, were producing locomotives with two-speed clockwork motors incorporating forward and reverse gears. A fairly simple clockwork locomotive of this period, by Issmayer of Nuremburg, Germany, dating from c1895, is shown at (3), *pages 34-35.*

One important factor leading to the generally increasing popularity of clockwork was that a clockwork-powered locomotive was far safer for children to handle than a steam-driven model, in which a methylated-spirit burner was

normally used to heat the water in the boiler, with the attendant risks to the user of burning or scalding.

FAMOUS MAKERS

In the period c1890-1900, also, a number of toy manufacturers all over the world—some of them still in production today—established themselves as leaders in the field of model railroads. In Germany, the firms of Gebrüder Marklin, Gebrüder Bing of Nuremburg, and, a little later, Georges Carette of Nuremburg, began production of steam- and clockwork-powered trains in the 1890s. Locomotives and rolling stock by both Bing and Carette, dating from about this period, are shown on *pages 34-35.* In the USA, the company founded in 1886 by Edward R. Ives at Plymouth, Conn., began to produce Gauge "0" railroad sets at Bridgeport, Conn., in c1901, while in New York (and later at Irvington, N.J.) Joshua Lionel Cowen's "Lionel" train sets appeared from c1908.

In Great Britain, the foremost name of the period was that of Wenman J. Bassett-Lowke. He had established a toy-making concern at Northampton in 1899, and within a year or two was negotiating an agreement under which he would market the products of the foremost German makers of railroad toys, notably Bing, in the United Kingdom. Bassett-Lowke's emphasis on the building of *scale* models was the greatest single influence on the shape of

model railroads to come. Before c1900, model locomotives were generally fairly basic representations of the "real thing", often quite realistic, but built to no particular scale. Under Bassett-Lowke's influence, makers began to specialize in locomotives built to standard gauges, the most common at this time being designated Gauge "1".

STANDARD GAUGES

At this point, therefore, it will be useful to summarize the standard gauges that will be encountered by the collector of railroad toys. We have adopted the system established in Bassett-Lowke's catalogs early in this century, in which the size of the gauge is expressed as the distance between the inner edges of the track. The standard gauges are:

Gauge "4":	2·8125in (71·44mm), but commonly known as "3-inch Gauge";
Gauge "3":	2·5in (63·5mm);
Gauge "2":	2in (50·8mm);
Gauge "1":	1·75in (44·45mm);
Gauge "0":	1·25in (31·75mm);
Gauge "00" or "H0":	0·625in (15·875mm).

Of these, only Gauge "1" and the smaller gauges will be encountered with any frequency: Gauges "2", "3", and "4" were never to gain comparable popularity (although they are now, of course, eagerly collected), mainly because of the space they required for a reasonable track layout. Also, of course, the cost of items in the larger gauges was significantly greater; for example, in the Bassett-Lowke Catalog for 1905-06, an "Express Clockwork Locomotive" of good quality, of the type made by Bing, is priced at £1 9s 6d (£1.47½p, $2.09) in Gauge "1"; £2 2s 0d (£2.10, $2.98) in Gauge "2"; £2 9s 0d (£2.45, $3.48) in Gauge "3"; and £2 15s 6d (£2.77½p, $3.94) in Gauge "4". In the same Catalog, the price of a "Scale Model Great Western Railway Locomotive" rises from £1 1s 0d (£1.05, $1.49) in Gauge "0", to £3 7s 6d (£3.37½, $4.79) in Gauge "2". Price variations for rolling stock are even more marked: the catalog price for a "Scale Model Coach" rises from 4s 0d (20p, 28c) in Gauge "0" to no less than £2 4s 6d (£2.22½, $3.16) in Gauge "4". Prices for lengths of track roughly double from Gauge "0" to Gauge "4".

The period of dominance of Gauge "1" was brief: by around 1914, Gauge "0" had become more popular, mainly because it was possible to create a more realistic Gauge "0" layout in a limited space. Within a few years, however, most major manufacturers had almost abandoned the production of steam-powered trains in Gauge "0"; and in c1922, rapidly recovering from the setbacks on its trade inflicted by World War I, the German firm of Bing began to introduce railroads in Gauge "00" or "H0" (the latter signifying "Half-0"), at first in clockwork and later powered by electric motors.

At first, Bing's "Miniature Table Railways"—see (1-6), *pages 58-59*—failed to find favor, since the range was limited and the early production models lacked the realism of Gauge "0" items. Thus, for some years, Bing itself, like other major makers in Germany, Great Britain (where the famous Hornby range began to appear in the 1920s), and the USA, continued to center its main efforts on Gauge "0".

By the mid-1930s, however, some impression had been made on the market by the German-made (with a British subsidiary, in conjunction with Bassett-Lowke) "Trix" series of electric-powered Gauge "00" railroads. Marklin and Bub in Germany, and some US makers, were also active in the smaller-gauge field, but the tide was finally turned in favor of Gauge "00" railroads largely through the activities of the British firm of Hornby (Meccano Limited, Liverpool), which set new standards in smaller-gauge realism with its "Hornby Dublo" (ie, "Double-0") range of the later 1930s.

Hornby launched its Dublo range in *c*1938. Items were originally offered in both clockwork and electric versions: the first models issued were the "Sir Nigel Gresley" 4-6-2 locomotive—for an up-dated version, see (16), *pages 50-51*—and eight-wheeled tender, with an articulated two-coach unit in LNER (London and North Eastern Railway) livery, and an 0-6-2 Tank Locomotive together with freight-train rolling stock. From the outset, Hornby Dublo locomotives had diecast bodies; tinplate bodies and diecast chassis were used for the rolling stock. A wide selection of items from the post-World War II Dublo range is shown on *pages 50-57*. The Dublo railroads' realism was enhanced, and their popularity strengthened, by the provision of a fine range of well-detailed accessories, including stations, lineside fixtures, figures, and, later, vehicles (Dublo Dinky Toys; see (22-25), *pages 50-51*, and elsewhere in this section, for examples).

ELECTRIC TRAINS

At this point it will be useful briefly to trace the development of electric-powered toy railroads. By the time of the introduction of the Hornby Dublo series in the late 1930s, mains electric supply that, by the use of a transformer to modify the domestic current to the required voltage, could be used to operate toy railroads, was available in most regions of Great Britain, Europe, and the USA. This, in doing away with the previous need of many "electric"

enthusiasts for batteries and accumulators, was the major factor in the increasing popularity of electric-powered trains from that time onward. Electric operation has always appealed to seekers after realism, since it means that a train can be run without the constant re-winding required by clockwork, and that its track-speed can be varied by the use of a simple switch-control.

However, electric-powered locomotives had, in fact, been available at least since the 1900s. Bassett-Lowke's Catalog for 1905-06 lists a typical good-quality electric locomotive of the period: the 2-4-0 "Charles Dickens", available in Gauges "1" and "2", powered by a 110-volt motor on the "three-rail" system (see below). Current from the domestic supply (then still fairly rare outside urban areas) could be modified via an incandescent lamp of suitable power or by the use of a purpose-designed "Regulating Resistance" apparatus, fitted with an automatic cut-out. "Charles Dickens" was priced at £3 3s 6d (£3.17½, $4.51) in Gauge "1" or £3 10s 6d (£3.52½, $5) in Gauge "2", and the "Regulating Resistance", with connector rail, at 17s 6d (87½p, $1.24). In the same Catalog was listed a "self-contained", accumulator-powered locomotive that could be run on conventional steam/clockwork track. Both the locomotives cataloged were of German make, probably by Bing; at the same period, in the USA, Lionel was producing electric-powered street cars and would soon begin to offer railroads proper.

Earlier electric trains powered by domestic current made use of the three-rail system, with a pick-up on the underside of the locomotive making contact with the "live" central rail. It was not until the 1950s that the two-rail system—one rail live, the other earthed—using locomotives with insulated axles became predominant, and added realism to the operation of models representing steam-powered locomotives.

Although electric trains appeared on the market in increasing numbers in the years before and after World War I, they were never as popular as clockwork railroads at this time. As stated above, it was not until the increasing availability of mains electricity coincided with the launch of the Hornby Dublo series, in the late 1930s, that the average enthusiast had both the power and, with Gauge "00", the space to build up a really convincing layout. Thus, it may be said that Hornby Dublo trains not only firmly established the popularity of Gauge "00", but also prepared the way for the eclipse of clockwork-powered trains by electric models.

After World War II, Hornby soon discontinued the production of scale or semi-scale railroad toys in Gauge "0", and this lead was followed by other

major makers. However, the trend to smaller gauges was not to end in Gauge "00". From the 1950s, some makers, among them Lima of Italy, Wren of Great Britain, and the "Mini-Trix" range, began to produce models in even smaller gauges, notably "TT" (0·5in, 12·7mm) and Gauge "N" (0·375in, 9·525mm). However, railroad toys in these mini-gauges are not as yet of interest to collectors, whatever the future trend may prove to be.

The post-1945 period also saw a great increase in the use of plastic in the construction of railroad toys: some of the later examples of rolling stock shown on the photographic spreads illustrate this trend. From around the 1960s, most makers used diecast and plastic, and tinplate became less common. Models in which plastic is combined with metal are genuinely collectable—and so, increasingly, are some wholly plastic items. One attraction of plastic for the toy railroad enthusiast, as distinct from the collector, is that injection-molding techniques permit the provision of excellent detail, enhancing their authenticity.

Above: *The Roman numeral on this Carette carriage indicates the maker's Gauge "II" size, with a distance of 54mm (2·125in) between the inner faces of the rails.*

Above left: *Carette tender of this maker's Gauge "I" (48mm, 1·89in), briefly the dominant gauge for model railways in the early years of this century.*

Left: *Sleeping car interiors by Marklin. The Gauge "2" example (top) of c1906 has a detachable interior; similar details appear on the Gauge "1" model of c1914.*

Above right: *The Hornby No 1 Engine Shed of the 1930s, shown here with a postwar tank locomotive No 101 of BR's London, Midland and Scottish Region.*

Right: *A young boy admires an American Flyer Lines train (see pages 48-49) in November 1945, when such luxuries had long been unavailable in Britain.*

COLLECTORS' THEMES

The newcomer to the field of collecting railroad toys may decide to specialize in items in one gauge; of one type: unpowered, steam, clockwork, or electric; of one period; or from one maker. His choice must, obviously, be influenced by considerations of location, space, and financial resources.

While items by such makers as Bing, Marklin, Hornby, and Bassett-Lowke are to be encountered in sale-rooms and dealers' shops in most cities, it may be difficult for a collector in Europe to find many examples of work by such US makers as Lionel, Ives, and American Flyer (see *pages 48-49*), or for US collectors to locate work by smaller European producers. The collector whose storage/display space is limited will not wish to acquire many larger-gauge items. The general trend of prices paid for early items by such famous names as Marklin and Bassett-Lowke will deter many: a Marklin Gauge "1" Armored Train, *c*1902-03, recently sold at auction in the UK for £9,000 ($12,780).

As with other toys, prices are dictated by the laws of supply and demand. Leaving aside very early and comparatively modern items, we would suggest that the average collector is likely to find the simplest field in Gauge "00" items of the post-World War II period. Post-1945 Gauge "0" non-scale locomotives (ie, "toy-like" models with few pretensions to realism) by Hornby and other European and US makers remain comparatively inexpensive, and, moving a little up-market, simple Gauge "1" locomotives, even by famous makers like Bing, may still be purchased for around £100 (around $140).

Condition is of great importance. Examine any item offered for sale for structural damage, missing parts, originality of parts (ie, have any been re-placed?), and for the cracks or blisters that herald metal fatigue on cast metal parts (especially on the wheels of Hornby items). Make sure that a locomotive's tender is present, if it had one—and that it is the correct tender. Look for signs of re-painting; only good restoration is acceptable. If you intend to

attempt a restoration, check which parts are available from modelers' suppliers and which must be specially manufactured at considerable cost. If you hope to run a locomotive—some collectors, of course, maintain their models only as static exhibits—check that the mechanism is in order, or can be made so, and that suitable track is available on which to operate it.

Ideally, railroad models should be displayed in running order on a permanent track layout, but this will be beyond the resources of many collectors. Second-best are shallow, glazed cabinets with strong shelving—model locomotives may be fairly heavy—with the specimens displayed on lengths of track of the correct gauge. Either way, conditions should be dry and an even temperature maintained; the mechanisms and wheels of the models should be kept slightly oiled. If it is absolutely necessary, the finish of tinplate items may be cleaned with mild soap and warm water and a final polish given with good-quality automobile wax and a clean, soft, dry cloth.

European and American "Floor Trains", 1860-1890

Among the earliest of all commercially-produced metal toys, dating from the second half of the 19th century, are tinplate and cast-iron trains of the kind shown here. Since they were usually push-along or pull-along toys and were not meant for operation on a track, they are generally known as "floor trains" or "carpet toys". With the increasing availability towards the turn of the century of steam- or clockwork-driven trains operating on rails and marketed as sets, carpet toy trains lost their popularity and were latterly only produced in the cheap and simple form of "penny toys". Carpet toy trains are still to be found at what are, considering their age and their historical value alone, fairly reasonable prices.

All the trains shown on this spread were photographed at the London Toy & Model Museum.

1 Carpet Locomotive by a British maker, c1890. This charming tinplate locomotive, which is hand-enameled and has a brass plate with the impressed designation "Express" affixed to the farther side of the boiler, is powered by a "Hall's Patent" mechanism. When the winding handle that forms an integral part of the rear wheel is wound anti-clockwise, a cord draws back and compresses a large-diameter coil spring (with a sealing washer at its forward end) inside the boiler. When the rear wheels are released, the locomotive is propelled forward and a whistle set in the smoke-stack is sounded by the air forced up the stack by the washer. Length:

10·75in (273mm). Scarce.
2-4 Platform Train by Faivre, France, c1885. This simple pull-along carpet toy is of tinplate with hand-enameled finish, and consists of three "platforms", or six-wheeled chassis, bearing a very basically designed locomotive and eight passenger coach units. No provision appears to be made for coupling: originally, wire hooks and loops may have been fitted, or the owner may have been expected to improvise couplings of wire or thread. Each of the three platforms is 9·5in (241mm) long. Limited.
5 Platform Train by Faivre; a smaller and even more simple version of the train shown at (2-4), by the same maker and again dating from c1885. The locomotive and two carriage units are mounted on a

four-wheeled platform. Length: 8in (203mm). Limited.
6-8 Pull-Along Locomotive, Tender and Carriages by Wallwork's, Manchester, England, c1890; a cast-iron floor train (but note the flanged wheels, presumably fitted for added realism) of British manufacture—American examples in this material being more common. The semi-scale 4-2-2 locomotive with the cast number "1893" (possibly the date of manufacture) is a reasonably faithful representation of a contemporary railway engine; it has a six-wheeled tender with the cast designation "Express". Simple couplings link these to a six-wheeled carriage (7), the central pair of wheels missing in this example, and a six-wheeled brake composite carriage (8), again with

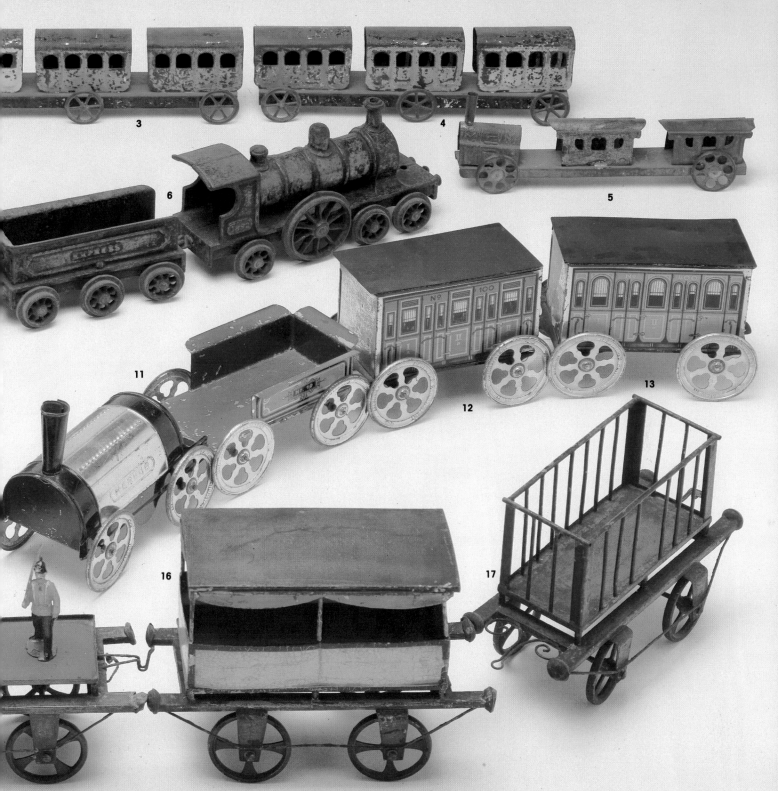

the central wheels missing. Note the words "Wallwork's Patent" cast along the chassis of the carriages. Limited.

9 Locomotive and Tender by J. & E. Stevens Company, USA; a pull-along toy (with pull-cord attached) of cast-iron construction, dating from about 1890. The 2-2-0 locomotive, with a cowcatcher and a high smoke-stack of the kind associated with American wood-burning locomotives, is a two-piece casting: the front wheels are of a wider gauge (3in, 76mm) than those at the rear (2.25in, 57mm). A matching four-wheeled tender and four-wheeled open wagon, both bearing the embossed letters "UPRR" (Union Pacific Rail Road), are attached by simple couplings. Well known for their cast-iron toys,

notably money banks, the Stevens brothers traded from 1869 onward in association with the pioneer tin toy manufacturer George W. Brown, as the Stevens and Brown Manufacturing Company of Cromwell, Connecticut. After Brown's death in 1889, the Stevens brothers continued business on their own account. Limited.

10 Floor Locomotive by Hess, Nuremburg, Germany, c1885. This tinplate locomotive, with its plated boiler, short chimney, and large, decorative, spoked wheels (note the patent marking and "Made in Germany" on the hub plates), is driven by a flywheel. The cast-iron flywheel, mounted on brackets on the rear platform of the locomotive, is spun by a sharp pull on a string wrapped round its

axle towards the center: power is transmitted via the ends of the axle, which rest on the locomotive's rear wheels. The Hess company, founded in 1826 and in production until the 1930s, was one of the pioneer manufacturers of metal toys in Germany. Length: 7.25in (184mm). Limited.

11-13 Floor Train by Hess, c1875; an earlier product of the maker noted at (10). This is a simple but most attractive pull-along toy of pressed tin; note the "rivet" details on the boiler. The 2.5in (63.5mm) gauge, 0-4-0 locomotive, with the embossed name "Merkur" ("Mercury"), pulls a rather oversized four-wheeled tender, numbered "No. 10", and First/Second Class enclosed four-wheeled carriages numbered "No. 100" (12) and

"No. 400" (13). The carriages have paper lithographed side details. Note the German patent wording and number around the wheel rims. Scarce.

14-17 Floor Train attributed to Lutz, Germany, c1860. This charming and elegant pull-along carpet toy, an early example of its kind, is of tinplate and diecast construction, with soldered joints; the finish is hand-enameled. The 2.25in (57mm) gauge, four-wheeled locomotive, with a high smoke-stack, a well-detailed boiler, a firebox with opening door, and diecast wheels, is linked by simple wire hooks to a four-wheeled tender, with raised "rivet" detail on its sides, a flat truck (15), a passenger coach (16), and a cattle truck (17). This toy is rare.

Rails for the assembly of circuits on which toy trains could be run in a realistic manner were in general production towards the end of the 19th century. The gauges (ie, the distance between the rails and, hence, between the wheels on the axle of locomotive or rolling stock) took some time to become standardized: in the early period, trains were made in a variety of large gauges, which were eventually standardized to Gauges "0" to "4", followed by the introduction, around 1922, of "table top" railways and the smaller Gauges "00" and "HO" of the type preferred today. (For a detailed explanation of "Gauges", see the introduction to this section on *pages 26-29.*) Most of the early large-gauge locomotives, as shown here, were of

the spirit-fired live-steam type. All the trains shown on this spread were photographed at the London Toy & Model Museum.

1 "3¾" Gauge (3.75in, 95mm) 2-4-0 Locomotive and Six-Wheeled Tender by Bateman, Great Britain, *c*1880. Note that Gauge "4", largest of the later standardized gauges, was 2¹³⁄₁₆" (2.8125in, 71mm). An excellent example of a spirit-fired live-steam locomotive, constructed of steel and brass. It bears a cast plate identifying it as an engine of the "L&NWR" (London and North-Western Railway) and it is a fine representation of a locomotive of the period. Note such details as the safety valve on the dome, hand rails along the boiler, springs beneath

the boiler, finely cast coupled driving wheels, and checkered footplate. The six-wheeled tender is similarly well detailed, with hand rails, springs, and a painted chassis. Overall length: 22.5in (572mm). Rare.
2 "3¼" Gauge (3.25in, 83mm) First/Third Class Passenger Coach by Stevens Model Dockyard Company, Great Britain, *c*1885. The hand-enameled detail of this six-wheeled carriage, in tinplate with soldered joints and finished in L&NWR livery, extends to pull-cords for the window blinds. Note the roof ventilators; the rather crude buffers are probably replacements for the originals. Length: 16in (406mm). Limited.
3 "3¼" Gauge (3.25in, 83mm) 2-2-2 Locomotive by Radiguet, Paris,

France, *c*1890. It is constructed mainly of brass: Radiguet, in production from 1872 to *c*1902, was noted for locomotives in this material. Incorporating its own tender, and thus of tank engine type, its detail includes a high chimney (or smoke-stack), a whistle and safety valve on the boiler top, and a drain tap on the boiler front. This spirit-fired live-steam locomotive belongs to a class generally known as "Piddlers" or "Dribblers", so called from their propensity to leave behind them a trail of water from their oscillating cylinders! Length: 9.5in (241mm). Limited.
4 "3⅝" Gauge (3.625in, 92mm) 2-2-0 Locomotive by a French maker, *c*1890. A fine example of a spirit-fired live-steam locomotive

with simple rear-mounted oscillating cylinders, built mainly of
brass. The detail is extremely
attractive, including a mahogany
front buffer beam and a boiler,
part-enameled to simulate lagging,
fitted with hand rails and, from
front to rear, a high chimney, a
pressure dome, a safety valve with
a lever-operated regulator, and a
whistle (the top part missing from
this example). Length: 12·25in
(311mm). Limited.

5 "4¼" Gauge (4·25in, 108mm)
2-2-2 "Express" Locomotive by
Stevens Model Dockyard Company, Great Britain, c1880.
Although a spirit-fired live-steam
"Dribbler" (with rear-mounted
oscillating cylinders), this is a "floor
train", not meant to run on rails. It is
somewhat crudely constructed of

tin and brass, with a high chimney,
pressure dome, and whistle (the
top part missing). Length: 14·75in
(375mm). Limited.

6 "2⅝" Gauge (2·625in, 67mm)
2-2-0 "Vulkan" Locomotive by
Ernst Plank, Nuremburg, Germany
(with the maker's early trademark
on the front of the boiler), c1890.
This is one of the earliest locomotives made by a firm founded 1866,
and is a spirit-fired live-steam
engine, with oscillating cylinders
mounted in front of the (rear)
driving wheels, of brass and tinplate
construction. Note the simple
five-spoked wheels, the large pressure dome, and the whistle; the
greater part of the narrow smoke-
stack is missing from this example.
Length: 7in (178mm). Scarce.

7 Gauge "1" 0-6-0 Locomotive,

possibly a British maker's proto-
type, c1890. Constructed mainly
of brass, this is a spirit-fired
live-steam locomotive with forward-
mounted oscillating cylinders
driving the front wheels. Detail on
the boiler includes hand rails, a
pressure dome, and a safety valve.
The central pair of wheels is
missing—possibly removed by a
former owner to enable the locomotive to negotiate tight turns on
the track. Length: 7·125in
(181mm). Scarce.

8 "3¾" Gauge (3·75in, 95mm) 2-4-0
"Express" Locomotive by the
British Modelling and Electric
Company, c1880. This spirit-fired
live-steam locomotive, of mainly
brass construction, has oscillating
cylinders driving the central pair of
wheels. The ribbed boiler is fitted

with a smoke-stack, pressure
dome, safety valve, and dome-
topped whistle. The front buffers
are obviously later items. Length:
11in (270mm). Limited.

9 A selection of the parts available
from Stevens Model Dockyard
Company, Great Britain, around
1890. The oscillating cylinder (top),
smoke-stack (left), and pressure
dome (right) were among the parts
that could be purchased to build or
refurbish a model locomotive.
Home assembly of toy locomotives
by railroad enthusiasts, using
parts like those shown here, was a
hobby followed in Great Britain
from around the late 1860s-early
1870s onward, but it does not
appear to have been a popular
pastime in other European
countries or in the USA.

By the early years of the 20th century, several toy manufacturers in Britain, Europe, and the USA were specializing in the production of toy trains in standardized gauges and with increasing realism of scale and design. The advance of standardization was such that the British firm of Bassett-Lowke Limited, Northampton, founded in 1899, was able to buy trains made in Germany by such manufacturers as Bing, Carette, and Marklin and market them successfully in the United Kingdom. It was, in fact, Bassett-Lowke's emphasis on scale models and the British firm's encouragement of the great German makers of the time to produce items in standardized gauges, that set the pattern for future development of toy railroads.

At this period, too, spirit-fired live-steam locomotives became less popular, as clockwork mechanisms improved—some incorporating two-speed motors, reverse gears, and other refinements—and electrically-powered railroad toys began to appear in both Europe and the USA. Of the trains of the type shown on this spread, the collector today is most likely to find examples in Gauge "1" (or in Gauge "0", as shown on succeeding spreads): trains in Gauges "2", "3", and "4" are comparatively scarce. All the trains shown on this spread were photographed at the London Toy & Model Museum.

1 Signal Box; a tinplate accessory of German manufacture, c1920.

Height: 3·875in (98mm).
2 Gauge "1" Ticket Office; a tinplate accessory of German manufacture, c1905. Height: 4in (102mm).
3 Gauge "1" 0-2-2 Locomotive by Issmayer, Nuremburg, Germany, c1895. A fairly basic clockwork toy with hand-enameled finish; its simple tinplate boiler is fitted with a tall chimney, a bell-shaped pressure dome, and what appears to be a support for a bell. Note that although it is fitted with buffers at the rear as well as at the front, this locomotive was originally supplied with a tender. Limited.
4 Gauge "1" "Pacific Express Line" Bogie Car by Issmayer, c1905; an example of an item produced for the US market, where Issmayer's products were popular. The lithographed detail of this tinplate

coach includes the figures of passengers, all different, on the windows. a most pleasing touch. Note access platforms with steps at either end, simple couplings, and clerestory roof. Limited.
5 Gauge "3" 4-4-0 Locomotive of Adams Flyer type, numbered "7096", by Gebrüder Bing, Nuremburg, Germany, c1904. This fine locomotive from Bing's extensive range was marketed in Great Britain by Clyde Model Dockyard Company: note the name "Clyde" inscribed on the brass rim of the wheel arch. A spirit-fired live-steam engine, it is of tinplate construction with brass fittings and steel wheels, and is finished in the green livery of the LSWR (London and South Western Railway). The detail includes a brass wheel on

the smokebox (with a bracket for a headlamp above it), chimney, pressure dome, part-concealed whistle, safety valve, and a one-piece hand rail. Note also the fluted connecting rods and spring buffers. Also worthy of note is the cast detail of springs and axle boxes on the six-wheeled tender. Limited.

6 Gauge "3" Eight-Wheeled Bogie Third Class Passenger Carriage by Bing, c1901. Like the Bing locomotive at (5), it has hand-enameled finish. Detail includes opening doors and—just visible here at the front end, but better seen on (7) below—steps on the carriage ends to enable railroad staff to light the interior lamps from the carriage roof. Limited.

7 Gauge "2" Passenger Brake Carriage, six-wheeled and close-coupled, by Bing, c1902. Like (6), it is hand-enameled and incorporates opening doors and steps to the roof. Limited.

8 Gauge "2" 4-4-0 North London Tank Locomotive by Bing, c1905. This spirit-fired live-steam engine, of hand-enameled tinplate and brass construction, is fitted with double-action slide valve cylinders and has a reverse mechanism operated from the cab. It is a faithful representation of a contemporary locomotive, with side tanks and a fully detailed boiler, having a whistle partly concealed within the cab. This was sold in Great Britain by Bassett-Lowke and was claimed to be one of the most popular "small gauge" locomotives in Bassett-Lowke's 1905-06 Catalog—in which it was offered in Gauge "1",

priced at £2 10s 0d (£2.50, $3.55); Gauge "2", as seen here, at £2 18s 6d (£2.92½, $4.15); and Gauge "3" at £3 7s 6d (£3.37½, $4.79). Limited.

9 Gauge "1" 2-2-2 "Lady of the Lake" Express Locomotive, numbered "531", by Carette, Nuremburg, Germany, c1905. A spirit-fired live-steam model, with oscillating cylinders, it is of tinplate and brass construction with enameled finish in the livery of the L&NWR (London and North-Western Railway). The boiler detail includes chimney, pressure dome, safety valve, whistle, and hand rails. With its matching six-wheeled tender, as seen here, this locomotive was offered for sale in Great Britain in the same Bassett-Lowke Catalog as noted at (8), at a price of

£1 12s 6d (£1.62½, $2.31). Limited.

10 Gauge "1" Six-Wheeled Third Class Brake Composite Carriage by Carette, c1912. Of tinplate, it is nicely finished but has non-opening doors. Like the Carette locomotive shown at (9), it is in L&NWR livery and, although a little later in date, is the type of carriage that would have been used with that locomotive. Again, it was sold in Great Britain by Bassett-Lowke, appearing in the firm's 1912 Catalog at a price of 4s 6d (22½p, 32c).

11 Signal Bell; a tinplate accessory by a German maker, c1906. This is a hand-operated version: when the crank is turned, the colored signal swivels to green and a bell rings. An automatic version, operated by weight of locomotive on track, was made. Height: 4·5in (114mm).

On this spread are shown locomotives and rolling stock made by the famous British company of Bassett-Lowke Limited, Northampton. Some are items produced by other makers for sale by Bassett-Lowke. All are shown on Bassett-Lowke's brass "permanent way" track, which featured wooden sleepers and ties.

1 Gauge "0" Baggage/Guards (Conductors) Van, made by E. Exley, Derbyshire, Britain, for sale by Bassett-Lowke, c1950. This eight-wheeled van, numbered "115", is a tinplate model of high quality, with such detail as underframes, steps at the ends (clearly seen on the right in the photograph) to give access to the roof, roof fittings including

ventilators, and door handles. It is finished in the green livery of Southern Region. Limited.

2 Gauge "0" 0-6-0 Standard Tank Locomotive, electric-powered, by Bassett-Lowke, mid-1930s. This example has undergone some modification: the number "19" is not as the original, numbered "946", and some minor details also differ. Nevertheless, it is a fine example of its type. The specification includes frames and superstructure of lithographed steel plate and turned cast-iron wheels. It was available in the livery of the London, Midland & Scottish Railway (LMS); London and North Eastern Railway (LNER); and Southern Railway (SR). This locomotive was cataloged in the late 1930s at a price of £2 2s 0d

(£2.10, $2.98) for the version powered by the "junior" 8-volt electric motor, or £2 6s 0d (£2.30, $3.27) with a 20-volt AC motor; it was also available with a clockwork motor. Limited.

3 Gauge "0" 12-Ton Covered Goods Wagon, numbered "91375", by Bassett-Lowke. Tinplate rolling stock with printed detail, of the type shown here—this example in LMS livery—was available from Bassett-Lowke from the 1930s to the 1950s.

4-5 Gauge "0" 2-6-0 Locomotive (5), numbered "33", and Six-Wheeled Tender (4), by Bassett-Lowke, mid-1930s. This example is electric-powered. The model was also available in clockwork or steam (and in LMS livery as well as LNER, as shown),

and in all cases was priced in the later 1930s at £5 5s 0d (£5.25, $7.45). After World War II, the price rose dramatically, reaching a maximum of more than £20 0s 0d (£20.00, $28.40) in the 1950s.

6 Gauge "0" 20-Ton Goods Brake Van, numbered "837354", by Bassett-Lowke; like (3), an example of the tinplate rolling stock with printed detail available from the 1930s to the 1950s.

7 Gauge "0" 4-4-0 Compound Locomotive, electric-powered, numbered "41109", and Six-Wheeled Tender, by Bassett-Lowke. This model was available before and after World War II. The specimen shown is finished in the black livery of British Railways, marking it as a post-War example. Pre-1939, it was made in LMS

(Below) Underside of Gauge "2" 0-4-0 clockwork locomotive by Marklin, c1900. Note the wide and powerful mainspring and heavy cogwheels, and brakes operating directly on wheels.

livery—or, says Bassett-Lowke's catalog "altered to GWR [Great Western Railway] style and colours at extra charge"—and was priced at £1 12s 6d (£1.62½, $2.31) if clockwork-powered, or between £1 17s 0d (£1.85, $2.63) and £2 10s 0d (£2.50, $3.55) depending on the power of the electric motor.

8 Gauge "0" 2-6-0 Locomotive, electric-powered, and Six-Wheeled Tender, by Bassett-Lowke, 1930s. As in (4-5), the finish has been modified: it bears the number "23", rather than the usual "866". Note that while it is basically similar to the model shown at (4-5), the design of the cab and firebox differ, and added detail here includes lamps at the front, rails on the cab, and "coal" in the tender. It is shown in Southern Railway livery, and

was also available in the mid-1930s, priced at £5 5s 0d (£5.25, $7.45) in either clockwork- or electric-powered versions, in GWR livery and style. The latter involved, as with (7), changes in design.

9 Gauge "0" Hydraulic Buffer Stops by Bassett-Lowke; made from the 1930s to the 1950s. This track accessory is fitted with nickel-plated spring buffers and has an enameled finish in the color of concrete. It was available for use with either brass "permanent way" track or with tinplate rails.

10 Gauge "0" 4-4-0 "Merchant Taylors" Locomotive and Six-Wheeled Tender, made by Gebrüder Marklin, Goppingen, Germany, for sale in Britain by Bassett-Lowke and dating from the early 1930s. The model shows

a Southern Railway "Schools Class" locomotive. As in (4-5) and (8), the finish of this electric-powered model has been somewhat modified: it bears the number "17" instead of the original "910". A late-type Marklin trademark cast on the cylinders is just visible in the photograph. Introduced in 1934, the model was listed in Bassett-Lowke's Catalog for November 1937 at £4 10s 0d (£4.50, $6.39) with a clockwork motor, £5 5s 0d (£5.25, $7.45) with an 8-volt DC electric motor, and £6 6s 0d (£6.30, $8.95) with a 20-volt AC electric motor. This is a particularly attractive locomotive— note especially the smoke-deflectors at either side of the firebox—and is very popular with collectors. Scarce.

1 Gauge "0" Passenger Brake Van by Gebrüder Bing, Nuremburg, Germany, dating from the famous company's final years in production, c1930-34. It is of close-coupled bogie type, with opening doors, and has a simulated teak finish in the contemporary livery of Britain's LNER (London and North Eastern Railway). It could be purchased separately or as part of a complete train set.

2 Gauge "0" First/Third Class Passenger Bogie Coach by Bing, an earlier version of the item of rolling stock shown at (1), with non-automatic couplings, dating from c1925-30. Again with simulated teak finish, in LNER livery, and with opening doors.

3 Gauge "0" 4-4-0 Freelance Tank Locomotive, produced in c1912-20 by Bing for the British firm of Bassett-Lowke Limited, and offered for sale in the latter's catalogs of the period. This clockwork locomotive is finished in Midland Railway maroon livery and was available also in other liveries. The forward/reverse gears and the brake can be operated by push-pull levers in the cab (note the large control knobs) or from the track, where pickups beneath the locomotive are triggered by hand-operated levers on special rail sections. Note that this example is shown on three such sections, with the levers clearly visible. The locomotive shown has undergone some restoration. Limited.

4 Gauge "0" 4-2-2 Midland Express Locomotive and Six-Wheeled Tender, numbered "650", made by Bing in 1920 for sale in Britain by Bassett-Lowke—at a price then of £2 2s 0d (£2.10, $2.98). This clockwork locomotive has forward and reverse gears operated from cab or track—see note at (3)—and solid front bogie wheels. Note that it has single driving wheels: at the time of production this system was obsolescent, and this may therefore be described as a somewhat retrospective model. Scarce.

5 Gauge "0" Number 1 Rotary Tipping Wagon, with "Sir Robert McAlpine & Sons" (construction company) transfers, by Hornby, Britain, dating from c1930. It was available in other finishes. Note that the chassis and couplings are of early type: link couplings, as seen here, were replaced on Hornby models in the 1930s by automatic couplings, which allowed shunting operations to take place.

6 Gauge "0" Number 2 Hydraulic Buffer Stops by Hornby, dating from before World War II. Note the long-travel spring-loaded mechanism.

7 Gauge "0" 4-4-0 "George the Fifth" Locomotive and Six-Wheeled Tender, numbered "5320", made by Bing in the 1920s for marketing in Britain by Bassett-Lowke (whose address is marked on the rear of the tender). This clockwork locomotive is finished in Midland Railway maroon livery: it was also available (and is more commonly encountered) in the black livery of the LNWR (London & North-Western Railway) and the green livery of the GWR (Great Western

Railway). The forward/reverse mechanism operates from the track or the cab (the third lever visible in the cab is for self-starting on the track). This was a popular model in the 1920s and is relatively common.

8 Gauge "0" Number 1 0-4-0 Tank Locomotive (note that the number on the tank is that of the wheel configuration) by Hornby, listed in the company's 1927-28 Catalog. Finished in LNER green, this clockwork locomotive was available also in LNER black or LMS (London, Midland and Scottish) maroon. It has cab-operated forward and reverse mechanism. Driven only by the front pair of wheels, this is an early example of its type, but is still fairly common.

9 Gauge "0" Railway Bridge/Viaduct by Bing, dating from the 1920s.

Note that two central sections and one end section are shown here: it was normally sold — at a price in Britain of 4s 3d (21½p, 31c) — together with one central section and two end sections.

Gauge "0" Number 2 Signal Gantry, "Home" or "Distant", made by Hornby during the 1930s and priced at 11s 6d (57½p, 82c) in the firm's 1938-39 Catalog. It has lever-operated signals (it was also available in an electric version) and detail includes an access ladder, diecast lamps, and celluloid warning panels. The largest of the Hornby signal accessories, it was intended for use, as shown, with double track. It is seen here with the Hornby "Flying Scotsman" (electric model, on clockwork track).

1 Gauge "0" Cement Wagon by Hornby, Great Britain, dating from the 1920s. The underframe is of the type made in the early pre-World War II period, with voided (ie, cut-out) detail of springs: on the later type, as shown at (2), this detail is in pressed tin. Note also that the earlier type has a somewhat shorter wheelbase. The wheels are nickel-plated—another feature of the earlier type. As shown, it has a hinged door in the roof. This wagon was also available with the lettering of the various British regional railway companies.
2 Gauge "0" Number 1 Side Tipping Wagon by Hornby, with a chassis of the late 1930s type—see note at (1). It is designed to tip to either side of the track. The wagon was available with "Robert Hudson Ltd"

transfers, or transfers for the McAlpine construction company.
3 Gauge "0" Pullman Bogie Coach by Bing, Germany, dating from the 1930s. It features opening doors, corridor connections, and an interior fitted with bench seats and tables. Dummy gas cylinders (coaches at that time were still gas-lit) are fitted to the underbody. It was sold in Britain by Bond's, Euston Road, London, at a price of 9s 6d (47½p, 67c) in 1934.
4 Gauge "0" 0-6-0 Six-Coupled Goods Locomotive and Six-Wheeled Tender, numbered "773", by Bing, Germany, dating from the 1930s. It is finished in Southern Railway green livery. The central pair of driving wheels on the clockwork-powered locomotive is unflanged, to allow it to negotiate

tight curves on the track. It is fitted with reversing mechanism and with a brake operated from the cab or track. This item was offered at a "special price" of £1 8s 6d (£1.42½p, $2.02) in Bond's 1934 Catalog, where it was stated that the locomotive "like its prototype will haul great loads . . . the mechanism is particularly powerful with new ⅝" [16mm] wide spring and wide cut gearing". Limited.
5 Gauge "0" Number 2 Level Crossing by Hornby, produced only in the pre-World War II period. As shown, this grade crossing is for use with clockwork double track: it was also produced with electric track and lighting.
6 Gauge "0" Platelayers Hut by Hornby, dating from c1930. This tinplate lineside accessory, priced

at 1s 2d (6p, 9c) in the 1938 Catalog, was popular and is therefore still fairly common.
7 Gauge "0" 0-4-0 Number 1 Tank Locomotive by Hornby, available in c1930 in Britain at a price of 15s 0d (75p, $1.06). Finished in LNER (London and North Eastern Railway) black livery and numbered "623", the clockwork locomotive is fitted with reversing gear and a brake. Note that a connecting rod is missing from the example shown and that it has fixed headlights; detachable lamps were fitted to later models. An earlier version of this model is shown at (8) on pages 38-39: compare, and note that the one shown here has oval buffers, while those of the earlier model are round, and that the earlier model has no headlamps.

This locomotive is shown on Hornby PPL2 Parallel Points (Left Hand), used to change the circuit from single to double track.

8 Gauge "0" Number 2 Special 4-4-2 Tank Locomotive by Hornby, numbered "2221", dating from c1935-40. The mechanism is four-coupled (ie, the clockwork drives the front pair of wheels, which in turn drive the rear wheels via connecting rods) and has forward and reverse gears operated from the cab or the track.

9 Gauge "0" 0-4-0 Locomotive and Four-Wheeled Tender, numbered "8851", made by Bing, Germany, for sale in Britain and available there at a price of 8s 6d (42½p, 60c) in 1929. Automatic couplings are fitted front and rear; the reverse gear of the clockwork mechanism

can be operated only from the cab, but the brake can be operated from both cab and track. This example is in LNER green livery.

10-11 Gauge "0" First Class Four-Wheeled Coaches by Bing, dating from the 1920s. With imitation teak finish, these coaches in LNER livery form part of a set with the locomotive shown at (9). The locomotive and tender, coaches, and eight curved rails to form a circuit, were sold in Britain in 1929 at an inclusive price of 16s 9d (84p, $1.19).

(Left) Number 5 Railway Accessories, Gradient and Mileposts, by Hornby, 1930s; tinplate, with original box. (Right) Gauge "1" (also used with Gauge "0") Station Staff by Crescent, Britain, c1950; diecast, with original box.

1 Gauge "0" 4-4-0 "Prince Charles" Locomotive and Six-Wheeled Tender, made by Bassett-Lowke Limited, Northampton, England, and dating from the early 1950s (ie, not long after the birth of the Prince of Wales, whose name it bears). This clockwork locomotive is finished in British Railways blue livery and is numbered "62078"; the model is more frequently to be found in British Railways green livery and numbered "62453". Made in both clockwork and electric versions, this was one of Bassett-Lowke's more basic models of the period (although still of a standard befitting the firm's reputation) and may still be obtained relatively inexpensively.

2 Gauge "0" Electric BO-BO Locomotive, numbered "BB-8051", by Hornby, France, dating from the post-World War II period. ("BO-BO" refers to the wheel configuration and signifies that the locomotive has two bogies, each with four wheels.) Note the overhead pantograph pickups and the automatic couplings at either end. The locomotive is finished in the livery of the SCNF (Société Nationale des Chemins de Fer Français; French National Railways). This is a product of the Meccano factory at Bobigny, France; during the period after World War II the Bobigny factory produced a range of locomotives independent of its British parent, and continued to make electric Gauge "0" locomotives at a time when the British company was producing Gauge "0" locomotives in clockwork only.

3 Gauge "0" Electric Locomotive, numbered "212", made by Buco, Switzerland, and dating from the period after World War II. The Buco company began production during the later war years and, Switzerland being a neutral country, gained some commercial advantage from the eclipse of German manufacturers. It continued to produce a good range of continental-type locomotives—like the example shown here, with its typical overhead pantograph pickups—and rolling stock until the mid-1950s.

4 Gauge "0" Metropolitan Locomotive by Hornby, Great Britain, dating from the 1920s. This is modeled on the locomotives then in use by the Metropolitan Railway, an electrified line serving London and its suburbs; note the lights fitted to the locomotive (and also to the coaches, which are not shown here), since part of the real line ran underground. This model has a concealed four-wheel mechanism, whereas the real locomotive had eight wheels. A reversing gear is fitted. It was available either clockwork-powered (later models only) or driven by a 4-volt, 6-volt, or (again later) 20-volt electric motor. The example shown is something of an oddity: originally electric, it has been refitted by an owner with a clockwork mechanism. The lights are powered by a battery, as was standard on the maker's clockwork version. This model was first announced in the issue of "Meccano Magazine" for December 1925, as an electric version to run on a 100/240 volt system; ie,

running directly from an AC or DC mains supply, with the aid of a rheostat with an adapter which transformed the current to the correct pressure by means of a 60-watt bulb. It was originally a very expensive item, priced at £5 10s 0d (£5.50, $7.81) for the set — comprising locomotive, two passenger coaches, rails for a 4-foot (1·22m) diameter circle, rheostat and adapter — or at £2 12s 6d (£2.62½, $3.73) for the locomotive alone, but the prices became lower as the model appeared in its various forms until the later 1930s. Limited.

5 Gauge "0" Viaduct (Electric) by Hornby, dating from the 1930s. It was priced at 8s 0d (40p, 57c) in 1935; the central section alone cost 5s 0d (25p, 35c).

6 Gauge "0" 0-6-0 Standard Tank Locomotive, numbered "68211" on cab and firebox, by Bassett-Lowke, Britain, dating from after World War II. This model was available in both electric (as shown here) and clockwork versions; its six-coupled mechanism incorporates a non-flanged central pair of wheels to facilitate the negotiation of tight bends on the track. Although a post-World War II example finished in British Railways black livery is shown, this well-detailed and popular model was also produced in the 1930s in the liveries of the contemporary British regional railway companies.

7 Gauge "0" Number 2 Special Pullman Composite Coach by Hornby, dating from the 1930s. This example is named, in the Pullman tradition, "Arcadia". Note the Mansell-type wheels; ie, solid cast metal wheels, as opposed to the hollow-pressed metal wheels more often fitted to rolling stock. Mansell-type wheels, which were claimed to be smoother-running and quieter in operation, were standard on Pullman cars; they were available as separate items — at a price of 3d (1½p, 2c) per pair in 1938 — for fitting to other rolling stock. The very pleasing detail of this car includes opening doors, roof ventilators, and celluloid windows with printed lamps; provision is made for corridor connections with other cars.

8 Gauge "0" Number 1 Water Tank (available also in a larger, Number 2, version) by Hornby. This accessory was produced both before and after World War II: the colors of the example shown indicate that it is a post-War version, when the red and green finish was standard. As seen, it incorporates a flexible filler tube and a chain-operated release valve.

9 Gauge "0" Trolley Wagon by Hornby; a model produced only before World War II and priced at 4s 0d (20p, 28c) in the 1938 Catalog. Note the bogie wheels and automatic couplings. It was also available complete with cable drums, in that case priced at 4s 6d (22½p, 32c) in the 1938 Catalog.

10 Gauge "0" PPR2 Parallel Points (Right Hand) by Hornby, made only in the period before World War II. This item was also available in an electric version, with a central rail for the current.

1. Gauge "0" 0-4-0 Type 501 Locomotive and Tender by Hornby, numbered "1842" and finished in LNER (London and North Eastern Railway) green livery. The clockwork reversing mechanism and brake operate from both track and cab. This popular, lower-priced, model was produced throughout the 1930s and appeared again after World War II. An early post-war model is shown, dating from before the nationalization of British railway companies in 1948; the model was later made in British Railways livery.

2. Gauge "0" Number 4 Railway Station in tinplate by Hornby, offered in the 1939 Catalog at a price of 10s 6d (52½p, 75c), or at 11s 9d (59p, 84c) with electric lighting. The example shown has slot-together platform extensions with the station name "Ripon"; these could also be purchased with the names "Margate", "Wembley", or "Reading". Note the lithographed exterior details and the ticket-office barrier. Length: 33in (84cm).

3. Gauge "0" Number 3 Platform Accessory: Fire Box, in tinplate, by Hornby, dating from the 1930s.

4. Gauge "0" Number 3 Platform Accessory: Station Seat, in tinplate, by Hornby, dating from the 1930s. See also (7).

5. Gauge "0" Number 3 Platform Accessory: Chocolate Machine, in tinplate, by Hornby, dating from the 1930s.

6. Gauge "0" Number 3 Platform Accessory: Naming Machine, in tinplate, by Hornby, dating from the 1930s. (In the real machine, a coin was inserted and the pointer moved to the desired letters in sequence; a lever was pressed for each letter, to a maximum of c12, and as the end-product the patron received a metal strip stamped with the selected name or message.)

7. Station Seat; as (4).

8. Gauge "0" 0-4-0 Type 101 Tank Locomotive, numbered "2270", by Hornby. This clockwork model was available both before and after World War II: an early post-war example, finished in LMS (London, Midland, & Scottish Railway) maroon livery, is shown here. The control rods for the forward/reverse mechanism and brake protrude from the cab. On post-War models, only the brake can also be operated from the track; on pre-War models, both brake and forward/reverse will operate thus. The finish of pre-War models is also superior, with a tinplate fairing beneath the rear of the cab, a brass hand rail, and additional details on the locomotive's firebox.

9. Gauge "0" Number 1 Lumber Wagon by Hornby, finished with LNER motif. This wagon was available both before and after World War II: a pre-war example, with an early-type underframe and non-automatic couplings (one of which is missing from this item), is shown.

10. Gauge "0" 4-4-2 "Flying Scotsman" Locomotive and Tender by Hornby, numbered "4472" and finished in LNER green livery. This electric-powered model (confirmed as such by the bulb in the center of the fire-box) ran on track with a

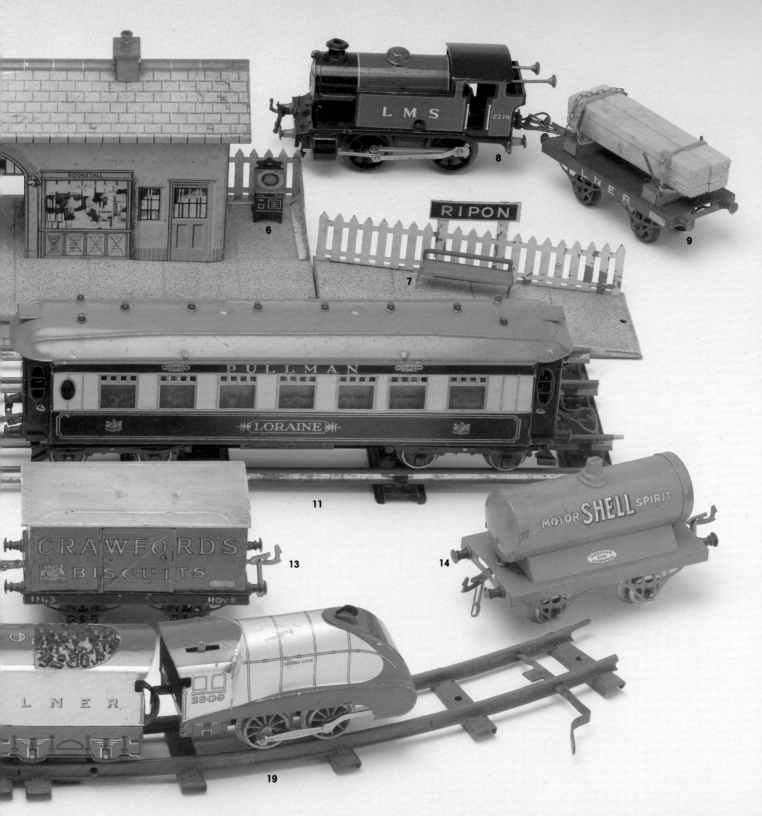

center-rail pickup. The example shown is 20-volt electric; it was available also in 6-volt electric and in clockwork. It was produced only before World War II (the earlier electric models having slightly smaller driving wheels) and was offered at a price of £1 12s 6d (£1.62½p, $2.31) in 1939. Compare this model with the more realistic (and much more expensive) version also produced in the 1930s by Bassett-Lowke, shown at (8) on *pages 46-47*.

11 Gauge "0" Number 2 Pullman Coach by Hornby: the most expensive of the Hornby coaches, priced at 13s 6d (67½p, 96c) in 1939, and produced only before World War II. Like all Pullmans, it is named; in this case "Loraine", but bogie coaches of this type were

available with other names and also as brake composites. It has Mansell-type wheels and is designed to take corridor connections; detail includes opening doors and celluloid windows with printed lamps.

12 Gauge "0" Number 1 Milk Traffic Van by Hornby; also available as Number 0 Milk Traffic Van, without the sliding doors of this example. Milk cans to fit within the van were available. The example shown has underframe and couplings of the early type and dates from before World War II.

13 Gauge "0" Biscuit Van, with "Crawford's Biscuits" advertising, by Hornby. This example features opening doors, hinged and with handles; later production models have sliding doors. Also, on the

example shown, an attempt has been made to paint out the "Hornby Series" label and the legends "1143" and "Hove" have been applied to the chassis, no doubt by an owner seeking to add realism to his layout. This van was produced only before World War II, and is now scarce.

14 Gauge "0" Petrol Tank Wagon for "Shell", by Hornby. The cutaway underframe and nickel-plated wheels distinguish this example as being rolling stock of early pre-World War II type.

15 Gauge "0" Number 2 Buffer Stops by Hornby; hydraulic type, with sprung buffers. These appeared in the Catalog at a price of 4s 11d (24½p, 35c) in 1939.

16 Gauge "0" Fiber Wagon (shown without load) by Hornby. This

example clearly illustrates the late-pattern underframe, with slots to accommodate the axle boxes; a pre-World War II feature. As shown, however, no axle boxes are fitted and the slots are therefore superfluous; this is a usual feature of pre-War rolling stock with this type of underframe.

17-19 Hornby Gauge "0" Number 0 0-4-0 "Silver Link" Streamlined Locomotive with Tender (19), numbered "2509", with "Silver Jubilee" Articulated Coach (17-18), numbered "1584" and "1585". This low-priced clockwork toy was sold as a set; the locomotive, non-reversing and with a brake lever protruding through the cab roof, was available as a separate item at a price of 3s 6d (17½p, 24c) in c1935-40. Limited.

1

2

3

7

(Below) Underside of the Gauge "0" 4-6-2 "Flying Scotsman" Locomotive and Tender by Bassett-Lowke, shown at (8). Note particularly the "spoon" pickups, for the electric motor to receive power from the center rail of the three-rail track, and the non-flanged central pair of wheels.

1 Gauge "0" 4-4-2 Number 2 Special Tank Locomotive, numbered "6954", by Hornby, Great Britain, dating from the 1930s—it was offered at a price of £1 1s 0d (£1.05, $1.49) in the 1938-39 Hornby Catalog—and not available after World War II. It has a four-coupled clockwork reversing mechanism and brake controlled from the cab (note protruding control rods) or track; an automatic coupling is fitted at the rear. The example shown is in LMS (London, Midland & Scottish Railway) livery; it was also available in the liveries of the other British regional railroad companies of the pre-War period.

2 Gauge "0" Number 2 Saloon Bogie Coach by Hornby, availabe in the 1920s and 1930s and priced

at 10s 6d (52½p, 75c) in the 1938-39 Catalog. This bogie coach, unsuited to operation on a one-foot radius curved track, is provided with corridor connections and has opening doors and celluloid windows with painted lamps. This example is in LMS livery; it was also available in LNER (London and North Eastern Railway) livery.

3 Gauge "0" 4-4-2 Number 2 Special Tank Locomotive by Hornby; as (1), but finished in the green livery of Southern (Railway). Note the aperture for the key, apparent in this left-side view of the clockwork locomotive, and also the cracks in the rear driving wheel. The latter is an illustration of metal fatigue: replacement wheels for these Hornby locomotives

are currently available. This item was available either individually or as part of a set that also included (4) and (5).

4 Gauge "0" Number 2 First/Third Class Passenger Bogie Coach by Hornby, dating from the 1930s and priced at 7s 0d (35p, 50c) in the 1938-39 Catalog. Finished in Southern Railway livery, the coach has Mansell-type wheels and a slide-off roof; printed detail includes windows and door-handles.

5 Gauge "0" Number 2 Passenger Bogie Coach, Brake/Third Composite, by Hornby, dating from the 1930s, when it was available as part of a set that also comprised (3) and (4). Like (4) it has Mansell-type wheels, a slide-off roof, and printed detail for doors and windows.

6 Gauge "0" Number COL2 Crossover Points, Two-Foot Radius, by Hornby; a left-hand set is shown, and these were sold as a pair with the right-hand set at a price in the 1932 Catalog (in which they constitute the most expensive item of clockwork track) of 12s 0d (60p, 85c). Hornby electric track is similar to the clockwork shown here, but has a center-rail for pickup. Note that double-track lengths are now more eagerly sought by collectors than single-track.

7 Gauge "0" 20-volt Electric 4-6-2 "Princess Elizabeth" Locomotive and Tender, numbered "6201" and finished in LMS livery, by Hornby. A prestige item, featured on the front of the 1938-39 Catalog issued by Hamley's, the

famous London toyshop, and priced therein at £5 5s (£5.25, $7.45), this was the finest and most expensive of the Hornby Gauge "0" locomotives, and was sold in a special presentation box. Advertisements featured approving comments by the engineer of the real "Princess Elizabeth", stressed the virtues of the electric motor, and recommended that the new drawn-steel track, with 3-foot (91cm) radius curves, should be used to permit maximum performance. This magnificent locomotive is now a very scarce and valuable collectors' item.

8 Gauge "0" 4-6-2 "Flying Scotsman" Locomotive and Tender by Bassett-Lowke Limited, Northampton, England. Introduced in 1933, and available in clockwork

or with electric motors of three different types (an electric version is shown here), this famous LNER (London and North Eastern Railway) locomotive was issued with three numbers: "4472", the pre-World War II number and the most common; "103", as shown; and "6103", the late version. Note the six-coupled mechanism, with non-flanged central wheels to facilitate the negotiation of curves in the track. Depending on its power unit, this model was on sale in 1937 at prices ranging from £4 4s 0d (£4.20, $5.96) to £4 13s 0d (£4.65, $6.60). Compare this expensive and accurately-detailed locomotive item with the cheaper, less realistic, Hornby "Flying Scotsman" that is shown at (10) on *pages 44-45.*

From around the mid-19th century, toy companies in the United States produced a wide range of locomotives and other railroad toys—as might be expected in a nation whose development was so profoundly affected by the railroads. In the early period, pull-along locomotives in cast iron (see examples on *pages 30-31*) were extremely popular, and these were followed by heavy gauge tinplate and clockwork trains, with electric-powered locomotives appearing early in the 20th century and entering their greatest period of popularity after World War I. As in other countries, the import of toys from Germany tended to slow the expansion of domestic manufacturers, especially before World War I, but in the representation of

indigenous locomotives the US makers were supreme (and were able, notably in the case of the Lionel Corporation, to establish an export market in Europe). Bearing in mind that the types of locomotives developed in America often differed considerably from those of Europe, this is perhaps hardly surprising. American-made toy trains—including the examples shown here, which date from a comparatively recent period—will naturally be more easily found by collectors in the United States than elsewhere, and it may be assumed that all the items shown here will rank as "scarce" or "limited" for collectors in Europe.

All the trains shown on this spread were photographed at the London Toy & Model Museum.

1-3 Gauge "0" "Flying Yankee" Diesel Train Set by the Lionel Corporation, New York, dating from around 1935. Well made and most strikingly finished in chrome and silver paint, this futuristically designed electric train set consisted in all of six units, of which three are shown here: the Locomotive (3), one Car (2), and the Passenger/Brake Car (1). Details are shown at (4) and (5). The Lionel company was founded in 1901 by Joshua Lionel Cowen and almost immediately began production of electric trams in various gauges. The first Lionel train set appeared around 1908 and, after c1920, Gauge "0" took first place in the company's output.
4 Inter-connecting Bogie Units from the Lionel "Flying Yankee" shown

at (1-3). The knobs on the tops of the units operate spring-loaded retainers which engage with the ends of the car units. In the 1930s, Hornby of Britain used bogie units to connect cars in this way in some Hornby Dublo models—but only between pairs of cars, not to interconnect a whole row of them.
5 Car Section from the Lionel "Flying Yankee"; note celluloid windows and chromed door rails.
6 Gauge "0" "American Flyer Line" 0-4-0 Locomotive and Four-Wheeled Tender by the American Flyer company, dating from the 1920s. The clockwork-powered locomotive, with a cow-catcher and cast boiler detail, is of cast iron finished in enamel: the weight of its body serves to give increased

traction. The tender is tinplate, with
lithographed finish. Locomotives of
this type were made by Ives before
the company's takeover by
American Flyer, Hafner, and Lionel
in the late 1920s.

7 Gauge "0" "American Flyer Line"
Bogie Baggage Car, complementary to the locomotive shown
at (6) and of the same date. It is of
tinplate construction, with attractive
lithographed detail, and also
features sliding doors.

8-9 Gauge "0" "Santa Fe" Diesel
Locomotive and Matching Unit by
Marx, New York, dating from
around 1940. Note that although
the two units appear to be identical,
only one has an electric motor: in
operation, the two are intended to
form the front and back of the train,
separated by rolling stock, the

unpowered unit being pulled or
pushed as required. They are of
tinplate construction, with details in
pressed tin and lithography; note
the electric headlights on the cab
fronts. Louis Marx and Company,
manufacturing also in Great Britain
from the early 1930s, was one of
the world's largest toy-making
concerns in the 1930s and 1940s.

10-11 Gauge "0" Diesel Locomotive
(11) and one of the two Cars (10)
making up the "Union Pacific"
"City of Portland" set by Lionel,
dating from around 1935. Note
that this electric train set utilizes
inter-connecting bogie units—see
the example shown at (4)—similar
to those used in the Lionel "Flying
Yankee" set shown at (1-3). It is of
heavy pressed-tin and diecast
construction; detail on the raised

cab of the locomotive includes an
electric headlamp, six exhaust
stubs on the roof, and a slatted
grille on the streamlined apron that
takes the place of the cow-catcher
seen on earlier US locomotives.

12 Gauge "0" 0-4-0 "N.Y.C. & H.R."
Electric Locomotive, numbered
"3253" and with the additional
transfer "The Ives Railway Lines",
by Ives, Connecticut, dating from
the early 1920s. This is a late
example of the output of a famous
American maker: Ives produced
steam- and clockwork-powered
floor trains from the 1880s onward
and Gauge "0" sets from 1901,
eventually being swallowed up by
the Lionel Corporation in 1930.
The electric-powered locomotive
shown here is of heavy tinplate
construction, finished in enamel

with hand-lined windows, and is a
well-detailed model of an
American urban line locomotive.

13-14 Gauge "0" Bogie Coach
"Saratoga" (13), numbered
"No.129", and Bogie "Buffet" Car
(14), numbered "No.130", "The
Ives Railway Lines"; like the locomotive shown at (12), by Ives,
early 1920s. Note the attractive
lithographed detail of these
tinplate coaches.

15 Platform Clock with movable
hands; a large-gauge tinplate
accessory by an unidentified
American maker, dating from the
1930s. Height: 7in (178mm).

16 Grade Crossing Alarm, with electrically-operated warning bell; a
large-gauge tinplate accessory by
an American maker, dating from
the 1930s. Height: 9in (229mm).

Among the items of rolling stock illustrated here and on the following pages, where the Hornby Dublo range is shown, are several items of plastic or part-plastic fabrication. In most cases these represent a continuation of the tinplate and diecast ranges. Note that although all items are shown on three-rail track, some are properly suited only to two-rail track.

1 Gauge "00" Goods Brake Van, numbered "B950350" (and, like other items shown on this spread, with further identification letters and/or numbers); Hornby Catalog Number 4311, issued in various forms in c1959-64. Available in brown, as shown, or gray, with automatic couplings, this is a later, plastic, item.

2 Gauge "00" Gunpowder Van, numbered "B887002"; Hornby Catalog Number 4313, dating from the early 1960s. Again, a later item of plastic construction, with automatic couplings and in the standard finish.

3 Gauge "00" "Bogie Bolster" Wagon, numbered "M 720550"; Hornby Series D1, c1953-56. A diecast item.

4 Gauge "00" Bogie Tank Wagon, numbered "5710" and with "ICI" (Imperial Chemical Industries) markings; Hornby Catalog Number 4685, early 1960s.

5 Gauge "00" Low-Sided Wagon, with wooden "Liverpool Cables" drums; Hornby Series D1, c1954-58. A diecast item.

6 Gauge "00" Insulated Meat Container, for use with Low-Sided Wagon (5); dating from the 1950s; wood with printed paper covering.

7 Gauge "00" 2-6-4 Tank Locomotive, numbered "80033"; Hornby Catalog Number 2218, c1959-64. Note the well-detailed valve gear on this two-rail electric locomotive, which was available only in British Railways black livery.

8 Gauge "00" 2-8-0 Heavy Goods Locomotive and Tender, numbered "48073"; Hornby Catalog Number 2224, issued c1960-64. Note that the forward-central pair of wheels on this two-rail electric model is non-flanged.

9 Gauge "00" Breakdown Crane "No 133"; Hornby Catalog Number 4620, c1959-64. Of diecast construction, with metal couplings, the crane has an operating jib; it is shown complete with the small trucks (cars) carrying its outriggers and the larger wagon which accommodates the jib when the crane is traveling.

10 Gauge "00" Six-Wheeled Passenger Brake Van, numbered "M32958"; Hornby Catalog Number 4076, early 1960s; with tinplate body and plastic roof.

11 Gauge "00" 0-6-0 Diesel Shunting Locomotive, numbered "D3302"; Hornby Catalog Number 2231, c1960-65. Note the single connecting rod on this two-rail electric model, in British Railways green.

12 Gauge "00" "Saxa Salt" Wagon; Hornby Catalog Number 4465, early 1960s. This item has a plastic body and metal couplings.

13 Gauge "00" Ventilated Van, numbered "B757051"; Hornby Catalog Number 4325, c1960;

plastic, with metal couplings.

14 Gauge "00" Pullman Coach, Brake/Second Class, "Car No 79"; Hornby Catalog Number 4037, early 1960s. An all-plastic item with detailed interior.

15 Gauge "00" Pullman Coach, Second Class, "Car No 74";

Gauge "00" Three-Rail Electric Rails for Hornby Dublo. Top to bottom, left to right: EDA½, curved half rail; ED1A, curved rail; EDA2, large radius curved rail; EDCR, diamond crossing, right hand; ISPL, isolating switch points, left hand; ISPR, isolating switch points, right hand; IBR¼, isolating rail; UBR, uncoupling rail; EDBS, short straight; EDB1¼ straight quarter rail; EDB1½, straight half rail; EDB1, straight rail.

16 Gauge "00" 4-6-2 "Golden Fleece" Streamlined Locomotive and Eight-Wheeled Tender, numbered "60030"; Hornby Catalog Number 2211, c1959-61. Two-rail electric locomotive.

17 Gauge "00" Corridor Coach, Brake/Second Class, numbered "E35173"; Hornby Catalog Number 4053, early 1960s; tinplate and plastic.

18 Gauge "00" Corridor Coach, First/Second Class, numbered "E15770"; Hornby Catalog Number 4052, other details as (17).

19 Gauge "00" 4-6-2 "City of London" Locomotive and Six-Wheeled Tender, numbered "46245"; Hornby Catalog Number 2226. Two-rail locomotive, c1959-60.

Hornby Catalog Number 4036, other details as (14).

20 Gauge "00" Mineral Wagon, numbered "B550200"; Hornby Catalog Number 4656, c1962-65. A plastic item.

21 Gauge "00" Open Wagon; Hornby Catalog Number 4660, c1958-62. A plastic item.

22 Ford Prefect; Dublo Dinky Toys Number 061, c1958-60. This range of diecast vehicles was introduced in the Catalog for December 1957. Length: 2·28in (58mm).

23 Volkswagen Delivery Van; Dublo Dinky Toys Number 071, c1960-65. Length: 2·13in (54mm).

24 Royal Mail Van; Dublo Dinky Toys Number 068, 1959-64. Length: 1·89in (48mm).

25 Bedford Articulated Flat Truck; Dublo Dinky Toys Number 072, 1959-64. Overall length: 4·57in (116mm).

Gauge "00" Trains by Hornby Dublo, Britain, 1950s-1960s

Reference should be made to the introductory note on *pages 50-51*.

1 Gauge "00" "Power Petrol" Tank Wagon; Hornby Series D1, *c*1953-59. This wagon has a tinplate tank and a diecast chassis.

2 Gauge "00" "ICI" (Imperial Chemical Industries) Chloride Tank Wagon; Hornby Catalog Number 4675, 1960-64. It has a plastic tank and a diecast chassis.

3 Gauge "00" "Esso" Fuel Oil Tank Wagon, with "Esso Petroleum Company Limited" transfer; Hornby Catalog Number 4680, 1959-64. The tank is tinplate; the chassis is diecast.

4 Gauge "00" "Mobil" Tank Wagon; Hornby Catalog Number 4677, 1957-64. The tank is tinplate; the chassis is diecast.

5 Gauge "00" "Traffic Services Ltd" Tank Wagon (based on a wagon used to carry chemicals to Europe; note the additional small transfer "No Naked Light"); Hornby Catalog Number 4679, 1960-64.

6 Gauge "00" 2-8-0 Freight Locomotive and Six-Wheeled Tender, numbered "48109" and finished in British Railways black livery; Hornby Catalog Number 2225, 1959. This two-rail electric model has its two central pairs of wheels non-flanged, to facilitate the negotiation of tight curves on the track. Note particularly that on all two-rail electric models in the Dublo range the bogie (truck) wheels of locomotives and the wheels of tenders and other rolling stock are made of plastic. Price in 1959: £4 1s 6d (£4.07½, $5.79).

7 Gauge "00" Restaurant Car; Hornby Catalog Number 4049, *c*1959-61. In British Railways livery, this coach has a tinplate body, a plastic roof, and perspex windows. Note the basic interior detail.

8 Gauge "00" First Class Sleeping Car, numbered "W2402"; Hornby Catalog Number 4078, 1961-64. Again in British Railways livery and with a plastic roof.

9 Gauge "00" First Class Coach, numbered "M3002"; Hornby Catalog Number 4062, 1962-64. In British Railways livery, with a plastic roof and perspex windows.

10 Gauge "00" Passenger Brake Van, numbered "E81312"; Hornby Catalog Number 4075, 1960-64. In British Railways livery, this van has a plastic roof and perspex windows.

11 Gauge "00" British Railways Pullman Coach, named "Aries"; Hornby Catalog Number 4035, 1961-64. This car has a plastic body, a well-detailed plastic roof, perspex windows, and interior detail of tables, seats, and lamps.

12 Gauge "00" 4-6-2 Locomotive (with nameplate "Dorchester", surmounted by that British city's coat of arms), numbered "34042", and Six-Wheeled Tender; Hornby Catalog Number 3235, 1961-63. A three-rail electric model in British Railways green livery; the locomotive is diecast.

13 Gauge "00" British Railways Suburban Coach, Brake/Third Class; Hornby Catalog Number D14, 1956-57. The body, which has lithographed detail, and roof are tinplate; windows are perspex.

14 Gauge "00" 0-6-0 Tank Locomotive, numbered "31337";
Hornby Catalog Number 2206,
1961-64. This is a two-rail electric
model finished in British Railways
black livery.

15 Gauge "00" Deltic Diesel-Electric
CO-CO Locomotive, numbered
"D9012" and named "Crepello"
(after a famous racehorse); Hornby
Catalog Number 2234, 1962-64.
The designation "CO-CO" refers
to the wheel configuration and
signifies that the locomotive has six
wheels on each bogie. Finished in
British Railways green livery.

16 Gauge "00" 1000BHP Diesel-
Electric BO-BO (ie, with four wheels
on each bogie) Locomotive,
numbered "D8017"; Hornby
Catalog Number 2230, 1959-62.
Two-rail electric model.

17 Gauge "00" "Prestflo" Bulk Cement
Wagon; Hornby Catalog
Number 4626, 1961-64. The body
is plastic.

18 Gauge "00" Southern Suburban
Brake/Second Class Coach,
numbered "S43374"; Hornby
Catalog Number 4026, 1959-64.
The body is tinplate and the
windows perspex.

19 Gauge "00" Southern Suburban
First/Second Class Coach,
numbered "S41060"; Hornby
Catalog Number 4025, 1959-64.
Again, with a tinplate body and
perspex windows.

20 Gauge "00" Diesel-Electric CO-BO
(ie, with six wheels on the front
bogie and four wheels on the rear
bogie) Locomotive, numbered
"D5702"; Hornby Catalog
Number 2233, 1961-63. This two-

rail electric model is finished in
British Railways green livery.

21 Gauge "00" Passenger Fruit Van,
numbered "W2910" and with
further identification markings;
Hornby Catalog Number 4305,
1960-64. The body of this van is
made of plastic.

22 Gauge "00" Horse Box, numbered
"S96412"; Hornby Catalog
Number 4316, c1961-64. With a
well-detailed plastic body, featuring
opening half-doors and a hinge-
down ramp, this item is finished
in the green livery of Southern
Region, British Railways. It was
sold complete with a plastic horse
(not shown here).

23 Gauge "00" Utility Van, numbered
"S2380S"; Hornby Catalog
Number 4323, 1961-64. Again,
with a plastic body finished in

British Railways Southern Region
green livery.

24 Commer Van; Dublo Dinky Toys
Number 063, 1958. This and the
following items are from the range
of vehicles in the Hornby Dublo
scale, first introduced in the 1957
Catalog. This example was
priced at 1s 9d (9p, 13c) in 1958.
Length: 2·125in (54mm).

25 Austin Lorry; Dublo Dinky Toys
Number 064, 1957-62. Length:
2·5in (63·5mm).

26 Austin Taxi; Dublo Dinky Toys
Number 067, introduced in March
1959 — when it was one of the more
expensive models in the range.
Length: 2·375in (60mm).

27 Morris Pick-Up; Dublo Dinky Toys
Number 065, 1957-60. This was
one of the first models in the range.
Length: 2·125in (54mm).

Reference should be made to the introductory note on *pages 50-51*.

1 Gauge "00" Corridor Coach, First/Second Class, numbered "W15870"; Hornby Catalog Number 4050, issued *c*1960-64. This coach has a tinplate body finished in British Railways livery, perspex windows (through which the basic interior detail can be seen), and a plastic roof.

2 Gauge "00" Restaurant Car, numbered "W 1910"; Hornby Catalog Number 4070, mid-1960s. All other details are as (1).

3 Gauge "00" Second Class Coach, numbered "W3984"; Hornby Catalog Number 4061, early 1960s. All other details are as (1).

4 Gauge "00" Corridor Coach, Brake/Second Class, numbered "34290"; Hornby Catalog Number 4051, early 1960s. Again with a tinplate body, plastic roof, and perspex windows.

5 Gauge "00" 4-6-0 "Cardiff Castle" Locomotive and Six-Wheeled Tender, numbered "4075"; Hornby Catalog Number 2221, *c*1960-64. This two-rail electric model is finished in the green livery of Western Region (British Railways). This locomotive was first issued in a three-rail electric version in the later 1950s and was then named "Bristol Castle". Because the tender incorporated spring-loaded pickups for the three-rail track (rather than having spoon-type pickups attached to the motor of the locomotive itself, as in earlier models), it was permanently connected to the locomotive.

6 Gauge "00" Driving Trailer Coach, numbered "S. 77511"; Hornby Catalog Number 4150, *c*1962-64. This is a two-rail electric model (note that although it is not itself powered, it represents a powered coach) with a tinplate body finished in the green livery of Southern Region (British Railways). It has a plastic roof and perspex windows.

7 Gauge "00" Driving Unit, numbered "S.65326"; Hornby Catalog Number 2250, issued *c*1962-64 and complementary to the Driving Trailer Coach shown at (6), this Unit being the powered element.

8 Gauge "00" Through Station (ie, a way station, as opposed to a terminus); Hornby Series D1, issued in the 1950s. This is of diecast metal construction: three pieces are shown—the central section, with the station building, and two end ramps—and further sections were available.

9 Gauge "00" "Esso Royal Daylight" Tank Wagon; Hornby Series D1, issued in the mid-1950s. The tank is tinplate and the chassis diecast.

10 Gauge "00" "Shell Lubricating Oil" Tank Wagon; Hornby Series D1, *c*1953-59. The tank is tinplate and the chassis diecast.

11 Gauge "00" "Power Ethyl" Tank Wagon, with trademark transfer; Hornby Series D1, *c*1953-54. Tinplate tank, diecast chassis.

12 Gauge "00" "Esso" Tank Wagon; Hornby Series D1, *c*1956-59. The tank is tinplate and the chassis diecast.

13 Gauge "00" "Royal Daylight" Tank Wagon; Hornby Series D1, issued

in the early 1950s. This example is slightly earlier than the similar model shown at (9) but, like that wagon, has a tinplate tank and diecast chassis.

14 Gauge "00" 0-6-2 Tank Locomotive, numbered "69550"; Hornby Catalog Number 2217. This example of a popular model, finished in British Railways black livery and intended for two-rail electric operation, dates from c1959-64, but the casting dates from before World War II.

15 Gauge "00" 4-6-2 "Canadian Pacific" Locomotive and Six-Wheeled Tender, numbered "1215"; Hornby Catalog Number EDL2, dating from c1958. Note that this three-rail electric model (with one spoon-type pickup just visible here between the second

and third pair of driving wheels) is based on the same casting as that used for the "Duchess of Montrose" locomotive (Hornby Catalog Number EDL12, introduced in the early 1950s to replace "Duchess of Atholl"), but with the smoke deflectors that featured on the British locomotive removed, with a cow-catcher replacing the front buffers, and with the addition of a headlight. This "Canadian Pacific" model was intended for the North American market; it is, in consequence, scarce in the United Kingdom and Europe.

16 Gauge "00" "Canadian Pacific" Caboose, numbered "437270"; Hornby Series D1, issued c1958 and complementary to (15). It is of tinplate construction and, again, is scarce outside North America.

17 Lancing Bagnell Platform Tractor and Trailer, with Driver; Dublo Dinky Toys Number 076, issued in 1960-64. This station accessory, like the vehicles shown on this spread, is from the range of vehicles and accessories in the Hornby Dublo scale first introduced in the 1957 Catalog. Length overall: 2·95in (75mm). Other station accessories in the Dublo Dinky Toys range included a Set of Six Passengers (Catalog Number 053) and a Set of Station Staff (Catalog Number 051).

18 Bedford Flat Truck; Dublo Dinky Toys Number 066, c1957-60. This was one of the first models issued in the Dublo Dinky range. Length: 4·2in (107mm).

19 AEC Mercury Tanker, with "Petroleum Products" and "Shell" and

"BP" trade-mark transfers; Dublo Dinky Toys Number 070, 1959-64. Length: 3·58in (91mm).

20 Land Rover and Horse Trailer; Dublo Dinky Toys Number 073, c1960-66. This model came complete with a horse (not shown here). Length overall: 4·05in (103mm).

21 Massey-Harris Ferguson Tractor; Dublo Dinky Toys Number 069, 1959-64. Length: 1·46in (37mm).

22 Gauge "00" Trackside Flower Border. Note that this diecast accessory is by an unidentified maker, not by Hornby.

23 Singer Roadster; Dublo Dinky Toys Number 062, 1958-60. Length: 1·97in (50mm).

24 Gauge "00" EDCR Diamond Crossing (Right Hand); three-rail Hornby Dublo electric track.

As has already been noted, the value of most collectable toys is considerably enhanced by the possession of the original packaging. Shown here is a wide range of Hornby Dublo packaging.

1 Hornby Dublo box with serial number "34070" (visible here on the upper side). Note that the boxes themselves have serial numbers, which are visible on a number of the examples shown here. This red-and-white version of the maker's usual striped motif, bears the later type of "Hornby" logo, and dates from around 1964.

2 Gauge "00" 4-6-2 "Golden Fleece" Locomotive and Eight-Wheeled Tender; Hornby Catalog Number 2211 (note that the Catalog Number also appears on the box), a two-rail electric model issued c1961-64. Red-and-white striped box (body of box is plain red, as in similar boxes on this spread) with color illustration of locomotive on the lid.

3 Blue-and-white striped box with color illustration on yellow panel, for Gauge "00" 4-6-2 "Dorchester" Locomotive and Tender; Hornby Catalog Number 3235, a three-rail electric model issued c1961-63.

4 Red-and-white striped box with color illustration on yellow panel, for Gauge "00" 4-6-2 "Barnstaple" Locomotive and Tender; Hornby Catalog Number 2235, a two-rail electric model issued c1961-64.

5 Gauge "00" Bogie Bolster Wagon; Hornby Catalog Number 4610, c1961-64, with red-and-white striped box.

6 Red-and-white striped box with serial number "31226" and color illustration, for Gauge "00" "City of London" Locomotive and Tender; Hornby Catalog Number 2226, a two-rail electric model, that was issued c1959-60.

7 Gauge "00" Meat Container, of wood covered with printed paper, for use with Low-Sided Wagon; c1956-58, with blue-and-white striped box.

8 Gauge "00" "Saxa Salt" Wagon; Hornby Catalog Number 4665, c1959-60, with red-and-white striped box bearing line illustration.

9 Red-and-white striped box with serial number "31218" and color illustration, for Gauge "00" 2-6-4 Tank Locomotive; Hornby Catalog Number 2218, a two-rail electric model issued c1962-64.

10 Red-and-white striped box with line illustration for Gauge "00" Goods Wagon (steel type); Hornby Catalog Number 4640, c1961-64.

11 Red-and-white striped box with line illustration for "Gauge 00" Standard Wagon; Hornby Catalog Number 4670, c1959-60.

12 Gauge "00" 0-6-2 Tank Locomotive; Hornby Catalog Number 2217, a two-rail electric model, c1960-64, in red-and-white striped box, serial number "31217", with color illustration.

13 Red-and-white striped box, serial number "36620", with line illustration for Gauge "00" Breakdown Crane; Hornby Catalog Number 4620, for two- or three-rail operation, issued c1961-64.

14 Red-and-white striped box with color illustration for Gauge "00"

2-8-0 Locomotive and Tender; Hornby Catalog Number 2224, a two-rail electric model issued *c*1960-64.

15 Gauge "00" 0-6-0 Diesel-Electric Shunting Locomotive; Hornby Catalog Number 2231, a two-rail electric model, *c*1960-64, with red-and-white striped box, serial number "31231", with color illustration of locomotive.

16 Red-and-white striped box with line illustration for Gauge "00" Ventilated Van; Hornby Catalog Number 4325. The model was introduced in 1958, but this box dates from the period 1961-64.

17 Gauge "00" Low-Sided Wagon with wooden "Liverpool Cables" drums; Hornby Series D1, *c*1955-56, with blue-and-white striped box.

18 Red-and-white striped box, serial number "31206", with line illustration, for Gauge "00" 0-6-0 Tank Locomotive; Hornby Catalog Number 2206, a two-rail electric model issued *c*1959-64.

19 Red-and-white striped box, serial number "32043", with line illustration, for Gauge "00" Goods Brake Van; Hornby Catalog Number 4311, issued *c*1961-64.

20 Gauge "00" "Esso" Tank Wagon; Hornby Catalog Number 4676, *c*1959-60, with red-and-white striped box.

21 Gauge "00" Gunpowder Van; Hornby Catalog Number 4313, 1962-64, with red-and-white striped box.

22 Red-and-white striped box, serial number "31233", with color illustration on yellow top panel, for

Gauge "00" Deltic Diesel-Electric Locomotive; Hornby Catalog Number 2234, a two-rail electric model issued *c*1962-64.

23 Red-and-white striped box, serial number "31230", with color illustration, for Gauge "00" 1000BHP Diesel-Electric Locomotive; Hornby Catalog Number 2230, a two-rail electric model issued *c*1959-62.

24 Red-and-white striped box, serial number "31233", with color illustration on yellow panel, for Gauge "00" CO-BO Diesel-Electric Locomotive; Hornby Catalog Number 2233, a two-rail electric model issued *c*1961-64.

25 Gauge "00" "ICI" Bogie Tank Wagon; Hornby Catalog Number 4685, *c*1962-64, with red-and-white striped box.

26 Red-and-white striped box, serial number "31221", with color illustration, for Gauge "00" "Cardiff Castle" Locomotive and Tender; Hornby Catalog Number 2221, a three-rail electric model that was issued *c*1960-64.

27 Gauge "00" Electric Motor Coach Brake/2nd (note manufacturer's "Tested" label); Hornby Catalog Number 2250, a two-rail electric model issued *c*1962-64. Shown with red-and-white striped box, serial number "31250", with color illustration on yellow top and bearing another form of the later "Hornby Dublo" logo.

28 Red-and-white striped box with standard "Hornby Dublo" logo, dating from *c*1959-62; compare with the logo on the later packaging shown at (1).

The wellknown British Gauge "00" range by "Hornby Dublo" is illustrated on the preceding spreads (*pages 50-57*), but this, introduced in 1938, was by no means the first of the smaller systems. Although Gauge "0" railroads were increasingly popular from the early years of the 20th century, and predominant by the 1920s, small-gauge systems soon began to receive consideration. Around 1922, Gebrüder Bing of Nuremburg, Germany, produced a "Miniature Table Railway" set in Gauge "00": it was quickly included in the British Bassett-Lowke catalog. In the later 1920s, Stephan Bing and other German toy makers took over the Förtner & Haffner company, changing its name to "Trix" and embarking on a

series of electric-powered Gauge "00" railroads that were well-established by the mid-1930s (with a British subsidiary in conjunction with Bassett-Lowke). Other manufacturers in Germany (notably Marklin and Bub) and the USA also entered the market.

After World War II, Gauge "00" railroads rapidly increased in popularity, and Hornby's renunciation of Gauge "0" in favor of smaller-gauge railroads was shared by the majority of its competitors worldwide. In the 1960s-1970s, notable small-gauge railroad makers included Fleischmann, Hornby, Liliput, Lima, Marklin, and Rivarossi. Since that period, however, plastic has increasingly replaced metal in the construction of model railroads.

1 Gauge "00" Island Platform by Gebrüder Bing, Nuremburg, Germany, *c*1922. A tinplate accessory from an early "Miniature Table Railway" set.
2 Gauge "00" 2-4-0 Tank Locomotive by Bing, *c*1922. Finished in London & North-Western Railway (LNWR) livery, this tinplate locomotive is shown with its (removable) key in place for winding its clockwork motor: by 1924, sets were available with 4- to 6-volt electric motors.
3 Gauge "00" Third Class Coach (left) and Third/Brake Coach (right) by Bing, *c*1922. Both are in tinplate, with lithographed finish.
4 Gauge "00" Railroad Tunnel by Bing, *c*1922. Many of Bing's more expensive "Table Railway" sets included a tinplate tunnel.

5 Gauge "00" Telegraph Poles and Railroad Signals by Bing, *c*1922: further tinplate accessories of the kind included in larger sets.
6 Gauge "00" Station by Bing, *c*1922. Consisting of three tinplate sections, this "country wayside station" (Bing catalog) has considerable period charm.
7 Gauge "HO" 2-8-2 Tank Locomotive, numbered "65014", by Fleischmann, West Germany, *c*1960. The body of this well-detailed, electric-powered model of a continental locomotive is diecast metal.
8 Gauge "00" Bogie Freight Car by Trix, made in Great Britain in the late 1950s. This tinplate item in US style — note the roof walkway — was probably intended for the American market.

9 Gauge "H0" Express Bogie
Coach by Marklin, West Germany,
c1960. This fine tinplate model of a
continental railroad coach, with
both pressed and printed detail is
shown on a section of tinplate
track, also by Marklin.

10 Gauge "00" Bogie Caboose,
numbered "482690", by Trix,
made in Great Britain in the late
1950s. Like (8), this tinplate
conductor's van was intended for
the US market.

11 Gauge "00" 0-4-0 "Trix Express"
Passenger Locomotive, numbered
"20 051", and Six-Wheeled Tender,
numbered "5391", by Trix,
Nuremburg, Germany, c1938.
The "brush" fittings for the
electric-powered tinplate
locomotive to make contact with
the electric track are evident.

12-13 Gauge "00" First Class
Passenger Coach (12) and Bogie
Coach with Sliding Doors (13), by
Trix, c1938. These tinplate coaches
in continental livery formed part of
a set with the locomotive at (11).

14 Gauge "00" "Esso" Tank Wagon
by Trix, probably British-made,
c1950. This tinplate item has both
printed and applied detail.

15 Gauge "00" Schlafwagen
(Sleeping Car), numbered
"20164", by Trix, West Germany,
c1960. This tinplate bogie car has
celluloid windows and printed,
pressed, and applied detail.

16 Gauge "00" Telegraph Poles and
Signals by Bing, c1922; as (5). The
larger sets included up to five
telegraph poles and five lever-
operated signals (note spring clips
at bases, for fixing to track).

17 Gauge "H0" "Internationale
Schlafwagen Gesellschaft"
(International Sleeping Car
Company) Sleeping Car by
Marklin, c1960; see also (9). The
printed detail of this fine tinplate
coach includes the destination
board "Roma-Basel-Köln".

18 Gauge "00" "Mitropa"
"Speisewagen" (Restaurant
Car), numbered "20163", by
Trix, made in West Germany,
c1960. Like (15), a well-detailed
tinplate car.

19 Gauge "00" 45-Ton Bogie Well
Wagon, numbered "41900", by
Trix, made in Great Britain in the
1950s. This is a well-detailed
model, incorporating a cable
drum secured on the wagon by
chains and cords.

20 Gauge "00" 12-Ton "Charringtons"

Open Wagon, numbered "451",
by Trix: a further example of a
British-made item of rolling stock
in tinplate, dating from c1950.

21 Gauge "H0" 4-6-2 Locomotive,
numbered "01 182", and Eight-
Wheeled Tender, by Fleischmann,
West Germany, dating from
the 1950s. An electric-powered
model, this is finished in black
"DB" (Deutsche Bundesbahn,
German Railways) livery; its
detail includes smoke deflectors
(one missing), fluted connecting
rods, and cab ventilators.
Like the locomotive at (7), it
has a diecast body.

22 Gauge "H0" 4-6-2 Locomotive,
numbered "01 097" (note maker's
name above number), and Eight-
Wheeled Tender, by Marklin, West
Germany, c1960.

From the first appearance of toy railroad "sets" around the turn of the century, makers have produced accessories of various kinds to enhance the realism and add to the attraction of their ranges.

1 Gauge "0" No 2 Signal Cabin by Hornby, Great Britain, dating from the 1920s-1930s. The roof and back of the tinplate building are hinged to open (as shown here) so that a "lever frame" could be fitted and operated. This system offered by Hornby allowed points and signals along the track to be worked from the cabin via linking rods. This item (also produced in a cheaper "No 1" version) was priced in the early 1930s at 4s 6d (22½p, 32c).

2 Gauge "2" Crane Car by Marklin, Goppingen, Germany, c1903. Note the printed legend "10 000 KI" on this hand-enameled tinplate model, indicating that the "real" crane lifted up to 9·84 tons (10,000kg). Limited.

3 Gauge "0" "New Street" Station by Gebrüder Bing, Nuremburg, Germany, c1930. Produced for the British market, this most attractive model of a main-line station is constructed of tabbed and slotted tinplate. The station building, two extension sections, and one end section are shown. Note the many advertising signs. Bing used the same pressing, with appropriate variations in detail, to make stations for the continental market. Lengths: (station building section) 13·2in (33·5cm); (extension) 13·2in (33·5cm);

(end) 5·9in (15cm).

4 Gauge "2" "Central Station" by Marklin, Germany; produced for sale in Britain: appropriately finished versions were made from the same pressing for the continental market. With a hand-enameled finish, the station is of pressed tinplate construction with soldered joints, and features such detail as glazed windows, opening doors, and simulated porcelain telegraph insulators at the building's corners. Within the building are sockets for two candles, to provide the realism of interior lighting and smoke from the chimneys. Note the base for a lamp (missing from this example) at the corner of the platform. Length: 14·2in (36cm). Scarce.

5 Gauge "0" Station by Wells Brimtoy, Great Britain, c1950. In complete contrast to (3) and (4), this simple tinplate station relies almost completely on brightly-colored printed detail for its effect. Length: 9·55in (24·25cm). This item is common.

6 Gauge "0" Signal Box by Hornby, Great Britain, 1930s. In lightweight tinplate with printed detail, this simple, two-dimensional accessory is from Hornby's low-priced "M" Series Station Set. It was also sold in the 1930s as a separate item, priced at 0s 4d (2p, 3c). Length: 3·44in (8·75cm). Common.

7-9 Advertising Signs (7-8) and Station Name Boards (9), probably British-made and dating from the 1930s, when they could be purchased in packeted assortments. These tinplate signs for the

CENTRAL STATION

Waiting room

Telegraph

SMITHS
BLUECOL
the SAFE Anti-freeze

EVER READY

READ THE
NEWS
OF THE
WORLD
BEST
SUNDAY
PAPER

WAKEFIELD
PATENT
Castrol
MOTOR OIL

WILLS'S
CAPSTAN

TOO GOOD TO MISS
KLG
SPARKING PLUG

VIROL

WILLS'S
GOLD FLAKE
CIGARETTES

NEW STREET

BOVRIL

OXO
FOR
COOKING & DRINKING

WILLS'S
WOODBINES

Player's
Please

enhancement of station buildings are now popular with collectors of advertising material, as well as toy collectors. Fairly common.

10 Gauge "0" Station by Hornby, Great Britain: like (6), an "M" Series item of simple lightweight tinplate construction with printed detail, priced at 1s 0d (5p, 7c) in the 1930s. The example shown has a tinplate canopy: it was available also without this feature. Length: 9·74in (24·75cm). This item is common.

11 Gauge "0" Wayside Station by Hornby, Great Britain, 1930s: another "M" Series item in lightweight tinplate, using the same platform as (10). It was priced in the 1930s at 0s 8d (3p, 4c). Length: 9·74in (24·75cm). This item is common.

12 Gauge "0" Watchman's Hut, Railway Accessory No 7, by Hornby, Great Britain, 1930s. This attractive lineside accessory in tinplate came complete with a brazier, a shovel that hooked to its side, and a poker hooked to its back (the last-named not seen here). Common.

13 Luggage, No 1 Accessories Series, by Hornby, Great Britain, 1930s. The set of tinplate baggage included a strapped-up suitcase (lid only shown here), a trunk and basket (as shown), another suitcase, and a porter's handcart (not shown). The accessories are seen here with a Gauge "1" figure of a Porter, hollow-cast, with movable arm. Common.

14 From left to right on platform: two Traveling Trunks, diecast; Guard,

hollow-cast, by John Hill & Co, London; five Hornby No 2 Milk Cans, tinplate; Station Master, hollow-cast, by John Hill & Co; and (foreground) Railway Passenger, hollow-cast, by John Hill & Co. All date from the 1930s. Common.

15 Lady Passenger by Britains, Great Britain, 1930s. A hollow-cast Gauge "1" figure from Britains Railway Series (Cat No 806).

Jib Crane by G.G. Kellermann and Company (trademark "CKO") of Nuremburg, West Germany, dating from after 1950. This attractive railroad accessory in lightweight tinplate is shown here lifting a Gauge "0" container made by Hornby, Great Britain, pre-World War II. Height of crane tower: 16·93in (43cm).

Automotive Toys

Appearing in the late 19th century, the automobile soon caught the imagination of a public far larger than that which could ever hope to own such a machine in reality. Thus, it was not long before toy manufacturers sought to take advantage of the widespread fascination with the newfangled "horse-less carriage" or "gas buggy".

By the early 1900s, metal (as well as wooden) toys representing automobiles, trucks, and public utility vehicles—some powered by clockwork, spirit-fired steam engines, or even by electricity—had appeared in sizes ranging from the small "penny toy" to the child-carrying "pedal car" or "kiddie car" (although most early pedal cars were of wood). Of course, "road" or "transport" toys in metal were in existence well before the coming of the internal combustion engine (and such toys as wooden carts date from the very earliest times). From around the mid-19th century, toymakers produced many horse-drawn vehicles in metal; notable examples including the robust cast-iron road toys of US makers, such as the horse-drawn fire engines shown on *pages 90-91*.

TINPLATE CLASSICS

The production of automotive toys (ie, those representing powered vehicles) paralleled the rapid development of motor transport throughout the world. Although scale models were not early in evidence, such famous toymakers as Gebrüder Bing, Nuremburg, Germany, produced tinplate automobiles which were reasonably faithful representations—with detailed radiators, hoods, etc— of the more famous automobile marques of the early period, such as Mercedes and De Dion. Tinplate automobiles of the pre-1914 period are now generally rare and valuable. Of the various examples shown on the photographic spreads, the Limousine by Georges Carette of Nuremburg, shown at (4), *pages 66-67*, may be singled out as typical of the high-quality toys of the early period. Although it does not represent a specific marque, it incorporates such refinements as opening doors, a baggage rack, headlamps and side-lights, beveled glass windows, rubber-tired wheels, a working brake, and forward and reverse clockwork mechanism. A number of these early examples carried "realism" to the extent of working (oil-burning) headlamps.

As well as the rapid development of motor transport, the period 1900-1914 saw the birth of motor sport, with the running of a number of ambitious road races (notably the Peking-Paris event of 1907), and the beginning of circuit racing (Brooklands, the world's first purpose-built motor race track, was opened near Weybridge, Great Britain, in 1907; the first 500-mile event at the famous Indianapolis track in the USA was run in 1911). Toymakers were quick to follow this trend also, well knowing that the speed, thrills, and noise of motor racing would always appeal strongly to children! The earlier models to appear were mainly of road-racing automobiles: the "Paris-Berlin" Racing Car by Günthermann, shown at (3), *pages 66-67*, which dates from the very early years of the century, is an excellent example of its genre.

TRUCKS AND BUSES

Next to appear, as the internal combustion engine began to replace the horse in commercial applications, were toys based on commercial and public utility vehicles. By c1910, a limited number of toy trucks were available: an early example, the Tipping Truck by Bing, shown at (6), *pages 84-85*, dates from c1908. However, it was not until after the great increase in motor transport that followed World War I that toy trucks became widely available (although they were never to rival automobiles in popularity), and early examples of commercial vehicles are greatly prized by collectors.

Of all automotive toys of the early period, buses are perhaps the most attractive of the commercial/public utility vehicle ranges. Toy motor buses appeared as early as c1902, notably from Bing, while in the USA the Lionel company marketed an electric-powered

Above: *By December 1948 metal toys were available again in Britain, to the evident delight of this youngster in a London store. The pedal car is by Leeway; compare with the later example shown on page 121.*

Top: *Dinky Toys of the 1940s and 1950s: Mersey Tunnel Police Van, Daimler Ambulance, Morris Series E Telephone Service Van, Royal Mail Van, and black and two-tone Taxis of two eras, along with Telephone Box and Pillar Boxes. The pillar box in the center is a late-1930s "GR" type.*

Above left: *A selection of American diecast automobiles of the 1930s by Manoil, early rivals to Tootsietoy. The futuristic bodies are on two types of chassis, with and without front headlamps, and are unusual in having wooden wheels.*

street-car before 1908. "Lehmann's Autobus", shown (in a later version) at (11) on *pages 88-89*, first appeared before World War I. One of the most attractive features of toy buses, from the early period to recent years, is the fact that they often incorporate in their finish lithographed or printed advertising signs of the period in which they were produced: see the many examples on *pages 86-89*. As will be later noted, the presence of advertising slogans on a toy vehicle may considerably enhance its value as well as its general interest.

Toys showing motorized fire appliances also began to appear before World War I. As noted in the case of racing automobiles, the excitement and noise of fire engines must have exerted a strong fascination on juvenile buyers, since "fire toys" have always been among the most popular models in the "commercial" category. No really early example of a motorized fire appliance is shown in this book—although these exist, they are very scarce—but the cast-iron, pull-along model of a motorized unit by a US maker, and the tinplate, clockwork-driven fire vehicle by Distler, Germany, shown at (6) and (5) respectively on *pages 90-91*, are reasonably typical of the earlier "fire toys".

POST-WORLD WAR I

German toymakers had led the way in the production of automotive toys, but after World War I economic problems combined with lingering anti-German feeling abroad to produce a temporary eclipse of the German toymakers' production and exports, and a consequent increase in the production of automotive toys by other European and US makers. Among the makers to emerge during this period, the names of Wells and Brimtoy (later to amalgamate) and Lines Brothers Limited (Triang), Great Britain, Rossignol, Citroën, Jep (earlier J de P), and CIJ, of France, and Buddy "L", Kingsbury, and Structo, of the USA, are all to be particularly noted.

By the mid-1920s, German makers had generally succeeded in re-establishing themselves in world markets, with such companies as Tipp and Bub attaining greater recognition for their products at this time. However, one famous name that was not to reappear after World War I was that of Georges Carette: as a Frenchman working in Germany, Carette was forced to cease his activities during World War I and never returned to production; some of the former Carette range was taken over by Karl Bub.

It is not possible, in the space available here, individually to note all of the makers known for their products during the 1920s. Three makers, however, demand special mention because certain items from their ranges are now particularly sought after by collectors.

KINGSBURY, USA

In the USA, the name of the Kingsbury company became prominent in the 1920s, both because of the considerable extent of its production and because of the good quality and robust construction of its toys. Kingsbury (which ceased to produce toys during World War II) is now perhaps best remembered for its series representing "record cars": the automobiles that competed for the world's land speed record in the 1920s and early 1930s. Kingsbury's fine version of the "Napier Campbell" "Bluebird II", in which Malcolm Campbell captured the record for Great Britain in 1928, is

shown at (1) on *pages 76-77*; the company also produced equally notable models of Henry Segrave's "Sunbeam 1,000 HP" and "Golden Arrow". It should be noted that a similarly distinguished range of "record cars" was produced at the same period, some of the models being of the same automobiles, by the German maker Günthermann: see (5), (9), and (10) on *pages 78-79*.

CITROËN AND JEP

The great names in the production of automotive toys in France at this period included those of Citroën and Jep. The Citroën automobile company began to issue models of its products, for sale in dealers' showrooms as well as in toyshops, in 1923, the first issue being the 10CV "Torpedo". The company's aim was partly promotional: it hoped that children would be led to regard Citroën as being synonymous with "automobile" —with a favorable effect on sales when the juvenile customers grew up! The popularity of these detailed models— note the Citroën B14 Sedan, shown at (10), *pages 68-69*—had the effect of causing other toy manufacturers to put less emphasis on purely visual appeal and more on accurate detail, making scale of increasing importance. In 1927, Citroën added to its range construction kits with parts from which a chassis could be built, and in 1928 it began to manufacture diecast miniatures. By 1933, Citroën's toy production had reached an annual level of 576,000 diecast vehicles and 274,000 tinplate models, the latter ranging in size up to pedal cars. The production rate decreased after 1935 (although the JRD company continued to produce a limited range of Citroën toys until after World War II).

The French toymaking company now usually known simply as "Jep" was founded in 1889 as the Société Industrielle de Ferblanterie (SIF). The company was known as Jouets de Paris (J de P) from 1928, and as Jouets en Paris (JEP, or Jep), the name by which it is now commonly known, from c1932 until production ended in 1965. Its products were fairly undistinguished until the issue of its series of sedans and touring cars in the later 1920s. Although the most famous examples of Jep's range are the finely-detailed models, almost scale models, of such luxury automobiles as the Rolls Royce Phantom I, see (5), *pages 68-69*, and the Hispano Suiza Tourer, see (5), *pages 76-77*, the company also produced a wide variety of excellent but less expensive models, such as the Avions Voisin Sedan shown at (3), *pages 68-69*. Note also, on *pages 76-77*, several examples of another "classic" French automotive toy: the Alfa Romeo P2 Racing Car by Compagnie Industrielle du Jouet (CIJ) of Paris.

THE 1930s AND AFTER

The 1930s saw continued production by the major makers noted above (although Bing ceased production around 1933), together with the emergence of a market for "constructor" automobiles. Citroën's early entry into this field is noted above, and kits from which toy automobiles or, less often, commercial vehicles, could be assembled by an older child were issued in Britain by Meccano and in the "Ubilda" range—see (1-3), *pages 86-87*—by Burnett Limited (later Chad Valley), and in Germany by Marklin. In the USA, the Structo company—with its famous slogan "Structo Toys Make Men of Boys"—varied this style by issuing finished vehicles with nut-and-bolt construction (generally simpler than that of Meccano or Marklin) that enabled them to be dismantled and re-assembled: see *Inset, pages 68-69*.

The considerable increase in the production of toy military vehicles in the 1930s, especially in Germany, is described in the notes on "Soldiers and Military Toys" *(pages 144-147)*. However, one German firm of this period worthy of mention is Schuco (Schreyer and Company), a firm still active in the production of mechanical toys. Schuco's Mercedes Grand Prix Racing Car of the 1930s—see (11), *pages 78-79*—rates as a modern classic and, because of its long production life both before and after World War II, is relatively common.

The production of toy vehicles in tinplate continued, but on a reduced scale, after World War II (note that German-made toys of the immediate post-War period will usually be found marked "Made in US Zone"). Among the notable European makers of the post-1945 period are Wells Brimtoy, Chad Valley, and Mettoy (a firm established pre-1939, but best known for its post-War products), in Great Britain; Arnold and Schuco in West Germany; and the huge Marx company of the USA.

From the 1950s onward, however, the center of production for tinplate automotive toys—indeed, for tinplate toys of all kinds—increasingly shifted to Japan. Japanese makers had long had such models in production, but from the 1950s their export marketing became so efficient and their prices so competitive, that, faced with a diminishing market for tinplate, affected both by the coming of plastics and the increasingly stringent safety legislation concerning both construction and finish of metal toys, European and US makers virtually abandoned the tinplate toy. The Japanese makers, however, continue to produce tinplate toys of good quality: notable examples are on *pages 70-75* and *82-83*.

Although the diecast automotive toy had early origins—"penny toys" were made by the diecast process as well as in tinplate from around the turn of the century—it was not until the mid-1920s that the diecast toy firmly established itself. The first important name in the production of diecast automotive toys was that of the US company Tootsietoy, which introduced a range of diecast automobiles and other vehicles around 1926. Somewhat later models from Tootsietoy's range, dating from the 1930s, are shown at (38-41), *pages 106-107*. A US company active on a rather smaller scale in the 1930s was Manoil, whose limited range of diecast automobiles in 1:43 scale, typically in "futuristic" shapes—see photograph on *page 62*—was unusual in that the vehicles had wooden wheels.

From the point of view of many collectors, in Britain, Europe, and the USA alike, the most important name in the field of diecast models is that of Dinky Toys (Meccano Limited; under control of Lines Brothers Limited from 1964). The Dinky Toys range, produced over a period of some 45 years, is so large (including railroad accessories, farm figures and equipment, ships, and airplanes, as well as automotive models), so well-documented, and offers so many variations in style and color, that it constitutes a rich field for collectors and offers a variety of specialities.

Above: *Corgi Classics were introduced in the late 1960s. Shown here with boxes and contemporary publicity material are a 1927 3-liter Bentley, a red 38hp Daimler of 1910, a yellow 1910 Renault, and a blue Model "T" Ford of 1915.*

Left: *The Wells Brimtoy factory in November 1936, with a large pile of autos waiting for polishing before being packed for the Christmas market.*

Right: *These diecast clockwork autos of the early 1950s by the German maker Prameta—a Jaguar XK120 fixed head coupé (left) and a Buick 405—have provision for speed and direction settings. An original key in the form of a driver is also shown.*

DINKY TOYS

"Hornby Modelled Miniatures", from which the Dinky Toys range was to evolve, were announced in *Meccano Magazine* (see *pages 192-193*) in December 1933. The maker's early emphasis was on the railroad and farm items in the range: the first six automotive toys —two automobiles, two commercial vehicles, a tractor, and a tank—being designated "Modelled Miniatures No 22". In April 1934, however, the range was renamed "Dinky Toys" and its items were numbered. The automotive models, receiving the numbers 22A-22F, would become known to collectors as the "22 series", and each succeeding year saw the addition of new models in new series. At about the same time as the British parent company, the Meccano subsidiary at Bobigny, France, also began to produce Dinky Toys. Many collectors are of the opinion that the style and finish of French-made examples is superior to that of British-made models.

There is, unfortunately, insufficient space available here to enter into a description of the various Dinky Toys

series, of the many stylistic variants, and of the complex system of numbering and re-numbering of models over the years. The reader is directed to the reference works listed in the *Bibliography, pages 200-201* (the title by C. Gibson, covering the period up to 1964, is especially recommended), and to the brief explanations given in some of the captions for the photographic spreads on which Dinky Toys are shown *(pages 100-113)*. Note particularly the items shown on *pages 100-101*, where a number of later versions of models from the earlier series are illustrated.

Notable competition to Dinky Toys in the earlier period came from Triang (Lines Brothers), which, under the "Minic" trademark, produced from 1935 until the 1950s a most attractive series of small, clockwork-powered vehicles in tinplate. Competitors in the diecast field included the British makers Crescent (see *pages 104-105*) and Spot-On *(pages 106-107)*. Especially after the takeover by Lines Brothers in 1964, Dinky Toys became increasingly sophisticated in the face of competition from Corgi (Mettoy) *(pages 104-105)*, and "Matchbox" *(pages 94-97)* and "Models of Yesteryear" *(pages 98-99)*, both from Lesney, of Great Britain; Marklin *(pages*

106-107) of Germany; and Solido *(pages 102-103)* of France. However, the increasing trend towards "electronic" toys in the 1970s meant that even the most determined attempts at realism—working suspension, detailed interiors, jeweled headlamps, detachable wheels, and other detail—by diecast makers failed to maintain the interest of the juvenile market. As a result, such famous makers as Dinky Toys, Lesney, and Corgi were to cease operations in the 1980s.

COLLECTING DIECASTS

It will be apparent from the information given above that diecast automotive toys offer one of the widest ranges for the collector, who may decide to specialize in vehicles by a single maker, of a single type (eg, sedans, sports and racing cars, trucks, buses, etc), or of a single marque; even, in the case of ranges as large as those offered by such makers as Dinky and Lesney, in the casting and color variations of a single series of vehicles.

Currently, the most popular items appear to be vehicles that bear advertising signs and slogans. In the case of diecast toys (advertising signs on tinplate vehicles, notably buses, are mentioned above), advertising first appeared

on the Dinky Toys Delivery Vans of the "28 series", issued from 1934 onward. These are now scarce and expensive, and it should be noted that the "2nd type" and "3rd type" castings of the "28 series" advertising vehicles are known to be particularly susceptible to metal fatigue: they should be carefully examined for telltale cracks and blisters if a purchase is contemplated. A good selection of post-World War II Dinky advertising vehicles is shown on *pages 108-109*. An abundance of advertising vehicles was issued in the post-War period by Lesney, Corgi, and other makers, as well as by Dinky, but in buying post-War diecasts of any kind, remember that possession of the original box will almost always enhance the value of the vehicle itself.

All models offered for sale should be carefully inspected for signs of repainting and repair. A refurbished item may be fairly difficult to distinguish (especially if it is offered with an original box), since replacement transfers remain available, along with replacement tires and certain other (reproduction) spare parts. On pre-War models, original tires may have perished, either becoming soft and developing "flats" or becoming brittle and crumbling. Note that pre-War Dinky Toys in original condition will usually (although not invariably) have white tires, while tires of post-War examples are usually black or, in the case of some Dinky Supertoys, gray.

There is a somewhat uncertain line to be drawn between diecast models that are genuinely toys, with real "play value", and finely-detailed, fairly fragile, scale models intended mainly for adult automobile buffs. Examples of the latter type have appeared in increasing numbers in recent years, coincident with the decline in toy diecast production: the collector must be guided here by his own judgment.

An excellent collection of the largest automotive toys, pedal cars, or "kiddie cars", is shown on *pages 114-121*; note the short introduction to this category on *page 114*. Simply because of their size, and current cost, these will probably remain the province of a limited number of collectors. It should be noted, however, that most pedal cars encountered by the collector will either have been restored or, because they were intended for "active play" and normally received hard usage, will need restoration.

Both tinplate and diecast automotive toys should, ideally, be displayed in glazed cabinets. Whatever the method of storage and/or display, they should be preserved at an even temperature, to guard against metal fatigue, and should be kept out of direct sunlight, which will fade paint finishes, resulting in a poor appearance which will detract from both appeal and value.

These tinplate automobiles of the early 20th century have all the visual appeal of their full-size counterparts and, like them, are eagerly sought after by collectors and have become increasingly rare and expensive. Most are based on actual marques, although such parts as chassis, seats, and lamps were often designed to be interchangeable among the maker's various models. Many are of soldered construction with fine hand-enameled finish, featuring such details as beveled glass windows, working lamps, and rubber tires. They were, of course, toys for the well-to-do: the finer examples were sold before World War I at prices of up to £1 15s 0d (£1.75, $2.48) — perhaps a week's wages for a working man.

All the automobiles and accessories shown here were photographed at the London Toy & Model Museum.

1 Based on a Renault automobile of the pre-World War I period, this large and impressive Spanish-made car — the maker is possibly identified only by the initials "DL" — dates from around 1920. It has what was known in Europe as a "Berlin" body, in which the chauffeur — here a liveried figure with a bisque (porcelain) head — is exposed to the elements while the passengers travel in the luxury of an enclosed compartment. The toy is richly hand-enameled and features such detail as opening doors, glass windows, bell-type headlamps, radially-spoked wire wheels with rubber tires, and semi-

elliptic springing. Length: 22in (56cm). Rare.

2 Clockwork Car by Günthermann, Nuremburg, Germany, dating from around 1908. Loosely based on a landaulet type, with a rather unusual rectangular hood, it is of simple tinplate tab-and-slot construction, with pressed tin wheels and tires. The body is litho-graphed and detail includes opening doors and glazed windows. It features an automatic brake mechanism: a small spring-loaded wheel fitted centrally at the rear stops the axle via a cog-wheel when the car is picked up or when the clockwork mechanism is wound while it is off the ground. Length: 9·75in (25cm). Limited.

3 Paris-Berlin Racing Car by Günthermann, with an early

Günthermann trademark on the hood and dating from before 1905. This clockwork auto — note fixed key at rear — has a litho-graphed tinplate body, tinplate driver, and spoked wheels and tires of pressed tin. Length: 5·25in (13cm). Limited.

4 Clockwork Limousine by Carette, Nuremburg, Germany, dating from c1910: a magnificent toy from a range which represents the zenith of tinplate car production before World War I. This example from the top of the range is hand-enameled (it was available more cheaply with lithographed finish and lacking some of the refinements listed below); its detail includes a bolted-on top with baggage rack, opening doors, nickel-plated headlamps and side-lights, beveled glass

windows, "button-backed" seats, an operating brake and reverse mechanism, and radially-spoked wheels with white rubber tires. The liveried chauffeur is a composition figure. These Carette cars were made in three basic sizes— 8·5in (22cm), 12·5in (32cm), as seen here, and 16in (40cm), see (7)—with variations in finish and detail. Scarce.

5 Four-Seat Tourer (based on a Renault) by Bing, Germany, dating from c1905. Not so well proportioned as the Carette automobile at (4), this clockwork tinplate auto is nevertheless very well constructed, with hand-enameled finish, and features operating steering and brake. Detail includes a large detachable headlamp and two side lamps, and "button-backed" seats

of pressed tin. Note particularly the umbrella basket at the rear: this is usually missing from surviving examples. Length: 9·25in (23·5cm). Limited.

6 Clockwork Landaulet by Bing, Germany, dating from c1906. A tinplate auto with a most attractive hand-enameled finish (note the bright-work louvers on the hood), this has operating steering via a single crown wheel and bar. Detail includes a composition chauffeur, a single centrally-mounted head-lamp, and white rubber tires on diecast wheels. Length: 7·375in (18·5cm). Limited.

7 Clockwork Limousine by Carette, Germany, the largest from the range that included the automobile shown at (4), dating from c1910. This is one of the cheaper models

from that range, with lithographed coachwork, a tabbed and slotted roof, tinplate chauffeur, and pressed tin wheels and tires; it has a beveled windshield but no side windows. However, the doors open, headlamps and sidelights are fitted, and the brake operates. Length: 16in (40cm). Scarce.

8 De Dion Two-Seater Runabout by Bing, Germany (with Bing trade-mark just visible on the trunk), dating from c1905. Tinplate with a hand-enameled finish, the auto is clockwork-driven and has adjustable steering. Detail includes a centrally-mounted headlamp, "button-backed" upholstery in pressed tin, and diecast wheels with rubber tires. The model was made in four sizes; this example, 8·375in (21cm) long, being the

second-largest. Limited.

9 Rear-Entrance Tonneau by Carette, Germany, a clockwork-driven auto of lithographed tinplate, dating from c1908. It carries a driver and passengers of hand-enameled tinplate and includes in its detail lamps mounted on the windshield pillars, a glass windshield, operating brake, and diecast wheels with rubber tires. Length: 12·5in (32cm). Scarce.

10 Street Lamp, an oil-burning diecast accessory, probably made by Bing, Germany, and featured in Britain in Bassett-Lowke's Catalog issued in 1906.

11 Fuel Pumps, tinplate accessories by Charles Rossignol (the "CR" trademark is seen on the bases), Paris, c1920. Heights: (left) 3·25in (83mm); (right) 4·25in (108mm).

All the automobiles and accessories shown on this spread were photographed at the London Toy & Model Museum.

1 Citroën B14 Sedan by André Citroën, France, dating from *c*1927. This impressive tinplate model, driven by a battery-operated electric motor, was one of the largest in the range produced by the famous automobile manufacturer from 1923 onward —an inspired way of promoting its "real life" output by fixing the name of Citroën firmly in the minds of the motorists of the future! It is, indeed, a close copy of the real thing, with opening doors, windows that wind up and down, working suspension and steering, electrically-operated headlights,

and a two-tone paint finish. This was the first model in the Citroën range—which extended from pedal cars to small diecast toys—to have rubber tires. A taxi version of this most impressive automobile was also available. Length: 21·5in (55cm). Scarce.

2 Clockwork Limousine by Karl Bub, Nuremburg, Germany, dating from the early 1930s; a rather more "toy-like" example than the Citroën shown at (1). Of lightweight tinplate construction, it has simulated balloon tires (note the "Dunlop"

Robustly-constructed clockwork-powered auto by Structo, USA, dating from the early 1930s. Note the famous slogan on the trademark transfer on the radiator: "Structo Toys Make Men Of Boys"!

legend) on "artillery-type" wheels of pressed tin, extremely simple headlights, and wide bumpers. Larger versions, with opening doors, a tin chauffeur, and other refinements were also produced. Length: 14in (36cm).

3 Avions Voisin Sedan by Jouets de Paris (J de P), France, dating from c1930. Note that in c1932 the maker's name was changed to Jouets en Paris (JEP), and it is as "Jep" that the company is generally known. This tinplate car is typical of the fairly wide range of Jep sedans and tourers: note the well-modeled radiator, pierced for the key to the clockwork mechanism. Other details include an electric spotlamp mounted on the windshield pillar, operating steering, and single-sided wheels

and tires of pressed tin. A klaxon mounted on the running-board and the license plate "7392-JdeP", set well back beneath the radiator, cannot be seen in the photograph. Length 13·25in (34cm). This item is limited

4 Ford Model "T" by Bing, Germany, dating from c1922. This simple model in lightweight tinplate of one of the most famous automobiles of all time is clockwork-driven and, like the original on which it was based, is finished in black! Length: 6·375in (16cm).

5 Rolls Royce Phantom I by Jouets de Paris—see note at (3)—dating from c1928. This magnificent model was the masterpiece of the Jep range and is generally acknowledged to be one of the finest of all tinplate autos. Clock-

work-driven, with forward and reverse gears and a working brake, it has electric headlamps. Note the cantilever springs, just visible in front of the rear mudguard; other detail includes a sprung front bumper, front windshield and auster screen, fully detailed radiator grille, and rubber tires. It is shown here with its key, which incorporates a wrench in its handle, in place for winding. Length: 19·75in (50cm). Scarce.

6 "Roll-Top" Coupé by Günthermann, Nuremburg, Germany, dating from the 1930s. This tinplate auto is clockwork-driven (note the permanently-fixed winder just in front of the rear wheel) and features a canvas "roll-back" top with a hinged rear quarter of tin, opening doors and

trunk, and a tinplate chauffeur. The tin wheels are typical of Günthermann's autos. Length: 18in (46cm). Limited.

7 Two-Door Coupé by Tipp and Company, Germany, dating from the 1930s and a fairly typical example of the maker's range of tinplate vehicles. It features opening doors, a spare wheel on the (opening) lid of the trunk, and pressed tin wheels with simulated spokes and "Continental Record" tires. Note the fixed winder just in front of the rear wheel. Length: 16in (41cm). Limited.

8 Trafffic Policeman; a diecast accessory of French manufacture.

9-10 Street Lamps; simple tinplate accessories made by Charles Rossignol, Paris, to supplement the company's range of vehicles.

(Below) Fairlane "Ranch Wagon"
by ATC (Asahi Toy Company Ltd),
Tokyo, c1960. Friction-powered,
plated brightwork front and rear, a
celluloid windshield and rubber
tires. Length: 15·75in (40cm).

Fine tinplate interpretations of
American automobiles, like those
shown here and on the following
spreads, may well rank as
Japanese makers' major contri-
bution to the world of metal toys.
The larger autos of this kind are
already scarce, for they were
made, for the US market, in limited
numbers and in styles that
matched the many model changes
among real automobiles in the
1950s and 1960s. Thus, for
collectors, size as well as quality
will be a criterion of desirability.

1 Coupé (probably based on a
Mercury) by Haji (Mansei Toy
Company Ltd), Tokyo, dating from
the mid-1960s. This two-door,
four-seater automobile is friction-
powered and features opening
doors, plastic windows, plated
brightwork and a detailed interior.
Length: 11in (28cm). Limited.

2 Coupé (probably based on a
Dodge) bearing the trademark
"ET" (Japanese maker), dating
from the mid-1950s. This two-door
auto in a style typical of the 1950s
is friction-powered. It has a tinted
plastic windshield, printed interior
detail, and rubber tires. Length:
11·8in (30cm). Limited.

3 Automobile by ATC (Asahi Toy
Company Ltd), Tokyo, dating from
c1960. An attractively-detailed
model: note dual headlights,
heavily-chromed bumper and
radiator grille, applied two-tone
trim, printed dashboard in interior,
and printed hubcaps over rubber
whitewall tires; friction-powered.
Length: 12·6in (32cm). Limited.

4 Ford Mustang (2+2 "Fastback") by an unidentified Japanese maker, dating from c1970. Friction-powered, it features plated radiator, bumpers and brightwork, pressed tin detail on the hood, and dished and perforated hubcaps over rubber tires. Length: 10·8in (27·5cm). Limited.

5 Cadillac Fleetwood 60 Special by an unidentified Japanese maker (the trademark "Y" is just visible on the rear window), dating from the mid-1960s. This is an extremely impressive friction-powered model of a luxury auto of 1962; well-detailed, with a tinted windshield, printed interior detail. Length: 21·65in (55cm). Scarce.

6 Mercury Cougar by Bandai, Tokyo, c1970. This is a battery-operated model, with wheels for

variable steering concealed beneath the chassis. Closely based on the real auto, the two-door, four-seater model features sculptured wheels, printed interior detail, and rearlights mounted on the lid of the trunk. Length: 10·2in (26cm). Limited.

7 Chevrolet Corvette by Taiyo, Japan, c1970. The realistic detail of this battery-powered model of a two-seater "fastback" sports car extends to simulation of detachable top sections of the real auto. The lever just visible beneath the radiator controls variable-steering wheels. Length: 10·2in (26cm). Limited.

8 Chevrolet Camaro by an unidentified maker (probably Japanese), dating from the late 1960s. The body is tinplate and the top black plastic. A single variable-

steering wheel is concealed beneath the chassis of this battery-powered model. Length: 10·6in (27cm). Limited.

9 Mercury Cougar Coupé by Asakusa, Tokyo, c1970. Compared to the smaller Bandai version at (6), this features more detail (although lacking the trunk-mounted rearlights), including wing mirrors, a windshield and quarterlights of tinted plastic; friction-powered. Length: 15·35in (39cm). Limited.

10 Rambler Station Wagon by Bandai, Tokyo, dating from the late 1950s. This unpowered push-along toy features a built-in roof-rack, plastic windshield and windows, printed interior detail, plated brightwork, and rubber whitewall tires. Length: 10·8in (27·5cm). Limited.

11 Pontiac Firebird (note name of model on license plate) by Bandai, Tokyo, dating from the late 1960s. Its friction drive produces an "exhaust note" when in operation. This model of a two-door, four-seater coupé has a plastic windshield and windows, printed interior detail, plated brightwork, and sculptured wheels. Length: 10·04in (25·5cm). Limited.

12 Lincoln Continental Convertible Coupé by Bandai, Tokyo, dating from the mid-1950s. Friction-powered, this automobile has additional detail in pressed tin and features most attractively printed seating. The steering-wheel is operational and the wheels have detailed hubcaps over rubber whitewall tires. Length: 11·6in (29·5cm) Scarce.

Although they vary in quality and are, in general, rather more "gimmicky" than the fine Japanese-made models of US automobiles shown on *pages 70-71,* there are very few collectors who, if offered these tinplate Police Cars and other models, would not immediately respond "Ten-Four!": the affirmative phrase made famous in the 1960s by the internationally-shown TV series *Highway Patrol.*

1 Cadillac (note name on license plate) "Police Patrol" Car by Yuoni, Japan, dating from around 1960. A large and impressive model, with the distinctive tailfins of its period and an array of lights and sirens, this has good detail. both printed and applied. The latter includes a large flashing light and two smaller

warning lights on the top, fender-mounted sirens, tinted plastic windshield and rear windows, a detailed interior with plastic steering-wheel, and rubber tires. The trunk opens to give access to the batteries that power the auto and its lights and sirens; a realistic ignition key, shown here in place (note swivel cover for keyhole), is used to turn the power on and off. Length: 17·9in (45·5cm). Limited.
2 "Police Patrol Car" (based on a Ford) by SAN, Japan, dating from the 1950s. Battery-powered (note control lever on side), this rubber-tired auto has a top-mounted flashing light and a divided plastic windshield—behind which a squad of pressed-tin patrolmen are just visible. Note the prominent badge

and mascot on the hood. Length: 10·04in (25·5cm). Limited.
3 "Highway Patrol" Car by a Japanese maker (note trademark —"R" in red shield—on hood), dating from around 1960. This friction-driven, rubber-tired auto (modeled on a Chrysler) is fairly basic—almost all its detail is printed—but it incorporates an amusing novelty: as the car moves, the pressed-tin arm of a printed patrolman moves as if firing at a fugitive. Note that the legend on the hood is printed upside down. Length: 8·27in (21cm). Limited.
4 "Highway Patrol" Car (based on an Oldsmobile) by Ichiko, Japan, dating from the 1960s. Friction-driven (the mechanism producing a "siren" note), with a battery-

operated light mounted on the hood, this model has a tinted plastic windscreen and rear window, a spring aerial, printed interior detail, and rubber tires. Its novelty feature is a trunk-mounted "Speed Meter" (bearing the maker's trademark), intended, in the real thing, to warn drivers against excessive speeds. Length: 12·8in (32·5cm). Limited.
5 Cadillac "Highway Patrol" Car by Bandai, Tokyo, 1960s. The auto is friction-powered, with a battery to operate the top-mounted flashing light and siren sound (note control switch on trunk). A well-detailed model, with tinted plastic windshield and rear window, fender-mounted siren and rear-view mirror, and plastic loudspeakers atop. Length: 16·93in (43cm). Limited.

(Below) Cadillac Police Car by
Yuoni, Japan, c1960; compare
with the Cadillac by the same
maker at (1). Friction-powered,
this fine tinplate auto features
battery-operated lights and tinted
plastic windshield and windows.
Length: 18·1in (46cm). Limited.

6 Police Pursuit Car (in US-style
finish but based on a British "E"
Type Jaguar) by Nomura Toys,
Japan, mid-1960s. Friction-
powered, it has a plastic windshield
and rear window, a top-mounted
plastic light and fender-mounted
siren, printed interior with plastic
steering-wheel, and rubber-tired
wheels with printed spokes.
Length: 11in (28cm). Limited.

7 Station Wagon of Chrysler type
by an unidentified (probably
Japanese) maker, c1960. Friction-
powered, it has a plastic windshield
and rear window and rubber tires.
Length: 11·4in (29cm). Limited.

8 Camper by a Japanese maker,
dating from the 1960s, when it was
apparently marketed as an
individual item. Somewhat gaudily
finished, it features opening top

ventilators and has rubber tires.
Length: 9·25in (23·5cm). Limited.

9 "Phantom" Automobile by Tipp
and Company, West Germany, a
"dream car" dating from the
1950s. This futuristic auto is
clockwork-powered (note control
lever in door), with batteries to
power its lights concealed beneath
the hinged lid of the trunk. The
hardtop is detachable. Length:
13·8in (35cm). Scarce.

10 Delta-Bodied "Dream Car" by an
unidentified Japanese maker,
dating from the 1950s. With a rear
end styled to suggest jet propulsion,
this battery-powered coupé
features plated headlights set into
the radiator grille, a tinted plastic
windshield, and pivoted, folding
aerials mounted on the trunk.
Length: 11in (28cm). Scarce.

British Automobiles in Tinplate by Japanese Makers, 1950s-1960s

Although all these tinplate automobiles by Japanese makers represent British-built sports cars, the toys were made primarily for the US market and most of the examples shown here have left-hand drive. In general, all the toys shown on this spread, although not "Common", will be more easily found in the UK and USA than the Japanese-made autos shown on the two preceding spreads.

1 Aston Martin DB6 GT (note name on license plate) by ATC (Asahi Toy Company), Tokyo, late 1960s. This friction-powered model is right-hand drive and has a well-detailed body, with tinted plastic windshield and rear window, printed interior detail with plastic steering-wheel, and simulated wire wheels with rubber tires. Length: 11in (28cm).

2 Aston Martin DB5 by Gilbert, Japan, c1965. The battery-powered auto is modeled on the Aston Martin that "starred" in the James Bond movie *Goldfinger*, and incorporates some of its special features: an ejector seat; machine guns (with "flashing" mechanism) in the front fenders, and a retractable "bullet-proof" shield set into the trunk. Length: 11·4in (29cm).

3 Austin Healey by Bandai, Tokyo, c1960. This friction-powered roadster of simple tinplate construction has basic printed detail and simulated wire wheels. Length: 8·27in (21cm). Limited.

4 Austin Healey by Bandai, c1960, using the same tinplate pressing as

(3), but with a superior finish. A left-hand drive model, with a removable plastic top, it is friction-powered. Length: 8·27in (21cm). Limited.

5 M.G.A. 1600 by ATC (Asahi Toy Company), dating from c1960. Again with left-hand drive, this is a friction-powered model with a wealth of detail: license plates front and rear, plastic headlights and foglights, a plastic windscreen with an applied B.M.C. (British Motor Corporation) rosette, and a flock-upholstered cockpit. Length: 9·65in (24·5cm).

6 Lotus Elan (marked thus on base, but in fact displaying all the characteristics of the Lotus Elite) by Bandai, c1963. Friction-powered, with a removable plastic top, it has printed interior detail

with a plastic steering-wheel (right-hand drive), and simulated wire wheels with rubber tires. Length: 8·46in (21·5cm).

7 Jaguar XK 140 by Bandai, c1955. This friction-powered roadster features pressed-tin detail of air intakes and has rear-wheel "spats", a divided-frame perspex windshield (broken), and printed interior detail. Like (9), it has disk-type wheels bearing the name "Jaguar". Length: 9·65in (24·5cm).

8 Jaguar XK 150 by Bandai, late 1950s. Note the one-piece windshield with roadster-type side-screens, the printed interior detail (including gear-shift), over-riders on front and rear bumpers, and printed wire wheels with rubber tires. Length: 9·45in (24cm). Limited.

9 Jaguar XK 140 FHC (Fixed Head Coupé) by Bandai, mid-1950s. It closely resembles (7), by the same maker, but has a non-removable top. Length: 9·65in (24·5cm).

10 Jaguar "E" Type by Tomiyama, Japan, early 1960s. Note headlight fairings, printed interior with plastic lady driver (left-hand drive), and simulated folded soft-top; friction-powered. Length: 12in (30·5cm).

11 Jaguar XK "E" Type FHC by Bandai, early 1960s. This battery-powered model has additional wheels for variable steering beneath its chassis. Length: 10·43in (26·5cm).

12 Jaguar "E" Type by an unidentified Japanese maker, mid-1960s. A well-proportioned, friction-powered model. Length: 11·2in (28·5cm). Limited.

Cadillac Convertible by Bandai, Japan, c1960. This battery-powered auto (batteries in opening trunk) features working lights and an operating column-mounted gear shift. Length: 16·93in (43cm). Limited.

13-14 M.G. TF; two friction-powered models by Bandai, early 1950s. Although they appear near-identical, apart from color finish, there are significant differences. On (13) the body and fenders are separate pressings; (14) is a one-piece pressing. On (13) the windshield folds flat and the upholstery detail is pressed tin; (14) has a fixed windshield and printed upholstery. Length: 8·46in (21·5cm). Limited.

15 Triumph TR3 (note name on trunk) by Bandai, mid-1950s. This friction-powered auto has a most attractive "competition" finish. It is fitted with a fold-down windshield (tin frame only), and has printed upholstery detail and simulated wire wheels. Length: 8·27in (21cm). Limited.

In this close-up view of the "second type" Alfa Romeo note particularly the brake drums, shock absorbers, starting handle and "Pneu Michelin" tires which do not appear on the unsubsidized "third type".

In this close-up view of the front interior of Jep's Hispano Suiza (with the windshield and auster shield removed) note particularly the gear shift (left) and brake lever (right) that protrude through the floor in a realistic manner.

1 "Napier Campbell" "Bluebird II" World Land Speed Record Car, by Kingsbury, New Hampshire, USA, dating from the late 1920s-early 1930s. Models of the "Bluebird" cars in which Sir Malcolm Campbell captured world land speed records for Great Britain in the 1920s and 1930s were produced by a number of makers, notably Günthermann of Germany and Kingsbury of the USA, both firms being noted for their specialization in "record cars" at this period. Shown here is Kingsbury's model of "Bluebird II", in which Campbell set a record of 206·96mph (332·99km/h) at Daytona Beach, Florida, USA, on 19 February 1928. (Günthermann produced a model of "Bluebird III", in which Campbell set new

records in 1931 and 1932.) The car is constructed of heavy-gauge tinplate—note the side-mounted radiators—and has disk wheels fitted with "Dunlop Cord" rubber tires. The figure of the driver is cast-iron. It is fitted with a powerful clockwork motor which is wound from the underside of the car with a large, non-removable, disk-shaped key. Note that the example shown in the illustration above has been repainted. Length: 18·1in (46cm). Limited.

2 Alfa Romeo P2 Racing Car by Compagnie Industrielle du Jouet (CIJ), Paris, France. Introduced in the mid-1920s and in production for some years, this model was available until the mid-1930s, and is generally acknowledged to be one of the finest of all tinplate toys.

The example shown is of the "second type": it has treaded "Michelin" tires, whereas the "first type" had smooth, large-section balloon tires. Note that this specimen has been repainted and now bears the number "6": examples in original finish are (it is believed) always numbered "2" —and see further remarks on color finishes at (3) and (4). The superb detail includes leather straps and accurately-modeled louvers on the hood, a fine-mesh radiator grille with a replica Alfa Romeo badge above and a starting-handle below, opening filler caps, detailed suspension, operating handbrake, and front-wheel steering. Note the shock absorbers and brake drums on the wire-spoked wheels. The aperture

for the key to wind the powerful clockwork motor is visible near the tail. The model was originally priced at £1 5s 0d (£1.25, $1.77). Length: 20·9in (53cm). Limited.

3 Alfa Romeo P2 Racing Car by CIJ: a further example of the "second type"; this view showing the exhaust pipe. Like (2), this specimen has been repainted: it bears the number "4" instead of the original "2". The Alfa Romeo was originally issued in a choice of three color finishes, corresponding to the national racing colors of France (blue), Italy (red), and Germany (white, or silver). By the time of the "second type" in c1929, however, this very popular model was also available in green, lilac, and a number of other colors. Limited.

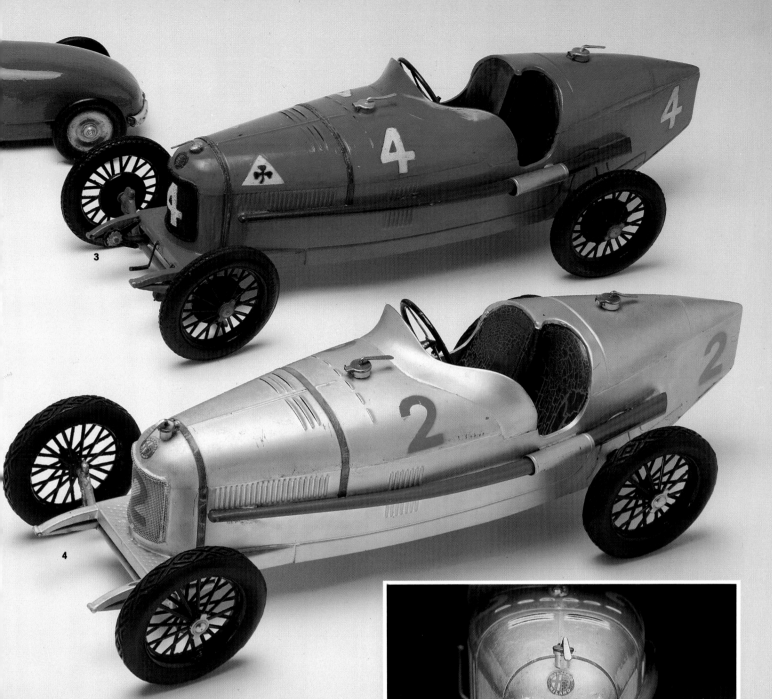

Left: Comparison of the "second type" (left) and "third type" Alfa Romeo P2 wheels. Note the eared "knock-off" wheel nuts. The front view of the "third type" (right) shows detail of the rack-and-pinion steering, operating from the steering wheel.

4 Alfa Romeo P2 Racing Car by CIJ: a "third type" model dating from the mid-1930s and, in comparison with (2) and (3), lacking such detail as the starting-handle, brake drums, and shock absorbers. However, this example is in its original finish, numbered "2" and, in this case, in the silver racing livery of Germany. Note that it has large-section rubber tires bearing no maker's name: (2) and (3) have "Michelin" tires. By the time this

version appeared, the tire and shock-absorber manufacturers who had formerly subsidised the toy as an advertisement for their products had withdrawn their support and, in consequence, the price of the toy had risen to £1 15s 0d (£1.75, £2.48). However, it would appear that, since the toy was comparatively expensive, it was better-preserved than most: although the Alfa Romeo is now eagerly sought by collectors, and may change hands at prices in excess of £750 ($1,065), examples in reasonable condition still appear regularly at auctions, swap-meets, and auto-jumbles. Limited.

5 Hispano Suiza Touring Automobile by Jep (Jouets en Paris), Paris, France, dating from c1929 — when, in fact, the maker was still known

as Jouets de Paris (J de P), the change to "Jep" being made in 1932. Jep's famous Rolls Royce Phantom I model of c1928 is shown at (5) on *pages 68-69*, and the almost equally fine automobile shown here is another "classic" automotive toy (and much scarcer than the Alfa Romeo P2). Constructed of tinplate, with soldered joints, it features such detail as a sprung front bumper, a fine-mesh radiator with the marque

name applied, working electric lamps, steering from the steering-wheel via a worm mechanism, an opening windshield and an auster (rear seat) shield, and disk wheels with brake drums, fitted with treaded rubber tires. Its powerful clockwork motor (note the long winding-shaft beneath the radiator) is fitted with operating levers for the brake and forward and reverse gears. Length: 20·47in (52cm). Rare.

Because racing and record-breaking cars appealed strongly to adult buyers as well as to children, toy manufacturers took some trouble to keep pace with developments in the world of speed. "Record" autos were particularly popular in the late 1920s and 1930s, when the world land speed record changed hands fairly frequently; after World War II, emphasis shifted towards motor racing.

All the automobiles shown on this spread were photographed at the London Toy & Model Museum.

1"Super Racer" by a Japanese maker; a large scale tinplate racing car based on the type driven on the motor speedways of the USA, such as Indianapolis, dating from the late 1950s. This car is of fairly good quality: note such detail as the tin windshield, exterior exhaust for a four-cylinder engine, and large section rubber tires (with larger diameter tires at the rear). Printed detail includes advertising for "Shell" and "BP" and for the Montlhéry (France) racing circuit. Length: 18.5in (47cm).

2"Super Racer" by Wo Co, German Federal Republic; very similar to the Japanese-made auto at (1) and again dating from the 1950s. Note, however, that the wheels, with simulated "knock-off" hubcaps, and the rubber tires, marked "Dunlop", differ considerably from those of (1). Again, "Shell" is advertised, also Monza (Italy) racing circuit. Length: 18.75in (48cm).

3"Railton" Record Car by a British maker, c1950, a tinplate, clockwork-driven model of a car used in record-breaking attempts by John Cobb before and after World War II. Note the facsimile autograph of the driver across the body. In this auto, known post-War as the "Mobil Special", Cobb raised the world land speed record to 394mph (634km/h) in 1947: the crossed flags on the nose indicate that this British auto made its record run at an American venue. Length: 10.125in (26cm).

4Racing Car by Mettoy Co Limited, Britain, c1950. Mettoy produced a large range of cheap, lightweight tinplate vehicles like this auto, with its simple clockwork mechanism (note fixed winder). The driver is barely three-dimensional; basic detail includes a cutaway windshield and pressed-tin wheels and tires with a rather unusual printed tread pattern. Length: 12in (30.5cm). Common.

5"Sunbeam Silver Bullet" Record Car by Günthermann, Nuremburg, Germany, c1930; a fine, tinplate, clockwork-driven model. Note the brake lever beside the cockpit. Günthermann made at least three versions of this auto: variations from the example shown include one with British and American flags on the nose cowling and the "Silver Bullet" legend on the hood sides, and a chromium-plated version (the latter is now scarce). Note that this car does not bear a Günthermann trademark: it is simply marked "Foreign". Length: 22in (56cm). Limited.

6M.G. Record Car by a British

maker, c1950; a friction-drive tinplate model of the auto in which Goldie Gardner (note facsimile autograph) set endurance records in Belgium. The model is fairly well detailed, with off-set cockpit and crossed British and Belgian flags on the nose, but is finished in red: the real car was in "M.G. green". Length: 9·875in (25cm).

7 "Bluebird" Record Car; a British maker's version, late 1930s, of the 1935 model (there were several "Bluebird" marques) of Sir Malcolm Campbell's land speed record auto. Models of the various Bluebirds were produced by British, American (Kingsbury), and German (Günthermann)—see (10)—makers. The dual rear wheels and streamlined body of this tinplate, clockwork-drive auto

are reasonably faithful to the original, but the cockpit, in reality slightly off-set, is in a central position. Note facsimile autograph on body. Length: 16in (41cm).

8 Racing Car by Jouets en Paris (Jep), France, c1950; a simple clockwork-driven model in light-weight tinplate from a company famed for its large and impressive toy autos of the pre-World War II period. The wheels are diecast; the tires (and also the driver's helmeted head) are rubber. Length: 12·25in (31cm).

9 "Golden Arrow" Record Car by Günthermann, Germany, c1929; another of this maker's range of record autos—see also (5) and (10). This fine tinplate model of the auto in which Sir Henry Segrave broke the land speed record in March 1929

has a separately-applied tinplate Union Jack on its tailfin, a strikingly faired hood, a brake for its clock-work mechanism (visible on far side of cockpit), and pressed tin wheels and tires. The tinplate driver is missing from this example. Length: 21in (53cm).

10 "Bluebird" by Günthermann, Germany (note "Foreign" marking beneath "Bluebird" legend), c1930; a smaller edition of the maker's standard 20in (51cm) version of one of Campbell's record automobiles, and showing an earlier "Bluebird" marque than the British-made example at (7). In tinplate, it is clockwork-powered (note the permanent winder forward of the rear wheel) and has lithographed British and US flags on its tailfin and radiator cowling.

Length: 12·375in (31·5cm) Limited.

11 Mercedes Grand Prix Car by Schuco, Germany, later 1930s. This ingenious little clockwork auto has exposed working differential and rack-and-pinion steering, and rubber-tired wheels with printed spokes: the sides of the wheels have different-colored spokes for timed wheel-changes! It is key-wound, but with a keyless winding facility, and was supplied with a tool kit. Available in various colors —here in the silver racing colors of Germany—and with different numbers, it was also produced after World War II; later models have unspoked wheels. Because of its long production life, this near-classic toy is still relatively common. Length: 5·5in (14cm).

1 Automobile, possibly modeled on a Horch or Mercedes coupé, by an unidentified German maker, late 1930s. Clockwork-powered, with "tear-drop" front fenders, fully-enclosed rear wheels, and a 'fastback' body, this toy stylishly captures in tinplate the characteristics of the high-performance automobiles built in Germany in the 1930s for use on the new *Autobahn* network. Length: 13·58in (34·5cm). Scarce.

2 Mercedes Type 196 Grand Prix Racing Car—see also (5)—by a West German maker (possibly Neuhierl), mid-1950s. Well-detailed, with plated exhausts and perforated hubcaps on rubber tires, it has five-position programable steering. The hood lifts up to give access to the batteries that power the auto.

Length: 9·65in (24·5cm). Limited.

3 Ferrari Sports Racing Car by Bandai, Tokyo, Japan, mid-1950s. Finished in Italian national racing colors, with the plated number "2" applied to hood and sides, it features a detailed cockpit and rubber-tired wheels with printed spokes. It is friction-powered. Length: 21cm (8·27in).

4 Racing Car by Memo, France, *c*1950. In lightweight tinplate, this simple toy is clockwork-powered, with pressed-tin hood louvers, exhausts, and wheels, and other detail, including driver in enclosed cockpit, printed. It is numbered in rear "808" (not visible in photograph); see also (6). Length: 7·68in (19·5cm).

5 Mercedes Type 196 Grand Prix Racing Car—streamlined version;

Touring Automobile by
Günthermann, Germany, 1920s.
Fenders and running-board are
missing, exposing the long winding
shaft of the clockwork. Length:
7·28in (18·5cm). Limited.

see also (2)—by an unidentified
West German maker, mid-1950s.
Friction-powered, it features an
operating steering-wheel. The
hubcaps are missing from the
rubber-tired wheels. Length:
10·43in (26·5cm).
6 Racing Cars by Memo, France,
c1950. Note the silhouetted tin
drivers and printed details of these
simple clockwork toys in
lightweight tinplate. The maker's
trademark is printed on the tail,
with the number "708"; see also
(4). Length: 5·9in (15cm).

7 "Galop" Racing Car by Lehmann,
Germany, c1930; a simple
clockwork auto of an earlier
period. The driver is a two-piece
pressing. Length: 5·61in
(14·25cm). Limited.
8 "Minia" Filling Station and
Automobile by Chad Valley, Great
Britain, 1950s. The two items of
printed tinplate were sold together
at a "pocket-money" price.
9-10 Motorcycle and Sidecar by an
unidentified maker, USSR, 1970s.
This brightly-finished tinplate toy of
Soviet manufacture is clockwork-
powered. It is seen at (10) without
its sidecar, to show further
pressed-tin engine detail. Length
(motorcycle): 8·46in (21·5cm).
Fairly common.
11 Automobile Association Patrolman
by an unidentified British maker,

late 1930s. This representation of a
figure once familiar on British
highways ("AA men" now use
yellow-painted vans) is clockwork-
powered and has most attractive
printed detail. Length: 7·68in
(19·5cm). Limited.
12 Competition Motorcyclist by an
unidentified British maker, late
1940s. A fairly similar pressing to
(11), but with non-voided (ie, tin
not cut away) areas between the
mudguard stays and forks. The
printed detail, including race
number "49" and license-plate "TT
3149", indicates that it represents
a competitor in the Tourist Trophy
(TT) event held annually in the Isle
of Man. Length: 7·68in (19·5cm).
13 BMW-type Racing Motorcyclist by
Technofix (Gebrüder Einfalt—note
license plate "GE 255"), dating

from c1948-50 and marked
(along exhaust pipe) "Made in
U.S. Zone Germany". Clockwork-
powered, it has most attractive
printed detail. Length: 6·99in
(17·75cm). Limited.
14 At first sight, this is identical with
(13), apart from color finish, but it
is a French-made copy dating
from the 1960s. It uses tabs to
secure mudguards, license plate,
etc, whereas (13) has rolled
edges. The pressed tin wheels and
tires differ considerably in printed
detail. Otherwise as (13).
15 Motorcyclist, probably of
Hungarian manufacture—note "L"
trademark on gas tank—dating
from c1970. Note the large
rubber-tired drive wheels on this
clockwork-powered toy. Length:
6·3in (16cm). Fairly common.

Tinplate motorcycles—see also *pages 80-81*—are increasingly popular with toy collectors. Many modern examples incorporate "novelty" features.

1 Venus Motorcycle by Nomura Toys (trademarked "TN"), Japan, 1960s. The machine is friction-powered: when the mechanism is started by a firm push, the colored balls in clear plastic cylinders beneath the gas tank move up and down to simulate piston action. Length: 9·06in (23cm).

2 Harley-Davidson Motorcycle by Nomura Toys, Japan, 1960s. Again friction-powered, but this time with brightly-colored "pistons" that pump up and down as the cycle moves. Note printed detail of springing on the forks, and treaded rubber tires. Length: 9·06in (23cm).

3 "MAC 700" Motorcycle by Arnold (trademark on front mudguard), West Germany, c1948-50. It has a clever novelty feature: as the clockwork-powered cycle moves away, the rider (with articulated joints, and pivoted at the handlebars) mounts, rides (as shown), dismounts, and remounts, until the clockwork is exhausted. Length: 7·68in (19·5cm). Limited.

4 "Silver Racer" by Tipp and Company, West Germany, 1950s. This clockwork-powered representation of a racing motorcycle and sidecar combination is given added realism by linking the front forks of the cycle and the feet of the sidecar rider to the clockwork motor (links visible in photograph), so that, as the cyclist steers a variable course, the sidecar rider alters position as if to "balance" the combination. Length: 7·09in (18cm). Limited.

5 Motorcycle and Sidecar by Tipp and Company, Germany, c1935-39. A pre-War example of this maker's work, clockwork-powered, and with the sidecar mounted on the right, indicating manufacture for the Continental or US markets. Length: 7·68in (19·5cm). Limited.

6 Motor Scooter by Technofix (Gebrüder Einfalt; note "Technofix" printed on front wheel and spare), West Germany, c1960. Friction-driven via dual rubber wheels, this model of a "gas economy" machine popular in the 1950s-60s has a driver and passenger of tin. Length: 6·3in (16cm).

7 Messerschmitt Tiger "Bubble Car" by Bandai, Japan, mid-1950s. Another "gas economy" vehicle of the 1950s-60s; a two-seat (tandem), four-wheeled auto with a hinged "bubble" top (plastic). Friction-powered, it has printed interior detail and rubber-tired wheels, with a rear-mounted spare. Length: 8·27in (21cm).

8 Messerschmitt by Bandai, mid-1950s: a variant on (7), using a similar pressing, but with only three wheels and no spare. Length: 7·87in (20cm).

9 Isetta "Bubble Car" by Bandai, late 1950s. This friction-powered toy shows the Italian-built auto that set the trend for vehicles of this type. It is a four-wheeled hardtop and, as in the real thing, the front is hinged for

opening. Length: 6·3in (16cm).

10 Renault 1060 4CV by "TM", Japan, 1950s. This model of a French-built sedan of the late 1940s has both friction and battery drive. Note the pressed-tin louvers in rear. Length: 7·09in (18cm).

11 Renault 1060 4CV by Yuoni, Japan, 1950s. This is friction-powered only, and features printed interior detail, a fender-mounted mirror, and—like (10), but note hub variation—rubber tires.

(Left) "Futura", by a Japanese maker, c1960; battery-powered "dream auto" with a hinged perspex top. Length: 11in (28cm). (Right) "Hot Rod" by Nomura Toys, Japan, c1965; battery-powered, with "vibrating" engine and "steering" driver. Length: 10in (25·4cm).

Length: 7·48in (19cm).

12 Three-Wheeled Truck by Bandai, Japan, 1950s. Probably made for the British market (right-hand drive), this vehicle is friction-powered and has a steerable front wheel. Note printed detail. Length: 10·2in (26cm).

13 Packard Hawk Convertible, "Electro-Synchromatic 5700", by Schuco (Schreyer and Company), West Germany, late 1950s. This finely-detailed toy, with working headlights, plastic windshield, plated bumper and trim, pressed and printed interior detail, and rubber whitewall tires, is battery-powered. It has provision for remote steering: note aperture for control cable in hood. Length: 10·6in (27cm). Limited.

Although most makers of toy automobiles also produced a range of commercial vehicles, such toys are generally felt to be of smaller interest to the collector of tinplate vehicles than automobiles are, since the commercial vehicle ranges were generally less extensive and incorporated fewer changes in style. An exception must be made, however, for commercial vehicles that bear well-marked advertising motifs. It should be noted also that toy commercial vehicles are more likely to be found in "play-worn" condition: many were designed for "active play" during which they were loaded with sand, etc. All the vehicles shown on this spread were photographed at the London Toy & Model Museum.

1 Pick-Up Truck, based on a Model "T" Ford, by "Buddy L" (The Moline Pressed Steel Company, East Moline, Illinois), USA, dating from the 1930s. This maker is chiefly known for the production of vehicles in heavy gauge sheet steel, like the example shown here; see also the Bus shown at (3) on *pages 88-89* and the Pumping Engine shown at (2) on *pages 90-91*. This vehicle has diecast "artillery type" spoked wheels and, like the original Model "T", is finished in black. Of extremely robust construction and obviously intended for "active play", it has little in the way of detail. Length: 12in (30·5cm).

2 "Sentinel Rigid Six Wheeler" Steam Lorry by Tipp and Company, Germany, c1930. This clockwork-driven tinplate vehicle was

produced in Germany as a promotional toy for the British company Sentinel, a manufacturer of steam wagons and other heavy plant. (It is worth noting that most of the real Sentinel wagons were four-wheeled; only a few six-wheelers were built.) It has a tipping body with a hinged tailgate, and pressed tin wheels and tires with lithographed detail of tread and spokes. Length: 20in (51cm). This truck is scarce.

3 Army Truck by Mettoy Co. Limited, Britain, c1940. Very much a wartime "utility" toy, this simple and cheaply-priced clockwork truck (note permanent winder) has a canvas canopy and is finished in camouflage of a kind more commonly associated with German than British military vehicles.

Length: 9in (23cm). A fairly common toy.

4 Motor Coach by Tipp and Company, Germany, c1928. This large tinplate vehicle, clockwork-driven, is attractively finished in red, lined with yellow and black, and has pressed tin wheels with lithographed spokes and "Dunlop Cord" tires; note also the lithographed spare tire at the rear. Other detail includes interior seating and battery-operated electric headlights. The same chassis was used by Tipp for other vehicles. Length: 17·5in (44·5cm). A limited item.

5 Mack "Coal" Truck by Arcade Models, an American maker, dating from c1930. Massively made in the cast iron long favored by American makers, this push-/pull-along toy

features a crank-operated tipping mechanism and has rubber tires (note dual tires at rear). A virtually indestructible toy, it has some cast detail—springs, radiator, "Mack" on cab door—but generally lacks the sophistication of its European tinplate contemporaries. Length: 10·125in (26cm).

6 Tipping Truck by Gebrüder Bing, Nuremburg, Germany, c1908. In excellent condition, this fine early example of a tinplate commercial vehicle has a hand-enameled finish, cast "artillery type" wheels with rubber tires, and a canvas canopy above the cab. It is clockwork-powered, with steering operating from the wheel and manually-operated tipping action. Length: 11·5in (29cm). A very scarce specimen.

7 Tipping Truck by Paya, Alicante, Spain, c1930. This clockwork-driven tinplate truck is attractively finished and derives a certain charm from the fact that the same simple tinplate silhouette of the driver appears above both doors. The spoked wheels are of pressed tin and the maker's trademark is visible on the near door. Length: 10in (25·4cm).

8 Pickup Truck by André Citroën, France, c1929. A fine model from this justly celebrated range—see note at (1), *pages 68-69*—this truck is based on the Citroën C6 chassis. It features opening doors, operating steering, and electric headlights, and has rubber tires. Note the detail of the radiator, with the Citroën chevrons and swan badge. As shown, it was sold complete

with a load of sacks, also bearing the Citroën chevrons. Length: 17in (43cm). Scarce. (A Road Sweeping Vehicle was produced on the same chassis; this is now very scarce.)

9 Trailer Truck by Wyn-Toy, Australia, c1950; note the maker's trademark on the cab door. This simple but effective toy is of pressed tin construction, with pressed tin wheels and a plated radiator. Length overall: 18·25in (46cm).

10 Gas Pump and Oil Cabinet Set by Tipp and Company, Germany, dating from c1920; a most attractive accessory—with considerable period charm for the present-day motorist! In those days, it was common for gas stations to offer for sale several brands of gasoline—and here

we see the familiar names of "Shell" and "BP" alongside the now-forgotten "Pratts". The glass globes of the fuel pumps are electrically lit by means of a battery concealed within the attractively-lithographed tinplate "Double Shell Motor Oil" cabinet, and the curved island on which the pumps and cabinet are mounted also incorporates "In" and "Out" signs. Length: 9·5in (24cm). Limited. (The water can shown in front of the set is a diecast garage accessory and was not made by Tipp and Company.)

11-12 Unlike Citroën—see (8)—most makers did not supply loads for their commercial vehicles. There must be few children who have not used composition blocks like these to load their vehicles.

Box for "Ubilda" Fire engine by Chad Valley, Great Britain. This vehicle construction kit, see (1-3) above, was made both before and after World War II.

1-3 "Ubilda" Fire Engine by Chad Valley, Great Britain, dating from c1950. Chad Valley produced a number of vehicle construction kits in its "Ubilda" series, among them the tinplate fire engine—based on a British-built vehicle of the 1930s—shown here, at (1), fully assembled. At (2), the larger components are shown, including the detachable escape, pressed tin wheels with printed tire-tread patterns, and a clockwork motor. At (3) are the smaller items supplied with the kit: axles, nuts, bolts, and monkey wrench. Length (finished model): 10·4in (25·5cm).

4 "Crumpsall Cream Crackers" Delivery Van (a novelty cookie tin) by Chad Valley, Great Britain, c1948-50. This item was produced for the British C.W.S. (Co-Operative Wholesale Society), a nation-wide chain of stores, whose monogram features in the wealth of lithographed detail. It originally contained soda crackers and, when empty, made an attractive toy. A clockwork motor drives the rear wheels; note the permanently-fixed winder. Chad Valley used the same pressing for its more common "Games" Van and its Mail Van. Length: 9·74in (24·75cm). Limited.

5 Tipping Truck by an unidentified British maker, c1948-52. In lightweight tinplate, with a tin driver, printed detail, and lever-operated tipping mechanism, this is fairly typical of low-priced clockwork toys made in Britain in the 1930s-40s. Length: 9.84in (25cm). Fairly common.

6 "Shell" Gasoline Tanker (with a Renault-type radiator) by Rossignol, France, c1935-40. Although lacking mudguards and lamps, this clockwork toy in lightweight tinplate has rudimentary detail of suspension and chassis, with printed detail that includes a gas can at the cab door. Length: 8·17in (20·75cm).

7 Trailer Truck by an unidentified British maker (marked only "Made in England" on mudguard), c1946-1950. A clockwork motor is concealed within the cab. It has simple tin wheels: note that the near-side front wheel of the trailer has detail printed off-center, a not uncommon fault in such cheaply-made toys. Length: 9·06in (23cm).

8 Tipping Truck by an unidentified British maker, dating from the

1930s-40s. It much resembles (7) in the shape of the cab and details of finish; the wheels, however, with printed "Dunlop" tires, are of what is believed to be an earlier type. Length: 7·68in (19·5cm).

9 "National Benzole Mixture" Gasoline Tanker by an unidentified British maker (again, with "Made in England" printed on the mudguard), dating from the late 1940s. This is another cheaply-made clockwork toy—note permanent winder in front of rear wheel—with pressed and printed filler-caps on the tank. Length: 6·5in (16·5cm).

10 "Pool" Articulated Gasoline Tanker by Mettoy, Great Britain, dating from the 1940s. ("Pool" gasoline represented the output in the 1940s of the major petroleum

companies, which, in Britain, "pooled" their resources during wartime.) Clockwork-powered, this has a suitably austere finish, with printed filler-cap detail, and the maker's name, atop the tank. Length: 7·87in (20cm).

11 "International Oil" Articulated Gasoline Tanker by Mettoy, Great Britain, dating from the 1940s: the same pressing as (10), but with a different finish. Again, a clockwork toy with printed detail of filler-caps —this time without the maker's name—on the tank. Length: 7·87in (20cm). Fairly common.

12 "Esso" Articulated Gasoline Tanker, British-made ("Made in England" printed on mudguard), dating from the 1940s. Although this clockwork toy bears no maker's name, it is likely , having

regard to the similarity of its pressing and size to (10) and (11), that it was made by Mettoy— perhaps for sale by another company or through special outlets. Length: 7·87in (20cm).

13 "Shell" Articulated Gasoline Tanker by an unidentified British maker (again, probably Mettoy), dating from the 1940s. It closely resembles (12) in size and pressing, but has more interesting printed detail on both the cab and tank. Length: 7·87in (20cm).

14 "Express Delivery" Van by Wells, Great Britain ("British Made" printed at base of radiator), dating from the mid-1930s. Wells produced the same vehicle in the livery of the "Carter, Paterson" haulage company. Length: 4·72in (12cm). Limited.

15 Light Truck by Paya, Spain, dating from the 1940s. A cheaply-made clockwork toy of lightweight tinplate; note the printed tin silhouette of the driver. Length: 7·58in (19·25cm).

16 "Campsa" Gasoline Tanker by Rico (note "RSA" trademark on cab door), Spain, dating from the 1940s. A simple clockwork toy of lightweight tinplate; note the perforated wheels. Length: 7·09in (18cm). Fairly common.

17 "Colis Express" Delivery Van by Memo (note maker's trademark printed on cab door), France, c1945-50. Another cheaply-made toy in lightweight tinplate, but with pleasing printed detail in *art deco* style. It has a somewhat over-sized permanent winder for its clockwork motor. Length: 5·81in (14·75cm).

Buses by European, Japanese, and US Makers, 1920-1960s

All the vehicles shown on this spread were photographed at the London Toy & Model Museum.

1 "General" Double-Deck Bus, tinplate, by Günthermann, Nuremburg, Germany, c1930. This British-style clockwork-driven bus, with an open cab (note pressed tin driver) and staircase, and a covered upper deck, has pressed tin wheels with lithographed spokes. It carries lithographed advertisements. Length: 9·25in (23·5cm). Scarce.

2 "General" Six-Wheeled Double-Deck Bus, tinplate, possibly British-made, c1929, for the wellknown British confectionery maker Huntley & Palmers, whose lithographed advertisement appears on the side. The top may

be removed to reveal (originally) a cargo of cookies—a popular marketing idea during the Christmas period. It is clockwork, the motor driving the rear pair of wheels, with a winder concealed beneath the body. The lithographed advertisements immediately above the side windows are "reversed": this was a feature of the real buses, where these messages were intended to be read from the inside. Note particularly the very attractive lithographed detail of individual passengers. Length: 9·5in (24cm). Very scarce.

3 Single-Deck Bus by Buddy "L" (The Moline Pressed Steel Company, East Moline, Illinois), USA, dating from the early 1930s. This company is noted for the manufacture of some of the largest

and toughest toy vehicles ever made—and this "Buddy 'L' Transportation Co" (legend on the destination board, above the cab) bus, of heavy gauge sheet steel, is a fine example. A pull/push-along toy, it features working steering, opening doors (note maker's transfer on the inner side), and interior seating. The cast metal wheels (dual at the rear) are detachable and two spares are carried, one on either side of the hood. Length: 29in (74cm). Scarce: especially as seen here with the original paint finish.

4 "Inter-State" Bus, numbered "109", by Strauss, USA, dating from the 1920s (before the purchase of the company by Louis Marx, as a step towards his toy-making empire). Made for the domestic market, this

open-topped double-decker in tinplate has clockwork driving the rear pair of pressed tin wheels. The finish, with lithographed detail of slatted seats, is rather unusual. Length: 10·125in (26cm). Scarce.

5 Six-Wheeled "Greyhound Scenicruiser" by a Japanese maker, 1960s. Made for the US market, this is a good example of latter-day tinplate toy production. Length: 14·5in (37cm). Fairly common, especially in the USA.

6 Four-Wheeled "Greyhound Scenicruiser", again by a Japanese maker (it bears a "Globe" trademark) for the US market, late 1960s. This is finished to a generally lower standard than the larger example at (5). Length: 8·75in (22cm). Fairly common.

7 Paris Bus (note lithographed

"Bastille Etoile" destination board) by a French maker, c1930. This cheaply-made push-along toy, with lithographed detail and printed passengers, is really a later equivalent of the "Penny Toys" of the pre-World War I period. Length: 3·5in (9cm).

8 "General" Six-Wheeled Double-Deck Bus, made in Germany for the British market, c1930. Although on a slightly smaller scale than the French bus shown at (7), this tinplate toy with lithographed detail is clockwork-driven. Length: 2·875in (7·3cm).

9 "General" Double-Deck Bus by Johann Distler, Nuremburg, Germany, c1929. This is a fine example of the work of a noted maker of cheaper tinplate toys. The British-style open-topped bus

—with the whimsical destination board "Route 29 To Toyland", large "Virol" advertisement, and small "reversed" advertisements above the windows—is clockwork-driven (note permanent winder) and has a staircase, wheels, and tires of pressed tin. Marketed as the "Fares Please" model, it incorporates a novelty feature: as the bus travels, the conductor moves backwards and forwards on the top deck as if collecting fares. Length: 8·625in (22cm). Scarce.

10 "General" Double-Deck Bus, numbered "K 200", by Gebrüder Bing, Nuremburg, Germany, mid-1920s; one of the more simple, but still very desirable, products of a famous maker. Clockwork-driven, it has artillery-type wheels with lithographed tire tread detail;

the "Wright's Coal Tar Soap" advertisement combines with other lithographed detail to give an accurate "feeling" of a London bus of the period. Length: 7·125in (18cm). Limited.

11 "Lehmann's Autobus", numbered "590", by Lehmann, Brandenburg, Germany, c1920. This tinplate double-decker was produced both before and after World War I and was a very popular model in both Europe and the USA. Clockwork-driven, it features spoked wheels (the rear pair larger than the front, with simple steering by turning the latter) and a pressed tin driver. Length: 8in (20cm). Scarce.

12 Double-Deck Bus by a German maker (without trademark), mid-1930s. This is a well-made tinplate model with pressed tin

wheels and tires, the rear pair driven by clockwork (note permanent winder). Length: 10·5in (27cm). Scarce.

13 "London Transport" Double-Deck Bus (based on a contemporary AEC bus) by Chad Valley, Great Britain, c1950. This tinplate model continues the tradition of novelty cookie tins into the 1950s: the detachable top gave access to a cargo of "Carr's Biscuits", and it was sold in both clockwork-driven (as shown, note winding shaft forward of rear wheels) and push-along forms. Length: 10in (25·4cm). Limited.

14 Double-Deck Bus, numbered "6", by Rico, Spain, probably 1950s; a very simple clockwork-driven toy in lightweight tinplate. Length: 6in (15cm). Fairly common.

Fire engines and other fire-fighting equipment are almost invariably finished in red. A collection of them may therefore seem to lack variety, but toys of this kind have always been popular with children—no doubt the clanging bells on many add considerably to their appeal! All the vehicles shown on this spread were photographed at the London Toy & Model Museum.

1 Fire Pump by Union, USA, dating from c1900. This fine toy of basically cast-iron construction features live-steam operation of a pump with twin cylinders of oscillating type. The spirit-fired brass boiler drives twin flywheels which operate the pump via con-rods. The smaller brass container visible beneath the

cylinders is the water reservoir and the nozzle that arches over the driver's head would originally have been fitted with a hose. The cast-iron driver should, of course, be urging on a team of horses. Length: 10·25in (26cm). Scarce.
2 Water Tower by Buddy "L" (Moline Pressed Steel Company, East Moline, Illinois), USA, dating from c1930. Made in the heavy gauge sheet steel favored by this manufacturer, this is an extremely tough pull/push-along toy, with an operating steering wheel and such detail as a bell above the radiator, headlamps and swiveling spotlamp, and a manually-operated tower with a pump worked by a lever (visible here in the "up" position) immediately behind the driver's seat. The pump, fed by the

large water tank (with the cap missing in this example) in the body of the vehicle, forces water up a channel in the tower, which is turned to direct the jet. The wheels and tires of the vehicle are diecast and it is finished (inevitably) in red enamel, with the maker's transfer below the pump base and a "CFD" (City Fire Department) transfer below the driver's seat. Length: 41in (104cm). Fairly scarce, especially outside the USA.
3 Horse-Drawn Fire Engine by R.W.S., USA, dating from c1890-1900. This large and impressive pull-along toy in cast iron, with a two-piece chassis, has detachable ladders and two detachable drivers. It is drawn by three galloping horses and the rear-most driver holds a wheel (non-operating on the

model) that, on the real engine, was used to steer the rear wheels to negotiate tight bends. Length: 28·5in (72cm). Scarce, especially outside the USA—and collectors are advised to beware of later copies of such classic American cast-iron toys.
4 Fire Chief's Auto by Günthermann, Nuremburg, Germany, c1930; note the maker's trademark on the trunk. A bell again features prominently on this clockwork-driven tinplate auto, with pressed tin firemen, artillery-type spoked wheels of pressed tin, and attractive lithographed detail and finish. Length: 7·125in (18cm).
5 Fire Pump, probably by Distler, Germany, late 1920s. The tinplate vehicle with its bright-finish boiler carries a crew of three pressed tin

figures; the wheels and tires are also of pressed tin. Clockwork-driven, it has an operating brake. Length: 8·125in (20·5cm).

6 Fire Pump by an American maker, *c*1920. This cast-iron pull-along toy is of two-piece construction and has attractive cast detail. Length: 8·25in (21cm).

7 Fire Pump by a Japanese maker, dating from after World War II. This simple tinplate vehicle, with a pressed tin driver and pressed tin wheels and tires, features a bell and a detachable ladder. Length: 5·5in (14cm). Common.

8 Fire Pump by an American maker, *c*1935 — a late date for a cast-iron toy. The cast detail is somewhat crude; note that the rubber tires are badly perished. Length: 4·875in (12cm). Fairly common.

9 Horse-Drawn Fire Pump by an American maker (possibly Kenton), *c*1900. This is a cheap and simple cast-iron pull-along toy of two-piece construction: the line of the joint can be clearly seen. Length: 9·5in (24cm). Limited.

10-12 Firemen and Fireguards: para-military figures in tin — including riflemen (10) and a bugler (12) — by a French maker, probably Faivre, dating from around 1900. Height of individual figure: 3·375in (8·5cm). Limited.

Hook-and-Ladder Fire Truck by Marx, USA, c1960. The trailer vehicle is tinplate with printed detail and has several plastic features, including windshield, spotlight, control panel, and driver. Length: 36·5in (91cm).

Tinplate Vehicles by "Minic", Great Britain, 1930s-1950s

A very successful alternative to Dinky diecast models was the series of clockwork tinplate vehicles made by Lines Brothers Limited, London, from the mid-1930s and, after World War II, into the 1950s, under the "Triang" and "Minic" trademarks. All the vehicles shown here are of the type generally known as "Minics" and are clockwork-driven.

1 Delivery Lorry; with chromium-plated radiator and front mudguards and pressed tin wheels; front-wheel drive. This vehicle, also made in a tipping version, was produced both before and after World War II—see also (7)—in various colors. A post-War example is shown here. Length: 5·5in (140mm).

2 Camouflaged Army Lorry—the same pressing as (1), but six-wheeled—made c1940. The camouflage finish here includes radiator and wheels, but it may be found with "blued" radiator, tires. Length: 5·5in (140mm). Scarce.

3 Jeep; a very popular model of the early post-War period. Production was large and many were exported to the USA; it may be found with "USA" on the hood rather than the Allied Invasion Star as seen here. Rear-wheel drive; it was made with plastic wheels with molded tread (two types) or with cast wheels and rubber tires. The finish may vary from olive drab to bronze-green gloss. Length: 3·125in (79mm).

4 Dustcart; a front-wheel drive vehicle made both pre- and post-War—a post-War example is shown. Note pressed tin wheels and the sliding covers over the partitioned interior. Length: 5·5in (140mm).

5 Breakdown Lorry; the only Minic to incorporate *two* clockwork motors: one driving the vehicle and the other operating the crane (the jib being raised or lowered manually by a handle on the left side). A post-War example, with diecast wheels and rubber tires, is shown. Length: 5·5in (140mm).

6 Shell-BP Petrol Tanker; front-wheel drive. Made pre- and post-War: the white rubber tires and long-shanked steering column of this example denote the pre-War type. Length: 5·5in (140mm).

7 Timber Lorry; as (1) but with a cross-member to support the load. On this post-War example, the wooden planks are in the original cellophane wrapper.

8-9 Vauxhall Town Coupé; post-War versions showing color variants. The front-wheel drive autos have wooden seats and plated radiators, bumpers, wheels, and windshields. The pre-War model had a baggage rack and was also issued with a plain radiator. Length: 5in (127mm).

10-11 Minic Racer No 1; post-War types showing color variants and (11) alterable angle of front wheels. The clockwork motor drives the rear wheels and is unregulated to give high speed. The cockpit cover and exhaust are plastic; the driver is printed paper. The pre-War model had an open cockpit with steering wheel on column, a windshield frame, and a voided

radiator grille. Length: 5·5in (140mm).

12 Royal Mail Van; pre-War example with rear-wheel drive, plain disk wheels with U-section rubber tires, and "GR" (King George VI) transfers. A version with "ER" (King Edward VIII) transfers exists. Length: 3in (76mm).

13 Ford Light Van; same pressing as (12), but with "Minic Transport" transfers and white rubber tires. A Ford Saloon Car, with the same chassis and front, was also made. Length: 3in (76mm).

14 Green Line Single-Deck Bus; a post-War type, with front-wheel drive. Note wooden seats; a destination board "Dorking" is above the cab and a "Bisto Kids" advertising transfer at rear. Length: 7·25in (184mm).

Ford Light Van; a pre-War model, shown by the gasoline can on the running board; see (13) above. Hole in box allowed for inspection of color without opening.

15-17 Vauxhall Tourer; post-War color variants. This model used the same chassis, radiator, and hood as the Coupé (8-9), but with a simulated folding soft-top and cutaway doors. Pre-War versions may be found with diecast driver and passengers; these are scarce. Length: 5in (127mm).

18-19 Carter Paterson & Pickfords Delivery Lorries; post-War examples showing both types of advertising transfers used. The model was also issued with railway company logos. Pre-War examples carry Carter Paterson advertisements only. Length: 5·5in (140mm).

20-22 Streamline Sports Car, based loosely on the Chrysler Airflow, showing on (20) transfer license plate "LBL 174" (LBL=Lines

Brothers Limited) at rear. Pre-War models have a different license-plate. A one-piece body pressing, with simulated folded soft-top and wooden seats. Length: 5in (127mm).

23 Minic Transport Van. Front-wheel drive like (18-19), it uses the same radiator and van compartment pressing but has a shorter wheelbase. The wheels are diecast, with balloon section tires. Color variants are found, but only post-War examples have cabs as shown. Length: 5·25in (133mm).

24-25 Vauxhall Cabriolet; post-War types. The body is the same as (8-9), with chromed top bars and rear window; the chassis, radiator, and hood are the same as (8-9) and (15-17). Length: 5in (127mm).

Diecast Vehicles by Lesney "Matchbox", Britain, 1950s-1960s

One of the most original marketing ideas in the post-War toy world was Lesney's "Matchbox" series, introduced in 1953: pocket-money priced diecast vehicles small enough to be packaged in a container resembling a standard British matchbox. Note that as items were added to the series and others dropped, existing identification numbers were reallocated.

1 Garage with opening doors; Lesney Matchbox (LM) Number A3 (Major Pack), dating from c1960. Length: 2·625in (67mm).
2 Wolseley; LM 57, issued 1959. Length: 2·125in (54mm).
3 Daimler Ambulance; LM 14, issued c1955-60, small size, 1st type. Length: 2in (51mm).
4 Daimler Ambulance; LM 14, c1962, larger size, 2nd type. Length: 2·25in (57mm).
5 Mobile Refreshments Bar, with lifting counter; LM 74, first issued 1959. Length: 2·625in (67mm).
6 Double Deck Bus, with "Visco-Static" advertising transfers; LM 5, issued 1960, 3rd type. Length: 2·625in (67mm).
7 Double Deck Bus, with "Matchbox" advertisements; LM 5, c1958, 2nd type. Length: 2·25in (57mm).
8 Double Deck Bus, with "Matchbox" advertisements; LM 5, issued 1954, 1st type. Length: 2in (51mm).
9 ER Foden Lorry; LM 20, issued 1955. Length: 2·25in (57mm).
10 ERF Horse Box, with opening side and ramp (not shown); LM 35, 1956. Length: 2·125in (54mm).
11 Jaguar 3.8 Mk II; LM 65, issued 1959, 1st type (later model had lift-up hood fitted). Length: 2·5in (63·5mm).
12 Aston Martin DB2/4; LM 52, issued c1963. Length: 2·5in (63·5mm).
13 Rolls Royce Silver Cloud; LM 44, 1957. Length: 2·75in (70mm).
14 Jaguar Mk 10; LM 28, issued c1964. Length: 2·75in (70mm).
15 Austin A50; LM 36, issued 1956. Length: 2·375in (60mm).
16 Ford Zodiac; LM 33, issued 1956. Length: 2·5in (63·5mm).
17 Ford Customline Station Wagon; LM 31, issued 1956. Length: 2·625in (67mm).
18 Hillman Minx; LM 43, issued 1957. Length: 2·625in (67mm).
19 Vauxhall Cresta; LM 22, issued 1955. Length: 2·5in (63·5mm).
20 Citroën DS 19; LM 66, issued 1958. Length: 2·5in (63·5mm).
21 Cadillac '60; LM 27, issued 1960.
Length: 2·75in (70mm).
22 Vauxhall Victor; LM 45, issued 1957. Length: 2·375in (60mm).
23 Ford Anglia; LM 7, issued 1961. Length: 2·625in (67mm).
24 Ford Prefect; LM 30, issued 1956. Length: 2·25in (57mm).
25 Morris Minor 1000; LM 46, issued 1957. Length: 2in (51mm).
26 M.G. TD; LM 19, first issue, 1955. Length: 2in (51mm).
27 Jaguar "D" Type Racing Car; LM 41, issued 1956, the first of three variants. Length: 2·25in (57mm).
28 M.G.A. Sports Car; LM 19 (second issue for this Number) issued 1959. Length: 2·25in (57mm).
29 Jaguar XK 140; LM 32, issued 1956 and also made in red. Length: 2·375in (60mm).
30 Maserati 4CLT Racing Car; LM 52, 1958. Length: 2·375in (60mm).

31 Aston Martin F1 Racing Car; LM 19 (third issue for this Number), issued 1961. Included driver (not shown). Length: 2·5in (63·5mm).

32 Bedford Car Transporter; LM A2 (Major Pack), issued c1960. Length: 6·5in (165mm).

33 Caravan; LM 23, 1st type, issued 1956. Length: 2·5in (63·5mm).

34 Caravan; LM 23, 3rd type, issued 1964. It has a detachable top. Length: 3in (76mm).

35 Caravan; LM 23, 2nd type, issued 1959. Opening door. Length: 2·625in (67mm).

36 Trolley Bus, with "Peardrax" advertisements; LM 56, issued 1959 and having a long production run. Length: 2·625in (67mm).

37 Leyland Royal Tiger Long Distance Bus; LM 40; issued c1961. Length: 3in (76mm).

38 Bedford "London to Glasgow" Coach; LM 21, large size, issued 1958. Length: 2·625in (67mm).

39 As (38), but small size, 1st issue, introduced 1955. Length: 2·25in (57mm).

40-41 British European Airway(s) Coaches, showing transfer variation; LM 58, issued c1959. Length: 2·5in (63·5mm).

42 Bedford "Dunlop" Delivery Van; LM 25, issued 1956. Length 2·125in (54mm).

43 Volkswagen Van, with "Matchbox International Express" transfers; LM 34, issued 1956. Length: 2·25in (57mm).

44 Commer Milk Delivery Truck; LM 21, 1961. Length: 2·25in (57mm).

45 Bedford Milk Delivery Truck; LM 29, 1956. Length: 2·25in (57mm).

46 Bedford "Evening News" Delivery Van; LM 42, first issued 1956. Length: 2·75in (70mm).

47 Commer Van, with "Nestlé's" advertisements; LM 69, issued 1959. Cab with sliding door. Length: 2·25in (57mm).

48-49 Bedford Removals Vans, with "Matchbox Removals Service" transfers; LM 17, issued c1955. Two color variations shown; it was also produced in pale blue. Length: 2·25in (57mm).

50 Commer Dustcart, with "Cleansing Department" transfers; LM 38, first issued c1956. Length: 2·625in (67mm).

51 Morris "Builders Supply Company" Pick-Up Truck; LM 60, issued 1959. Length: 2·25in (57mm).

52-53 Long Distance Removal Vans; LM 46. "Pickfords" transfers are missing from (52), issued in green

finish in c1961; (53) is in the earlier dark blue finish, issued c1960, complete with transfers. Length: 2·625in (67mm).

54 Petrol Tanker; LM 11, issued c1955, small size, 1st type—see also (56). Length: 2in (51mm).

55 Petrol Tanker; LM 11, issued 1960, larger size, 2nd type. Length: 2·625in (67mm).

56 As (54), but in red with "Esso" transfer at the rear, issued 1955. Length: 2in (51mm).

57 Coca-Cola Delivery Truck; LM 37, issued 1956. Note that the "uneven" load marks this as the 1st issue; the vehicle was also produced with an "even" load. Length: 2·25in (57mm).

58 Trojan Van, with "Brooke Bond Tea" transfers; LM 47, issued 1957. Length: 2·25in (57mm).

Diecast Vehicles by Lesney "Matchbox", Britain, 1950s-1960s

Some military vehicles are shown here as part of the "Matchbox" series. Note that military vehicles by other makers are shown on *pages 176-183,* in the section devoted to "Military Toys".

1 Military Ambulance (based on Fordson 4x4 ambulance of the 1950s); Lesney Matchbox (LM) Number 63, issued c1959. Length: 2·625in (67mm).

2 Saracen Troop Carrier, with revolving turret (based on Alvis 6x6 armored personnel carrier); LM 54, 1959. Length: 2·25in (57mm).

3 Military Personnel Carrier, with "invasion star" on hood (based on US Army half-track of World War II); LM 49, issued 1958. Length: 2·52in (64mm).

4 Saladin Armored Car (based on

Alvis 6x6 armored car); LM 67, issued 1959. A popular model with collectors. Length: 2·25in (57mm).

5 Military Scout Car (based on the 4x4 Ferret of the 1950s-60s); LM 61, 1959. Length: 2·25in (57mm).

6 Six-Wheeled Military Crane Truck (based on post-World War II 6x6 Scammell Explorer recovery vehicle); LM 64, issued 1959. Length: 2·625in (67mm).

7-8 Ten-Wheeled Tank Transporter (based on Thorneycroft Mighty Antar tractor and transporter unit) with Centurion Tank; LM M3 (Major Pack), issued c1960. Overall length: 6·1in (155mm).

9 Military General Service Truck (based on AEC Militant artillery tractor); LM 62, issued c1959. Length: 2·75in (70mm).

10 DUKW Amphibious General

Purpose Cargo Vehicle; LM 55, 1959. Length: 2·75in (70mm).

11 Hydraulic Excavator; LM 24, issued 1956. This is the 1st type, small size; a larger version of the model was later introduced. Length: 2·25in (57mm).

12 ERF Cement Truck; LM 26, 1956. 1st type, replaced by larger version of model in 1961. Length: 1·75in (44mm).

13 Bedford Tipping Lorry, with opening tailgate; LM 40, issued 1956. Length: 2·125in (54mm).

14 Mountaineer Dump Truck (with front-mounted snow-plow missing from this example); LM 16, 1964. Length: 3in (76mm).

15 Caterpillar Tractor; LM 8, issued c1955-57. Early type: see also (24), (25), and (26). Length: 1·5in (38mm).

16 Caterpillar Bulldozer (with driver's head missing from this example); LM 18, issued c1958, later type. Length: 2in (51mm).

17 Caterpillar Bulldozer; LM 18, 1955, 1st type. Length: 1·75in (44mm).

18 Earth Mover; LM MI (Major Pack), 1955. Length: 4·5in (114mm).

19 Prime Mover; LM 15, 1955, 1st type, shown with attached Transporter Trailer; LM 16, issued 1955. The two items were complementary. Lengths: (Prime Mover) 2·25in (57mm); (Transporter Trailer) 3in (76mm).

20 Harley Davidson Motorcycle and Sidecar; LM 66, issued 1963. Length: 2·875in (73mm).

21 Triumph Motorcycle and Sidecar; LM 4, 1959. Length: 2·25in (57mm).

22 Cement Mixer; LM 3, issued 1953—one of the first Matchbox

toys. Length: 1·5in (38mm).

23 Fordson Tractor; LM 72, issued 1959. Length: 2in (51mm).

24-26 Caterpillar Tractors (with tracks missing from these examples; see (15) for early type complete with tracks); LM 8. These three early types, issued c1955-57, show variations in both color and casting. Length: 1·5in (38mm).

27 Horse-Drawn Milk Float; LM7, issued 1955. Since this is a somewhat fragile model, it is one of the scarcer items of the 1st series. Length: 2·25in (57mm).

28 Fordson Articulated Cattle Truck, with opening tailgate; LM M7 (Major Pack), 1960. Length: 4·76in (121mm).

29 Bedford Tipper Truck, with opening tail flap; LM 3, issued 1961. Length: 2·52in (64mm).

30 Eight-Wheeled Tipper Truck, with "Douglas" transfers; LM 51, issued 1969. Length: 3in (76mm).

31 Ford Fairlane Police Car, with US Police transfers; LM 55, issued 1963, followed by a Ford Galaxie in c1966. Length: 2·64in (67mm).

32 Fordson Thames Wreck Truck/Breakdown Lorry; LM 13, issued 1959, 3rd type. Length: 2·5in (63·5mm).

33 Bedford Articulated "Wall's Ice Cream" Truck; LM M2 (Major Pack), issued 1955. Length: 3·875in (98mm).

34-35 Fire Engine with Escape (Dennis type); LM 9, issued c1955. Note radiator variation: (35) has smooth radiator. Length: 2·25in (57mm).

36 Fire Truck (based on Merryweather vehicle); LM 9, issued 1959. Length: 2·625in (67mm).

37 Fire Fighting Crash Tender; LM 63, 1964. Length: 2·375in (60mm).

38 Dennis Refuse Truck, with "Cleansing Service" transfers; LM 15, 1963. Length: 2·5in (63·5mm).

39 Diesel Road Roller; LM 1, issued 1953, 1st type. Note that canopy is missing from this example; the same model, with canopy and showing color variation, is shown at (41). Length: 1·875in (48mm).

40 Diesel Road Roller; LM 1, issued c1958, 2nd type model. Length: 2·25in (57mm).

41 Diesel Road Roller; see (39).

42 Mechanical Horse and Trailer; LM 10, issued 1958, 2nd type. Length: 3in (76mm).

43 Mechanical Horse and Trailer; LM 10, issued 1955, 1st type. Length: 2·25in (57mm).

44 Bedford Low Loader; LM 27,

issued 1956. Length: 3in (76mm).

45 Blue Circle Portland Cement Lorry; LM 51, issued 1958. Length: 2·5in (63·5mm).

46 Eight-Wheeled Foden Lorry, with "Ever Ready for Life!" transfers; LM 20, 1959. Length: 2·75in (70mm).

47 Dumper; LM 2, issued 1959, 2nd type. Length: 1·875in (48mm).

48 Dumper; LM 2, issued 1953, 1st type. Length: 1·5in (38mm).

49 Bedford Compressor Lorry; LM 28, 1956. Length: 1·75in (44mm).

50 Quarry Truck; LM 6, issued 1956, 1st type. Length: 2·25in (57mm).

51 Bedford Wreck Truck; LM 13, issued 1955. Length: 2in (51mm).

52 Tractor; LM 4, issued 1954. Length: 1·5in (38mm).

53 Land Rover; LM 12, issued 1955. Length: 1·625in (41mm).

Diecast "Models of Yesteryear" by Lesney, Britain, 1950s-1960s

In 1955, as an addition to an already extensive range of small diecast vehicles—see "Matchbox" series, *pages 94-97*—Lesney introduced "Models of Yesteryear", a series of vintage and veteran vehicles. The detailed models appealed not only to children but also to the growing number of adult diecast enthusiasts and, of course, to collectors, with whom they remain extremely popular. Note that on all models the tires, and some other details, are plastic. As with the "Matchbox" series, the identification numbers of deleted items were reallocated to new items in the range.

1 1912 Rolls Royce; Lesney Models of Yesteryear (MoY) Number Y-7 (Third Series), issued *c*1968. Scale 1:48. Length: 3·75in (95mm).

2 1930 Packard Victoria; MoY Y-15 (Second Series), *c*1969. Scale 1:46. Length: 4·25in (108mm).

3 1910 Benz Limousine; MoY Y-3 (Second Series), 1966; based on an example now preserved in the Daimler-Benz Museum, Stuttgart, West Germany. Scale 1:54. Length: 3·25in (83mm).

4 1912 Simplex (New York); MoY Y-9 (Second Series), 1968. Scale 1:48. Length: 3·75in (95mm).

5 1912 Packard Landaulet; MoY Y-11 (Second Series), 1964. Scale 1:50 Length: 3·25in (83mm).

6 1914 Stutz (Type 4E Roadster); MoY Y-8 (Third Series), issued in 1969. Scale 1:48. Length: 3·375in (86mm).

7 1908 Grand Prix Mercedes Racing Car; MoY Y-10 (First Series), issued in 1959. This racing automobile is modeled on the winning auto in the historic French Grand Prix of 1908. The scale of the model is 1:54. Length 3in (76mm).

8 1929 Le Mans Bentley; MoY Y-5 (First Series), 1957; modeled on the 4·5-liter British autos that dominated the 24-hour race at Le Mans, France, in the late 1920s and early 1930s. An improved model was introduced in 1963 (Second Series). Scale 1:55. Length: 3·125in (79mm).

9 1906 Rolls Royce Silver Ghost; MoY Y-10 (Third Series), issued in *c*1969. Scale 1:51. Length: 3·625in (92mm).

10 1914 Prince Henry Vauxhall; MoY Y-2 (Third Series), 1970. Scale 1:47. Length: 3·5in (89mm).

11 Type 35 Bugatti; MoY Y-6 (Second Series). The red finish of this model of one of the most famous racing cars of the 1920s indicates that it was issued *c*1967; see (12) for an earlier example. Scale 1:48. Length: 3·125in (79mm).

12 As (11) but finished in blue; this indicates that the model was issued earlier, *c*1962.

13 1911 Daimler; MoY Y-13 (Second Series), 1966. Scale 1:45. Length: 3·375in (86mm).

14 1904 Spyker; MoY Y-16 (First Series), 1961. The original was of Dutch origin. Scale 1:45. Length: 3·25in (83mm).

15 1907 Peugeot; MoY Y-5 (Third Series), 1969. Scale 1:43. Length: 3·5in (89mm).

16 1909 Thomas Flyabout; MoY Y-12 (Second Series), 1968. Scale 1:48. Length: 4in (102mm).

17 1911 Model "T" Ford; MoY Y-1 (Second Series). This very popular model of Henry Ford's "Tin Lizzie" was issued in 1965. The real Model "T" first appeared in 1908 and remained in production until 1927, by which time more than 15,000,000 had been built. The real auto was originally only available in black, but later could be had in other colors: the model shown here is finished in red. Scale 1:42. Length: 3in (76mm).

18 1911 Maxwell Roadster; MoY Y-14 (Second Series), 1965. Scale 1:49. Length: 3·25in (83mm).

19 1909 Opel Coupé; MoY Y-4 (Third Series), c1968. Scale 1:38. Length: 3·125in (79mm).

20 1913 Cadillac; MoY Y-6 (Third Series), 1968. Scale 1:48. Length: 3·375in (86mm).

21 4-4-0 "Santa Fé" Locomotive; MoY Y-13 (First Series), 1959. Note that this model was produced without the tender that complemented the real locomotive. The scale here is 1:112. Length: 3·5in (89mm).

22 Aveling and Porter Steam Roller; MoY Y-11 (First Series), 1959; modeled on a road roller produced in the 1920s by the company later known as Aveling and Barford. Scale 1:80. Length: 3·125in (79mm).

23 Allchin 7-NHP Traction Engine; MoY Y-1 (First Series), 1955; modeled on a machine built in 1925. The scale here is 1:80. Length: 2·625in (67mm).

24 Fowler "Big Lion" Showmans Engine with "Lesney's Modern Amusements" transfers; MoY Y-9 (First Series). This fine model of a fairground engine was issued in 1958 and remained in production until 1967. Color variations exist: the maroon body was later finished bright red. Scale 1:80. Length: 3·25in (83mm).

25 4-ton Leyland Van with "W&R. Jacob & Co Ltd" (biscuit manufacturers) transfers; MoY Y-7 (First Series), 1958; modeled on a vehicle produced during the World War I period. Scale 1:100. Length: 2·75in (70mm).

26 1907 London "E" Class Tramcar with "News of the World" (Sunday newspaper) and other transfers; MoY Y-3 (First Series), 1956. Scale 1:130. Length: 3·125in (79mm).

27 AEC "Y" Type Lorry with "Osram Lamps" transfers; MoY Y-6 (First Series), 1957; modeled on a vehicle built during the later World War I period. Scale 1:100. Length: 2·75in (70mm).

28 "B" Type London Bus with "Dewar's" transfers; MoY Y-2 (First Series), 1955; modeled on an omnibus of c1910. Scale 1:100. Length: 2·625in (67mm).

29 Sentinel Steam Wagon with "Sand & Gravel Supplies" transfers; MoY Y-4 (First Series), 1956; modeled on a vehicle of c1928. Scale 1:100. Length: 2·75in (70mm).

30 1926 Morris Cowley "Bullnose"; MoY Y-8 (First Series), 1958. This was modeled on a popular British runabout of the late 1920s: the real auto remains a favorite with British automobile enthusiasts and many are still carefully preserved in running order. Scale 1:50. Length: 2·5in (63·5mm).

1 Covered Wagon, Dinky Toys Number 25B, 25 Series; 3rd Type, with high mudguards and no sidelights. Note that this and the other 25 Series vehicles at (2), (3), (4), and (5) are all post-War examples, this one dating from 1946-47. Length: 4·13in (105mm).
2 Market Gardener's Van, 25F, 25 Series; 4th Type, 1947-50, with front mudguards/bumpers, and sidelights. Length: 4·33in (110mm).
3 Wagon, 25A, 25 Series; 4th Type as (2), issued 1947-50. Length: 4·33in (110mm).
4 Flat Truck, 25C, 25 Series; 3rd Type as (1), 1946-47. Length: 4·13in (105mm).
5 Tipping Wagon, 25E, 25 Series; 4th Type as (2), 1947-50. Note that it is shown partly tipped, but with hinged tailgate closed. Length:

4·33in (110mm).
6 Austin Devon, 40D, 40 Series. This and the other 40 Series autos at (7), (8), and (9) was produced post-War: the vehicles were introduced singly between 1947 and 1954, were renumbered in the mid-1950s, and were dropped from the range by 1960. They were available in various colors, including two-tone finish. Apart from the four cars shown here, the 40 Series included a Standard Vanguard Saloon (40E), Morris Oxford (40G), and Austin Somerset (40J). Length: 3·375in (86mm).
7 Hillman Minx, 40F, 40 Series. Length: 3·46in (88mm).
8 Triumph 1800 Saloon, 40B, 40 Series. Produced in two versions: the early type, 1948-49, had pillars supporting the rear axle; latter type

had axle fixed to baseplate. Length: 3·58in (91mm).
9 Riley Saloon, 40A, 40 Series. Length: 3·66in (93mm).
10 Bentley Coupé, 36B, 36 Series. This and the other 36 Series cars at (11), (12), (13), and (14) was produced both pre- and post-War, with variations, production beginning in 1938 and ending in 1950. The autos shown are post-War examples. The 36 Series, represented an advance on the 24 Series: all 24 Series autos had the same (Bentley type) radiator, but in the 36 Series "make" radiators—note "Rover" badge on (12)—gave added realism. Apart from the five autos shown, the 36 Series included a British Salmson Two-Seater (36E) and Austin Taxi (36G). Length: 3·66in (93mm).

Undersides of Frazer-Nash (38A): (top) post-War, black metal base, wheels with ridge simulating hubcap; (bottom) pre-War, bright base, smooth-sided wheels.

15   16   17   18   19

20   21   22   23   24

25   26   27   28

11 Armstrong Siddeley, 36A, 36 Series. Length: 3·82in (97mm).

12 Rover, 36D, 36 Series. Length: 3·7in (94mm).

13 Humber Vogue, 36C, 36 Series. Length: 3·58in (91mm).

14 British Salmson Four-Seater, 36F, 36 Series. Length: 3·78in (96mm).

15 Alvis Sports Tourer, 38D, 38 Series. The sports cars of the 38 Series, shown here and at (16), (17), (18), (19), (23), and (24), were announced in 1939, but only three (Frazer-Nash, Sunbeam Talbot, Alvis) were available in 1940, the rest appearing after World War II. Plans made before the War for a Triumph Dolomite model failed to materialize, and its intended Catalog number (38E) was allocated instead to the Armstrong Siddeley Coupé (drop-head tourer)

shown at (19). Note the introduction in this Series of perspex windshield: the Jaguar Sports Car (38F), shown at (23) has twin aero-shields. The pre-War price of these automobiles was 0s 10d (4p, 6c) each; post-War, they reappeared at 2s 9d (13½p, 19c). Length: 3.74in (95mmm).

16 Another example of the Alvis, 38D; but whereas (15) is the later type, this is the earlier type with plain wheels, a non-voided steering wheel, and a bright metal baseplate (see also *Inset).* Note also color variation: 38 Series cars were produced in many different color variations.

17 Sunbeam Talbot Sports Car, 38D, 38 Series, post-War example. Length: 3·62in (92mm).

18 Lagonda Sports Coupé, 38C, 38

Series. Length: 4·02in (102mm).

19 Armstrong Siddeley, 38E, 38 Series. Length: 3·78in (96mm).

20 Studebaker "State Commander" Coupé, 39F; one of the 39 Series of American autos announced in 1939 but not available until later. By this time (in fact, beginning with the 38 Series) Dinky was identifying vehicles by impressing the name of the model on the base-plate. Length: 4·06in (103mm).

21 Buick "Viceroy" Sedan, 39D, 39 Series. Note that this model—like (26) and several of the 38 Series—has separate headlamp castings. If examples are found with missing headlamps, it is possible to obtain replacements at specialist model shops which maintain stocks of reproduction Dinky parts. Length:

4·06in (103mm).

22 Lincoln "Zephyr" Coupé, 39C, 39 Series. Length: 4·17in (106mm).

23 Jaguar Sports Car, 38F, 38 Series. Note that the "lips" on the front fenders of this model are extremely fragile. Length: 3·15in (80mm).

24 Frazer-Nash BMW Sports Car, 38A, a 38 Series model. Length: 3·23in (82mm).

25 Oldsmobile Sedan, 39B, 39 Series. Length: 3·94in (100mm).

26 Packard "Super 8" Touring Sedan, 39A, a 39 Series model. Length: 3·94in (100mm).

27-28 Two examples of the Chrysler "Royal" Sedan, 39E, 39 Series. Note that (28) as well as being an earlier type (identifiable by bright metal baseplate) has a finish in a comparatively unusual color. Length: 4·17in (106mm).

1 Ford Vedette, 1953 Model; French Dinky Toys (FDT) Number 24X, issued 1954-56. This auto was also available in a taxi version (Number 24XT). Length: 4·1in (105mm).

2 Ford Vedette, 1949 Model Limousine; FDT 24Q, issued 1950-55. This was the first Ford from French Dinky Toys and may be found with variations to the base. Length: 3·9in (100mm).

3 Panhard PL17 Saloon; FDT 547, issued 1960-68. Three versions exist: in the first two types the doors are shown as opening from front to back; in the third type, seen here, the door handles are correctly placed. Length: 4·2in (106mm).

4 Peugeot 403 Cabriolet, made by Solido; one of the fine range of vehicles produced by this French company in the 1960s. Note that it

is shown without figure of driver. Length: 4in (104mm).

5 Alfa Romeo 1900 Super Sprint Coupé; FDT 24J, issued 1959 (and renumbered 527 later that year). Length: 3·97in (101mm).

6 Citroën 2CV, 1950 Model; FDT 24T, issued in 1952, renumbered 535 in 1959, and deleted from the range in 1963. Like the automobile it portrays, which has been popular with drivers all over the world for more than three decades, this is an extremely well-liked model. Length: 3·4in (87mm).

7 Simca Aronde; FDT 24U. This was produced in three versions: the example shown is of the 3rd type, with chromed wheels and top of different color to body, issued in 1958-59 (and by then renumbered 536). Length: 3·7in (93mm).

8 Simca Aronde, as (7), but of 1st type, issued 1953-55. In comparison with (7), note different radiator grille, painted wheels, and single color scheme.

9 Citroën DS 19, 1955 Model; FDT 530, issued 1963-70. Note opening hood and trunk, windows, jeweled headlights, and fully molded interior with steering column; suspension is fitted. Length: 4·3in (110mm).

10 Citroën DS 19, 1955 Model; FDT 24CP. This model was originally issued without windows in 1956-57. The example shown is of the 2nd type, with windows, issued 1958-59, renumbered 522 in 1959, and deleted in 1968. Dimensions as (9).

11 Peugeot 203 Sedan; FDT 24R. Issued in three versions from 1954,

with variations in size of rear window and to top interior: the auto shown is of early type, with small rear window. Renumbered 533 in 1959; deleted same year. Length: 3·89in (99mm).

12 Simca 5; FDT 35A, first issued in 1939 and a favorite with diecast collectors. The example shown is of post-War type, with black rubber tires, issued in 1948-49. Length: 2·4in (60mm). Limited.

13 Simca Versailles; FDT 24Z, produced as a successor to the Ford Vedette, (1) and (2), and issued 1956-58. Renumbered 541; deleted from range 1960. Length: 4·05in (103mm).

14 Citroën 11 BL; FDT 24N. Auto shown is the later type, with trunk, issued 1953-55. Length: 3·8in (97mm).

15 Citroën 11 BL, as (14), but earlier version, issued 1949-51, without trunk and with cast-on spare wheel and tinplate front bumper. Length: 3·7in (94mm). Limited.

16 Simca 8 Sport; FDT 24S, issued 1952-59 and then renumbered 534. Thick and thin windshield variants may be found. Length: 3·74in (95mm).

17 Peugeot 404 Pinifarina Cabriolet; FDT 528, introduced in 1966 and deleted from the range in 1971. A finely-detailed model, with jeweled headlights, the automobile is shown here without the plastic figure of a driver that was originally supplied. Length: 3·9in (100mm).

18 Peugeot 504 Cabriolet; FDT 1423, issued 1969-71. Well detailed but with very fragile windshield. Length: 3·86in (98mm).

19 Renault Floride Coupé; FDT 543, issued 1960-63, with plastic windows and a suspension system. Length: 3·82in (97mm).

20 Simca Chambord; FDT 24K. From its introduction in 1959 (renumbered 528 in that year), the model had plastic windows. It was withdrawn from the range in 1961. Length: 4·25in (108mm).

21-22 Plymouth Belvedere Coupé; FDT 24D, introduced in 1957, renumbered 523 in 1959, and deleted in 1961. Two examples shown, to show color variations. Length: 4·33in (110mm).

23 Lincoln Premier; FDT 532, issued 1959-65. Length: 4·65in (118mm).

24 Peugeot U5 Station Wagon; FDT 403, introduced in 1958, renumbered 525 in 1959, and deleted in 1962. Length: 4·17in (106mm).

Renault "Etoile Filante" Record Car by CIJ, France, c1957; a fine die-cast model from a company best-known for tinplate autos of an earlier period. Length: 3·75in (95mm).

25-26 Chrysler New Yorker Convertible; FDT 24A, introduced in 1956, renumbered 520 in 1959, and deleted in 1961. Two examples of this French-made model of a US automobile are shown; note variation in radiator grille. Length: 4·29in (109mm).

27 Buick Roadmaster; FDT 24V, introduced in 1954, renumbered 538 in 1959, and deleted from the range in the same year. Length: 4·3in (110mm).

28 Studebaker Commander Coupé; FDT 24Y, issued 1955-59, then renumbered 540, and deleted in 1961. The example shown is of the earlier type; the later type had the lower section of the front fenders and the lower part of the forward doors painted the same color as the top. Length: 4·25in (108mm).

Diecast Vehicles by British and French Makers, 1930s–1960s

Racing and sports cars are perhaps the most popular diecast models, and in this sector Dinky Toys faced stiff competition from other manufacturers—notably Crescent Toys, Britain, whose realistic series of eight racing cars and two sports racing cars, finely detailed and all in the same scale, are probably the most sought after of the company's products.

1 Mercedes 300SL Open Roadster; Corgi Toys Number 303S, announced in the 1962 catalog. With driver (not shown) and glidamatic spring suspension. Length: 3·75in (95mm).

2 M.G.C. GT; Corgi Toys 345; announced 1969. With jeweled headlamps, opening hood and doors. Length: 3·5in (90mm).

3 Mercedes-Benz Racing Car; Dinky Toys (DT) Number 237, introduced 1957. Length: 3·86in (98mm).

4 "Speed of the Wind"; DT 23E. Introduced in 1936, this model was based on George Eyston's distance record car. It was also produced post-War, and later renumbered. Various colors may be found. Length: 4·1in (104mm).

5 Connaught Racing Car; DT 236, introduced to the range in 1956. Length: 3·78in (96mm).

6 Mercedes-Benz 2·5-liter Grand Prix Car; Crescent Toys (CT) Number 1284. Like all the other Crescent racing and sports cars shown here, it dates from 1957. Length: 4·17in (106mm).

7 Ferrari 2.5-liter Grand Prix Car; CT 1286, introduced 1957. Note that the example shown has been repainted and has had new transfer details of numbers applied. Length: 3·94in (100mm).

8 Vanwall 2·5-liter Grand Prix Car; CT 1293, 1957: the scarcest of the Crescent racing auto set. Length: 4·5in (103mm).

9 Cooper Bristol 2-liter Grand Prix Car; CT 1288, introduced in 1957. Length: 3·3in (84mm).

10 Gordini 2·5-liter Grand Prix Car; CT 1289. Note that this example has been repainted and fitted with Corgi-type tires (compare with tires on other Crescent autos shown here). Length: 3·35in (85mm).

11 Connaught 2-liter Grand Prix Car; CT 1287, 1957. Length: 3·86in (98mm).

12 Maserati 2·5-liter Grand Prix Car; CT 1290, 1957. Note that this example has been repainted, with added detail to such features as the driver's helmet and filler cap. Length: 3·9in (99mm).

13 "D" Type Jaguar 3·5-liter Sports Car; CT 1292, 1957. Note that real cars of this type, famous for their victories at Le Mans, were obliged to fit a full-width windshield: an attempt to limit the ever-increasing speeds attained at Le Mans. This example has been carefully repainted with highlighted details. Length: 3·74in (95mm).

14 Aston Martin DB3S 2·9-liter Sports Car; CT 1291, 1957; an attractive model in American racing colors. Length: 3·74in (95mm).

15 B.R.M. MkII Grand Prix Car; CT 1285, 1957. Note that on all Crescent racing cars, the driver was cast as part of the base plate. Length: 3·86in (98mm).

16 Aston Martin DB3S Sports Racing Car; Dinky Toys (DT) Number 110, introduced in 1956 and available later. Note that this example is in competition finish; like the other models in the Dinky series shown here, the auto was also available in sports finish, with a different driver. Note that the models shown at (16-20) have separate diecast drivers and steering wheels, and that (17-20) have perspex windshields. Length: 3.43in (87mm).

17 Sunbeam Alpine; DT 107, introduced to the range in 1955. Length: 3.7in (94mm).

18 MG Midget (competition finish); DT 108; introduced 1955. Length: 3.27in (83mm).

19 Triumph TR2; DT 111, introduced 1956. Length: 3.3in (84mm).

20 Austin Healey 100; DT 109, introduced to the range in 1955. Length: 3.35in (85mm).

21 Streamlined Racing Car; French Dinky Toys (FDT) Number 23B. This model, which closely resembles the Renault Nervasport, was introduced in 1935; a post-War example is shown here. Length: 3.62in (92mm).

22 Talbot-Lago Racing Car; FDT 23H, introduced 1954. Note that it is smaller than the British Dinky Toys version, shown at (30). Length: 3.62in (92mm).

23 Ferrari Racing Car; FDT 23J, introduced 1957. Finished in Italian racing red; otherwise note similarity to British casting (31). Length: 3.94in (100mm).

24 Hotchkiss Racing Car; Dinky Toys Number 23B; a post-war example

of a model introduced in 1935. Note French Dinky Toys version at (26). Length: 3.78in (96mm).

25 Racing Car; DT 23A; a post-War example, with late-type tires, of an automobile introduced in 1934. Length: 3.7in (94mm).

26 Hotchkiss Racing Car; French Dinky Toys version of (24). Note cast wheels and tires, indicating early post-War issue (at a time of rubber shortage). This example has been repainted. Length: 3.78in (96mm). Limited.

27 Cooper-Bristol Racing Car; Dinky Toys (DT) Number 23G, introduced 1953. This is a late model, with plastic wheels and gray rubber tires. Length: 3.5in (89mm).

28 Alfa Romeo Racing Car; DT 23F, introduced 1952. Again, a later

example with plastic wheels is shown. Length: 3.94in (100mm).

29 H.W.M. Racing Car; DT 23J, introduced 1953, with a shorter production run than others in this series. Length: 3.9in (99mm).

30 Talbot-Lago Racing Car; DT 23K, see (22) for French version. Introduced in 1953, this auto was not included when the series was sold in gift sets. Length: 4.06in (103mm).

31 Ferrari Racing Car; DT 23H, introduced 1953—note French version at (23). The late model shown has a yellow triangle painted on the nose; earlier examples had the entire nose section painted yellow. Length: 3.98in (101mm).

32 Maserati Racing Car; DT 23N; introduced 1953. A later example is shown. Length: 3.7in (94mm).

Diecast Vehicles by European and US Makers, 1930s-1970s

1 Rolls Royce Silver Wraith by Spot-On, Great Britain; Catalog Number 103, issued c1960. Length: 5·125in (130mm). Limited.

2 Caravan by Dinky Toys, Great Britain; Cat No 30G, introduced 1936 and deleted 1940. Length: 3·19in (81mm). Limited.

3 Breakdown Van; Dinky Toys No 30E, introduced 1935, deleted 1940, reissued 1946-48. A pre-1940 example is shown. Length: 3·62in (92mm).

4 "Ecurie Ecosse" Car Transporter; Corgi Toys, Great Britain; Catalog No 1126, c1962-65. Length: 7·75in (197mm).

5 Lotus Elan; Corgi No 319, c1967. This hardtop model features a detachable chassis and opening hood. Length: 3·5in (89mm).

6 Lotus Elan S2; Corgi No 318, c1967. Open sports model with detachable chassis and opening hood. Length: 3·5in (89mm).

7 Marcos Volvo 1800GT; Corgi No 324, c1967, with opening doors and opening hood. Length: 3·625in (92mm).

8 Market Gardener's Van; Dinky Toys No 25F (1st Type), a 25 Series model, introduced 1934, deleted 1938. Note tinplate radiator without headlamps, characterizing 1st Type. It has been repainted. Length: 4·13in (105mm).

9 As (8), but 2nd Type, 1938-40. Note the cast radiator with headlamps. Voided chassis.

10 As (8), but 3rd Type, 1946-47. Note the ridged wheels. It has a non-voided (ie, not cut-away) chassis. Fairly common.

11 As (8), but 4th Type, issued 1947-50. This has a new chassis, with molded sump and transmission detail; and fuller front fenders, with a bumper bar and cast inner headlamps. Length: 3·98in (101mm). Common.

12 Double Deck Bus; Dinky No 29c, renumbered 290 in 1954. A post-war model with second-pattern radiator and straight front fender edges. Length: 3·98in (101mm). Common.

13 As (12); color variant. Common.

14 As (12), but with first-pattern radiator and rounded front fender edges; issued c1947-50.

15 Double Deck Bus; Dinky No 291, 1959-63. Length: 4·05in (103mm).

16 Double Deck Bus; Dinky No 290, c1959-63, with "Dunlop" transfer (sloping lettering) and third-pattern radiator. Length: 4·05in (103mm).

17 As (16), but c1957-60 issue, with "Dunlop" transfers (upright lettering); standard wheels; no roof number box.

18 Atlantean Bus; Dinky No 297. This model, issued c1962-78, is to be found with a variety of transfers. Length: 4·72in (120mm). Fairly common.

19 Jaguar "S" Type; Spot-On No 276, c1964-67. Length: 4·41in (112mm).

20 Aston Martin DB3 (thus cataloged; but in fact a DB2/4 Mark III); Spot-On No 113, c1959-63. Length: 4·125in (105mm).

21 Bristol 406 Sports Saloon; Spot-On No 115, issued c1960-63. Length: 4·56in (116mm).

22 Rover 3-Litre Saloon; Spot-On No 157, issued c1961-63. Length: 4·188in (106mm).

106

23 Jensen 541 Sports Saloon; Spot-On No 112, c1960-63. Length: 4·188in (106mm).

24 BMW 507 Sports Coupé by Marklin, West Germany; Cat No 8022. Issued in 1958. Length: 3·54in (90mm).

25 BMW 501 Saloon; Marklin No 8016, issued in 1957. Length: 4·13in (105mm).

26 Mercedes Benz 300SL Coupé; Marklin No 8019, 1958. Length: 3·66in (93mm).

27 Borgward Isabella Saloon; Marklin No 8015, 1957. Length: 3·82in (97mm).

28 Jaguar XK SS; Spot-On No 107, issued in c1960-63. Length: 3·625in (92mm).

29 M.G. Midget Mk II Sports Car; Spot-On No 281, c1966-67. Length: 3·25in (83mm).

30 M.G. "D" Type Midget; Spot-On No 279, c1965-67. The model has a diecast body and a plastic chassis. Length: 3·03in (77mm).

31 Sunbeam Alpine Convertible; Spot-On No 191, 1962-66. Length: 3·75in (95mm).

32 M.G.A. Sports Car; Spot-On No 104, issued in 1959-65. Length: 3·7in (94mm).

33 Daimler SP250 (Dart) Sports Car; Spot-On No 215, 1961-66. Length: 3·78in (96mm).

34 Vauxhall P.A. Cresta Saloon, Spot-On No 165, c1961-64. Length: 4·33in (110mm).

35 Armstrong Siddeley Sapphire 236 Saloon; Spot-On No 101, 1959-62. Length: 4·21in (107mm).

36 Humber Super Snipe Estate Car; Spot-On No 183, 1963-65. Length: 4·37in (111mm).

37 Hillman Minx Saloon; Spot-On No 287, issued in 1965-67. Length: 3·898in (99mm).

38 Streamlined Sedan by Tootsietoy, USA, mid-1930s. Length: 3·94in (100mm). Limited.

39 Graham Paige Limousine; Tootsietoy, 1930s. Note trunk-mounted spare. Length: 4·016in (102mm). Limited.

40 Graham Paige Ambulance; Tootsietoy, 1930s. It uses the same chassis as (39). This example has been repainted. Length: 3·82in (97mm). Limited.

41 Graham Paige Coupé; Tootsietoy, 1930s. This example has undergone some restoration. Length: 3·82in (97mm). Limited.

42 Austin "Seven" Tourer; Dinky Toys No 35D. A post-War example, issued 1946-48, is shown: the

version issued in 1938-40 had a wire-frame windshield. Length: 1·97in (50mm).

43 M.G. Sports Car; Dinky Toys No 35C. Post-War example, issued 1946-48, shown; originally issued c1936-40. Length: 2·05in (52mm).

44 Austin "Seven" Saloon; Dinky Toys No 35A. Post-War example, issued 1946-48, shown; also issued before World War II. Length: 2·008in (51mm).

45 Racing Car; Dinky Toys No 35B. A post-War example, with driver, issued 1946, renumbered 200 in 1954, deleted in 1957, is shown. Length: 2·24in (57mm). Common.

46 Civilian Motorcyclist; Dinky Toys No 37A. Post-War example, issued c1946-54, with dark tires. Length: 1·77in (45mm). Common.

Diecast "Advertising" Vehicles by Dinky Toys, Britain, 1940s-1960s

Dinky Toy vehicles bearing advertising transfers are both the most popular and the most valuable of the post-War range. Particularly notable are the large Guy Vans and the Foden Petrol Tankers, issued between 1949 and 1960, the larger vehicles being marketed as Dinky Supertoys. Value to the collector is much enhanced by clear, undamaged transfers, unchipped paintwork and, as with other toys, by the possession of the original box in good condition.

1 Guy Van with "Ever Ready" transfers; Dinky Supertoys (DS) Number 918, issued 1955-58. The vehicle has opening double doors at the rear, and the example shown has recessed commercial-type wheels. Length: 5·2in (132mm).

2 Petrol Tanker with "Esso" transfers; Dinky Toys (DT) Number 442, introduced c1952 and deleted c1960. Basically as the 25 Series gas tanker, but with an American Studebaker cab and streamlined tanker body with enclosed rear wheels. Length: 4·4in (112mm).

3 Oil Tanker with "Castrol" transfers; DT 441, originally issued as Number 30pa in c1952, renumbered in 1954, and in production until 1960. As (2).

4 Petrol Tanker; DT 30p, issued 1950 and in production—in red, as shown, or green—until 1952, when it was superseded by the tankers bearing advertisements. As (2).

5 Petrol Tanker with "National Benzole" transfers; DT 443, produced only in 1957-58 and one of the scarcest in the range. As (2).

Guy Warrior Van with "Heinz" transfers, issued 1960 and available for one year only. Compare with Big Bedford at (7), which bears earlier "can" transfer rather than "bottle" seen here. This Supertoy is very scarce.

6 Petrol Tanker with "Mobilgas" transfers; DT 440, first issued as Number 30p in 1952 on deletion of Petrol Tanker (4); renumbered in 1954. The "Mobilgas" tanker is also found with the transfer in blue on a white panel. As (2).

7 Big Bedford Delivery Van with "Heinz" transfers; DS 923. The vehicle was issued with the "can" transfer, as seen here, in 1955-58, and in 1958-59 with "bottle" transfer (as seen on Guy Warrior Van, *Inset*). Note that the van body, unlike that of the Guy vans shown at (1), (10), (14), (15), and *(Inset)*, has a rounded top. Length: 5·75in (146mm).

8 Austin Van with "BP" and (on left side) "Shell" transfers; DT 470, introduced 1954 and deleted 1960s. Length: 3·5in (89mm).

9 Leyland Comet Cement Lorry with "Blue Circle/Portland Cement" and (on left side) "Ferrocrete" transfers; DS 533, introduced 1953 and also issued as Number 933 in 1954 and Number 419 in 1956. Length: 5·59in (142mm).

10 Guy Van with "Golden Shred" transfers; DS 919, produced 1957-58. The example shown has a late-type cab, with strengthened license plate supports and recessed wheels. Length: 5·2in (132mm). Scarce.

11 Bedford Van with "Ovaltine" transfers; DT 481, issued 1955-60. Length: 3·27in (83mm).

12 Foden 14-ton Tanker with "Mobilgas" transfers; DS 504, issued 1953-54, renumbered 941, and deleted c1957. It was also produced as Number 942, with

"Regent" transfers. The second-type Foden cab and bold tread pattern tires of the example shown indicate late production. Length: 7·4in (188mm).

13 AEC Tanker with "Shell Chemicals Limited" transfers; DS 591, issued in this form 1952-55, then renumbered 991, and issued 1955-58 with transfer shortened to "Shell Chemicals"—see (4), *pages 112-113*. Length: 5·94in (151mm).

14 Guy Van with "Spratts" transfers; DS 514D, originally issued 1953-54. Recessed wheels indicate that the example shown is renumbered version, Number 917, produced 1955-56. Length: 5·2in (132mm).

15 Guy Van with "Slumberland" transfers; DS 514A, issued December 1949 and not renumbered. This example has

early type cab and wheels. As (14). Fairly common.

16 Bedford Van with "Kodak" transfers; DT 480, issued 1954-56. As (11).

17 Trojan Van with "Cydrax" transfers; DT 454, issued 1957-59. Length: 3·35in (85mm).

18 Trojan Van with "Dunlop" transfers; DT 31B, issued 1952-54 and then, as 451, in 1954-57. As (17).

19 Trojan Van with "Chivers Jellies" transfers; DT 31C, issued 1953-54, renumbered 452, and deleted in 1957. As (17).

20 Trojan Van with "Oxo" transfers; DT 31D, issued 1953-54. It was possibly allocated the new number 453, but is missing from the Dinky Toys 1954 Catalog. Certainly the scarcest of the Trojan range. As (17).

Diecast Commercial Vehicles by Dinky Toys, Britain, 1940s-1960s

Since both Dinky Toys and Dinky Supertoys are shown on this spread, as on some earlier pages, it is convenient to explain here the distinction between these series. In the case of Dinky Toys produced before c1939, commercial vehicles are in a smaller scale than cars; ie, a pre-World War II automobile and truck placed side by side, will be found to be roughly the same length. On resuming production after World War II, Dinky sought to add realism to its range by making commercial vehicles in a larger scale than autos. The first larger-scale commercial vehicles to bear the "Supertoys" description were introduced in 1947. The first group consisted of six models, the first in numerical order being Number 501, the Foden 14-ton Eight-

Wheeled Diesel Wagon—see (7) below. The same eight-wheeled chassis was used as the basis for the Flat Truck (Number 502) and Flat Truck with Tailboard (Number 503). The remaining items, again with a common chassis, were the Guy Four-Ton Lorry (Number 511), Guy Flat Truck (Number 512), and Guy Flat Truck with Tailboard (Number 513).

1 "A.B.C. Television" Mobile Control Room; Dinky Supertoys Number 987, issued 1962-69. The model was sold complete with the figure of a cameraman—not shown here. Length: 5·94in (151mm). Limited.
2 "A.B.C.-TV" Transmitter Van, with revolving aerial; Dinky Supertoys Number 988, issued 1962-68. Length: 4·45in (113mm). Limited.

3 "Dinky Auto Service" Car Carrier and Trailer; Dinky Supertoys Number 983 (also available as separate items: Carrier, Number 984; Trailer, Number 985), issued 1958-63. When sold as a set (ie, both items, but not including autos), this was the most expensive model in Dinky's 1962 Catalog, priced at £2 5s 6d (£2.27½, $3.23). The model is shown here in the loading position, carrying (left to right) AC Aceca Coupé (Dinky Toys Number 167); Aston Martin DB3S in touring finish (Dinky Toys Number 104); Austin Healey 100 Sports in touring finish (Dinky Toys Number 103). Length of model overall: 18·6in (472mm).
4 Big Bedford Lorry; Dinky Supertoys Number 522; introduced in 1952, renumbered

922 in 1954, again renumbered 408 in 1956, and dropped from the range in 1963. Length: 5·75in (146mm).
5 Trailer; Dinky Toys Number 551. Introduced to complement the larger vehicles in the range in 1948, this was renumbered 951 in 1954 and again renumbered 528 in 1956. Length: 4·13in (105mm).
6 "Dinky Toys Delivery Service" Pullmore Car Transporter; Dinky Supertoys Number 582, introduced in 1953. Shown here with its tin ramp in the loading position, this model had a long production life; it was renumbered 982 in 1954. It is shown here with (upper deck, left) Armstrong Siddeley (Dinky Toys Number 38E); (upper deck, right) Triumph 1800 Saloon (Dinky Toys Number 40B); (lower deck, left)

Standard Vanguard Saloon (Dinky Toys Number 40E); (lower deck, right) another Triumph 1800 Saloon. (Note that the Triumph 1800 Saloon is found in two versions: one has a pillar-mounted rear axle; the other has a base-mounted rear axle.) Length overall: 9·84in (250mm). Fairly common.

7 Foden 14-Ton Wagon; Dinky Supertoys Number 501. The example shown is of the first type, without a towing hook and with the early pattern cab, ridged wheels with herring-bone-pattern-tread tires (as used on Dinky's larger pre-War racing cars), and early type axle fittings. It was replaced by the second type in 1952. Length: 7·4in (188mm). Limited.

8 Bedford End Tipper; Dinky Toys Number 25M, introduced in 1948, renumbered 410 in 1954, and dropped from the range in 1963. The tipping mechanism is hand-operated via a spiral shaft. Length: 3·875in (98mm). Fairly common.

9 "Dinky Service" Breakdown Lorry; Dinky Toys Number 25X, introduced in 1950, renumbered 430 in 1954, and deleted in 1963. It was made in two color variants and is sometimes found with white lettering. Length: 4·84in (123mm).

10 Foden Flat Truck with Chains; Dinky Supertoys Number 505, introduced in 1952, renumbered 905 in 1954, and in production until 1964. The example shown has the later type cab and chassis: compare with (7) and (13). Length: 7·4in (188mm).

11 Leyland Comet Lorry; Dinky Toys Number 531, introduced in 1949, renumbered 931 in 1954, again renumbered 417 in 1956, and finally deleted in 1959. Length: 5·67in (144mm).

12 Bedford Articulated Lorry; Dinky Toys Number 521, issued in 1948, renumbered 921 in 1954, again renumbered 409 in 1956, and with a long production life. Length: 6·54in (166mm).

13 Foden Flat Truck; Dinky Supertoys Number 502, first issued in 1947 as one of the first six Supertoys. This example has a cab of early pattern—see (7) for a similar type—; (10) for the later pattern—in which form it was issued until 1952. The model was renumbered 902 in 1955. Length: 7·4in (188mm). Limited.

14 Fire Engine; Dinky Supertoys Number 555, introduced in 1952 and renumbered 955 in 1954. The ladder extends and can be rotated; note bells. Length: 5·7in (145mm). Fairly common.

15 Turntable Fire Escape; Dinky Supertoys Number 956, issued 1958 and in production until 1969. The extending ladder, mounted on a turntable, is operated by the handles visible at the rear. Length: 7·87in (200mm).

16 BBC Television Roving Eye Vehicle; Dinky Supertoys Number 968, issued 1959-64. Length: 4·33in (110mm).

17 BBC Television Extending Mast Vehicle; Dinky Supertoys Number 969—a companion model to (16) and, again, on issue 1959-64. Length: 7·68in (195mm).

Diecast Commercial Vehicles by Dinky Toys, Britain, 1940s-1970s

1 "British Railways" (Hire Service) Horse Box; Dinky Supertoys Number 581, introduced in 1953 and renumbered 981 in 1955. This large and impressive model, with its hinged ramp, had a long production life. Length: 6·89in (175mm).

2 Aveling-Barford Diesel Roller; Dinky Toys Number 25P, introduced in 1948, renumbered 251 in 1954, and deleted from the range in 1963. Length: 4·33in (110mm). Common.

3 Elevator Loader; Dinky Supertoys Number 564, introduced in 1952 and renumbered 964 in 1954. A working model: the loading ramp (a detachable tailgate is missing from this example) is lifted by the lever visible on the left and the load—sand, gravel, or the like—

raised on the endless chain (note cast detail on the exterior of the model) to pour down the chute into a truck, possibly that shown at (14). Length: 9·05in (230mm).

4 "Shell Chemicals" AEC Tanker; Dinky Supertoys Number 991, issued 1955-58. Length: 5·94in (151mm).

5 Jeep; Dinky Toys Number 25Y, introduced in 1952 and renumbered 405 in 1954. Length: 3·25in (83mm).

6 Motocart; Dinky Toys Number 27G, issued to complement Dinky's Farm Series in 1949 and renumbered 342 in 1954. Note the tipping back, all-metal wheels and tires, and cast detail of engine. Length: 4·33in (110mm).

7 Brink's Armored Security Van; Dinky Toys Number 275,

introduced in 1964 and deleted in 1969, when it was priced at 13s 11d (69½p, 99c). It has opening rear doors; note the decals (none too firmly applied on this example!) on the cab door and sides. Length: 4·76in (121mm).

8 Mighty Antar with Transformer; Dinky Supertoys Number 908, issued 1962-64. This used the same casting as the earlier Thorneycroft Mighty Antar Tank Transporter (Dinky Supertoys Number 660, introduced 1956) shown at (6) on pages 180-181. The Transformer is plastic; note that its trailer, with a spare tire at the front and twin hinged ramps at the rear, differs considerably from that shown with the Mighty Antar Low Loader at (9). Length: 13·19in (335mm). Scarce.

9 Mighty Antar Low Loader with Propeller; Dinky Supertoys Number 986, issued 1959-64. The Propeller is plastic. Length: 12in (305mm).

10 Blaw Knox Bulldozer; Dinky Supertoys Number 561, introduced in 1949, renumbered 961 in the Catalog for September 1954, and dropped from the range in 1964. The blade is raised and lowered by a lever on the driver's right; it is shown here in the raised position, with the lever near-horizontal. The caterpillar tracks are rubber. Length: 5·43in (138mm). Fairly common.

11 Coventry Climax Fork-Lift Truck; Dinky Toys Number 14C, introduced in 1949 and renumbered 401 in 1954. The lift is manually operated. Length: 4·25in (108mm). Fairly common.

12 Heavy Tractor; Dinky Supertoys Number 563, issued in 1948, renumbered 963 in 1954, and deleted in 1959. With rubber tracks, this uses the same casting as the Caterpillar D8 tractor of the Bulldozer shown at (10). Length: 4·57in (116mm).

13 Coles 20-ton Lorry-Mounted Crane; Dinky Supertoys Number 972, issued 1955-68. The crane body swivels; the angle of the jib is adjusted by the crank handle visible towards the rear of the body; the crane hook is raised and lowered by a similar crank handle on the opposite side. Length: 9·45in (240mm).

14 "Euclid" Rear Dump Truck; Dinky Supertoys Number 965, issued 1955-69. Note the transfers, including "Euclid" trademark, on

this robust model. The tipping action is worked by the crank. Length: 5·59in (142mm).

15 Weeks Tipping Farm Trailer; Dinky Toys Number 319, issued 1961-70: towed by Massey-Harris Tractor; Dinky Toys Number 27A, introduced in 1948 and renumbered 300 in 1954. The Trailer has tipping angles varied manually and controlled by a friction plunger, visible here. The Tractor shown here is an early example, with metal wheels and tires; later issues have plastic wheels with rubber tires. Lengths: (Trailer) 4·13in (105mm); (Tractor) 3·5in (89mm).

16 Massey-Harris Manure Spreader; Dinky Toys Number 27C, issued in 1949 and renumbered 321 in 1954: towed by Field Marshall

Tractor; Dinky Toys Number 27N, issued in 1953, renumbered 301 in 1954, and dropped from the range in 1965. The blades of the Manure Spreader are turned by an endless spring drive from its wheels; earlier examples have metal wheels and tires—the example shown is a later type, with plastic wheels and rubber tires. The Tractor, on the other hand, is of the earlier type, with metal wheels and tires. Lengths: (Manure Spreader) 4·45in (113mm); (Tractor) 2·95in (75mm).

17 Hay Rake; Dinky Toys Number 27K, introduced in 1953, renumbered 324 in 1954, and with a long production life. The blades are raised or lowered by means of the lever between the arms of the towing bar. Length: 3·03in (77mm).

18 Royal Mail Van; Dinky Toys Number 34B, first issued in 1938 (all examples having voided, ie, cut-out, rear windows) and re-issued in 1948-52 (examples with either voided or non-voided rear windows). It may also be found with a black top. Length: 3·25in (83mm).

19 Streamlined Fire Engine; Dinky Toys Number 25H, first issued in April 1936, re-issued after World War II, renumbered 250 in 1954, and deleted from the range in 1962. Note that a brass bell, missing from this example, should be suspended from the ladder. Some pre-World War II examples were provided with tinplate Firemen and were then numbered 25K, which is now very scarce. Length: 3·98in (101mm).

Pedal Cars by Triang (Lines Brothers Ltd), Britain, 1920s-1930s

The pedal car (sometimes called a "kiddie car" in the USA), propelled either by foot-operated cranks or bicycle-style pedals with chain drive, is almost as old as the automobile itself. However, most early pedal cars were made of wood, thus falling outside the scope of this book, and no really early models are shown on this and the three following spreads.

By the 1920s, metal had become the major constructional material for pedal cars (although wood was often used for body panels in the more elaborate models)—to remain so until ousted by heavy molded plastic from the 1960s onward. In Britain, particularly, the 1920s-1930s was the "golden age" of pedal cars: the most notable maker, Lines Brothers Limited,

produced under its "Triang" trademark a very wide range at prices varying from 17s 11d (89½p, $1.27) to £15 0s 0d (£15, $21.30). Quite recently, toy collectors' interest in pedal cars has been significantly increased by a number of specialized publications and, in Britain, by an exhibition of some 70 specimens at the National Motor Museum, Beaulieu, Hampshire, in December 1983-January 1984.

All the pedal cars shown on this spread are from the collection of Shaun Magee, Bishop's Waltham, Hampshire, Great Britain.

1 "Junior Model" Pedal Car by Triang (Lines Brothers Limited), Great Britain, dating from c1934. The license plate is "LIB.4242", the

letters indicating that this toy, a fairly simple example of its kind, was originally retailed by the famous store of Liberty, Regent Street, London. It features a fold-flat windshield, simulated headlamps, and simulated balloon tires (which are, in fact, of metal with a solid rubber rim). The row of slots running in an arc in the metal above the front fender was intended to allow the maker to fit the more elaborate fenders provided on the more expensive model based on the same body. Note that this example has been restored to its original condition; only the bulb horn is a later addition. Length: 32in (81·3cm). Limited.

2 "Bullnose Morris" Pedal Car by Triang: a most attractive

representation in metal with wood paneling of a very popular British-built "family" touring automobile of the 1920s. It bears the license plate "LB 3067"; "LB" standing for "Lines Brothers". An advertisement for this toy in the British humorous weekly *Punch*, dated 23 February 1927, quoted a price of £5 5s 0d (£5.25, $7.45)—which at that time represented a good weekly wage. For that sum, however, the purchaser obtained a toy of very high quality: it has bicycle-type chain drive and features a sprung bumper, an array of simulated head- and side-lights, a well-modeled radiator (with Lines Brothers' triangular trademark impressed on the upper part; it appears also on the running-board "mat") surmounted

(Below) "Citroën" Pedal Car by Triang, Great Britain, 1930s; with an all-steel pressed body. The original license plate and simulated headlights are missing; the mascot is a later addition. Length: 44in (111·8cm).

4

by a realistic filler cap and temperature gauge, an opening driver's door with handle, a battery-powered "starter" buzzer, a seat adjustable for height, a wood-rimmed steering wheel, and detachable disk wheels with solid rubber rims. A fold-down windshield was originally fitted, but is missing from this example. Length 49in (124·5cm). Limited.

3 The rear view of Triang's "Bullnose Morris" (2) reveals the pressed and printed detail of the applied dashboard (a feature of many Triang pedal cars), the applied "Four Wheel Brakes" sign and simulated warning light on the rear deck, and the rear-mounted baggage rack.

4 "Magna No 8" Pedal Car by Triang, dating from the mid-1930s. In describing this high-quality representation, in metal with wooden panels, of a British-built touring automobile, it is of interest to quote the maker's catalog: "A magnificent new Sporting Car . . . coach-built body fully sprung, ball-bearing back axle, opening side door, windscreen, dummy hood [soft-top] and lamps, Dunlop pneumatic tyres on tangent-spoked wheels, all bright parts chromium-plated . . ." To which may be added: a hand-brake (its knobbed lever visible in the photograph) and a well-modeled radiator surmounted by a mascot. It was priced at £5 15s 0d (£5.75, $8.16) in 1936. The spare wheel shown on this example did not feature in the original specification. Length: 53in (134·6cm). Limited.

Pedal Cars by British and French Makers, 1930s-1960s

All the pedal cars shown on this spread are from the collection of Shaun Magee, Bishop's Waltham, Hampshire, Great Britain.

1 "Brooklands No 8" Pedal Racing Car by Triang (Lines Brothers Limited), Great Britain, dating from the 1930s. Since children have always been impressed by very fast and powerful automobiles, most manufacturers in the field at some time produced pedal-powered racing cars. Among the best is this aluminum-bodied "Brooklands" racer, named after the famous British motor-racing circuit of the pre-World War II period, now closed, near Weybridge, Surrey. The "de luxe" version of the "Brooklands" auto is shown here: a cheaper model—

priced at £3 3s 0d (£3.15, $4.47)—was also made. This was called the "Brooklands No 6" and was shorter, had only one set of louvers in the hood sides, and was fitted with simulated pneumatic tires (in fact, solid), narrower than the 12·5in x 2·25in (31·75cm x 5·7cm) "Dunlop Cord" pneumatic balloon tires of the "de luxe" model shown here. The aluminum body and radiator of this auto were originally polished bright: the body has been repainted in "British Racing Green"; and the radiator enameled red; however, the red enameling of the chassis and wheel rims is in accord with the original finish (see below). Apart from the features mentioned in the quotation that follows, the racer has a padded seat and quickly-

detachable wheels (with spring-loaded plungers in the centers of the hubcaps). The bulb horn is a later addition—as is, of course, the figure of the famous "Michelin Man", seen here in the driving seat of a car with "Dunlop" tires! Triang's contemporary advertisement for this toy is worth quoting at some length: "Yes—its a Brooklands model car built by Triang engineers! They said—'Let's make this Brooklands car sporty

The "Brooklands No 8" Pedal Racing Car—see (1) above—features (below) in a Triang advertisement for the shorter-wheelbase version in "Meccano Magazine", February 1931. The "Rover Meteor" (above) was a medium-priced pedal car.

3

4

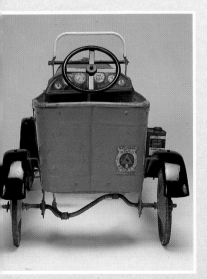

The rear view of the Tansad "Argyle" (4) shows the printed dashboard and the cranked rear axle. Note also the contemporary "National Road Safety Campaign" transfer on the rear deck, and the traces of a molded tread pattern on the solid rubber tires.

and splendid; let's make it strong and let's make it safe!' So they fitted it with a polished aluminium body and radiator and gave it a stunningly smart finish by covering the chassis and wheel rims with brilliant red enamel. Then they fitted it with a ball-bearing back axle, double-crank drive and real rubber pedals. And they added that long natty exhaust pipe [not visible in the photograph] because they knew you would like it. Now,

when is your birthday?" Length: 55in (139·7cm). Limited.

2 Pedal Racing Car, apparently based on a contemporary "Talbot-Lago" type, by an unidentified maker, probably French, dating from the 1960s. It has a body of pressed steel, with two rows of louvers applied on either side of the hood, and features a radiator grille of wire mesh and disk wheels. Length: 56·5in (143·5cm).

3 "Ferrari" Pedal Racing Car by an unidentified British maker, probably Triang, dating from the late-1950s-early 1960s. The positioning of the chromium-plated exhaust pipe suggests that this racer is modeled on a front-engined Ferrari of the late 1950s. Its simulated wire-spoked wheels, with detail of "knock-off" hubcaps,

are fitted with untreaded tires of solid rubber. The radiator grille originally fitted is missing from this example, which, unlike several of the pedal cars shown here, has not undergone restoration. Length: 44in (111·8cm).

4 "Argyle" Pedal Car by Tansad, Great Britain, dating from the 1930s. This automobile has an all-pressed-steel body, a printed radiator, fold-flat windshield, opening driver's door, and a seat with a padded back. It has disk wheels with solid rubber rims. Note that the "Red-X" gasoline can fitted to the running-board is non-original: Tansad autos with this feature normally fitted "Pratts" cans (while Triang pedal cars usually had "Shell"). Length: 33·5in (85cm). Limited.

Pedal Cars by British and French Makers, 1930s

1 "Bugatti" Pedal Racing Car by Eureka, France, dating from the early 1930s (the front axle is stamped "12/32", possibly indicating that the auto was made, or its design registered, in December 1932). The example shown was the cheapest and simplest in the French maker's "Bugatti" series. It features a well-modeled radiator, two sets of horizontal louvers on either side of the hood, and pressed-steel wheels with solid rubber rims bearing a molded tread pattern. It has been restored, but only the bulb horn is a non-original feature.

All the pedal cars shown on this spread are from the collection of Shaun Magee, Bishop's Waltham, Hampshire, Great Britain.

Eureka produced its "Bugatti" in a larger "touring" version, with the addition of fenders, lights, and a side-mounted spare wheel; and in a still larger version, which additionally featured an opening hood, perforated disk wheels fitted with pneumatic tires, and a "free-wheel" mechanism incorporated into its pedal drive. Length: 33in (83·8cm). Limited.

2 "Rolls Royce" Electric-Powered Automobile by Triang (Lines Brothers Limited), Great Britain, dating from the early 1930s. Note the Lines Brothers' triangular trademark on the cast step at the near side. This magnificent representation of one of the world's most famous automobiles — this example finely restored to near-original condition — was, it

need hardly be stated, the "top of the range"' of Lines Brothers' automotive toys. A Lucas 12-volt electric motor mounted on the rear axle is supplied with power by two 6-volt standard automobile batteries fitted beneath the hood. The retailer's publicity material claimed that the auto had a maximum endurance, before re-charging was needed, of 12-15 miles (19-24km) at a speed of 5mph (8km/h). The steering is fully operational, and power is controlled by a foot-pedal and a three-position gear shift: forward, neutral, and reverse. A hand-brake

Full-page advertisement for Triang pedal cars, "Meccano Magazine", July 1931. Note the "Buick Regal" as shown at (3) above.

3

4

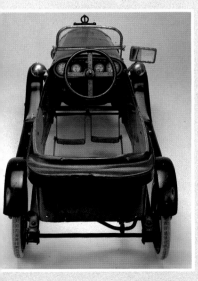

The rear view of Triang's "Buick Regal" (3) clearly shows the spring shackles of the suspension system, the treaded tires, the printed detail of the dashboard (note switch for electric lights, mounted below right), and the simulated soft-top. The two holes in the lower rear deck are for the retaining bolts of a baggage rack and trunk, missing from the example shown here.

acting on the rear axle is provided. The characteristic Rolls Royce radiator is chromium-plated, as are the working electric headlights, sidelights (mounted on either side of the lower windshield frame), and rearlights (not visible in the photograph). The opening hood of bright metal is provided with a row of louvers on either side; the body

panels are wooden. "Flag-type" direction indicators (the off-side one missing from this example) are fitted on either side of the windshield, and a button is provided for the electric horn. This automobile was certainly a toy only for the children of the richest and most indulgent parents: in the advertisement for it that appeared in *Hamley's News* in September 1933, it was priced at £31 10s 0d (£31.50, $44.73). Length: 80in (203·2cm). Rare.

3 "Buick Regal" Pedal Car by Triang, dating from *c*1931. This automobile has a pressed-steel body: it is shown in original condition, unrestored. It is a very well-detailed model, featuring suspension by half-elliptic springs, electric headlights and sidelights (note the

imitation "road tax disk" mounted below the near-side sidelight), a fold-flat windshield, a rear-view mirror, a padded seat, a simulated folded soft-top, and wire-spoked wheels with treaded tires of solid rubber. See also *Inset*. Length: 43in (109·2cm). Limited.

4 "Comet" Pedal Car by Triang, dating from *c*1931. A "first auto" for a young child, this simple model has a pressed-steel radiator, hood, and seat back, and a wooden chassis, seat, and steering-wheel rim. Its disk wheels have wired-on tires of narrow section. Note the license plate "LB 3067"; "LB" standing for "Lines Brothers". This was one of the cheapest pedal cars in the Triang range, priced at 17s 11d (89½p, $1.27) in 1931. Length: 33in (83·8cm). Limited.

1

2

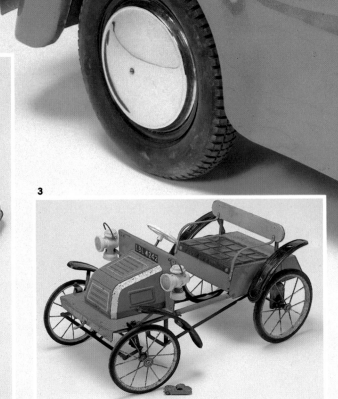

3

1 "Ford Zephyr" Pedal Car by Triang (Lines Brothers Limited), Great Britain, early 1950s. This has an all-metal body, with plated brightwork bumper bars, radiator grille, and hubcaps, and rubber tires. It features battery-powered headlights, an exterior-mounted handbrake, and a simulated column-mounted gear shift. Length: 48in (122cm).

2 "Marx-Mobile" Electric-Powered Automobile by Marx, USA, c1960. Battery-powered, the all-metal automobile, with brightly-printed finish and featuring the tail fins typical of the period, is controlled by the forward-reverse lever to the driver's right; the lever also has a "neutral", free-wheel, position. The foot-rests, (note driving position in maker's brochure) may be pushed

into the body. Also in the maker's brochure, note the dashboard detail, including a "real" ignition key. Length: 27in (68·5cm).

3 "De Dion" Pedal Car by Triang, Great Britain, 1960s. This "Vintage" automobile has a tubular metal chassis with a sprung rear axle; a pressed-steel body; plastic mudguards, steering-wheel, and side-lamps; and a plastic-upholstered, wooden-backed seat. The starting-handle mounted in the front of the body incorporates a "clicker" device, and the wheels are fitted with molded rubber tires. Length: 36in (91·5cm).

4 "Austin J (Junior) Forty" Pedal Car, often called the "Austin Joycar", by the Austin Motor Company Limited, Birmingham, Great Britain, built between 1950

and 1971. The red finish dates this as a later model—the same colors were used as on Austin's real autos of the period: light green and fawn on earlier models, and red, white or darker green on later ones. However, the "Flying A" mascot on the hood shows that it is not a very late example: in line with British laws prohibiting such projections on real autos, mascots were not fitted to late-production "Joycars". It is possible roughly to date examples from the chassis number

(Top) A publicity brochure of the 1950s for the Austin "J Forty" Pedal Car; see (4) above. (Bottom) "The Magic Motor Car", a British children's book of the 1920s, features Triang's Rolls Royce; see (2), pages 118-119.

stamped on the floor of the trunk. This pedal car is of unusually robust construction, since it is made of sheet steel of the same gauge as that used on Austin's real automobiles. Surplus material from Austin's production line was transported to a specially-constructed factory at Bargoed, Wales, where "Joycars" were built by disabled miners as part of a rehabilitation program. The "Joycar" features chromed bumpers, radiator grille, and hubcaps; battery-operated headlights and horn; a hood that

The end of production of the Austin "Joycar" is announced on the center-spread of the manufacturer's house journal, issued in May 1971.

opens to reveal an "engine" complete with spark plugs and leads; a felt-padded, leather-cloth-upholstered seat; a two-position interior handbrake; and pressed-steel wheels with Dunlop pneumatic tires. Total production over 21 years amounted to 32,100 "Joycars", and they are still fairly common. Length: 63in (160cm).

5 Pedal Car by Leeway, Great Britain, early 1950s. The chrome-plated brightwork radiator is of "Triumph Dolomite" type, but Leeway's designation for this toy was "Model 16/11". Its all-steel body has an opening door, and features include simulated head- and side-lights, pressed-steel "balloon-type" wheels with molded rubber tires, and a two-speed gear shift. Length: 45in (114cm).

Ships and Boats

Above: *Pre-war scene in a Nuremburg toy factory, possibly that of the Marklin company, where a tinplate ship receives its final coat of paint.*

Left: *A splendid clockwork liner, Carmania, by Marklin, c1905. An impressive 39in (99cm) long, it has lost its masts but is otherwise complete and in good working order.*

Produced in types ranging from rowing boats to battleships and in sizes ranging from a few inches to more than three feet (1m), toy ships and boats are among the most beautiful and desirable of all metal toys, as the selection illustrated on *pages 124-133* will show. The intending collector should be warned, however, that they are also among the most scarce and valuable.

Not only are many toy boats comparatively fragile (in terms of rigging and other detail), the "waterborne" examples are also particularly subject to accidental loss. A collector who assisted in the compilation of this book suggested, perhaps not wholly as a joke, that a profitable "salvage company" might be formed to raise the many sunken wrecks of classic tinplate boats that now lie on the bottoms of lakes and ponds in public parks all over Europe and the USA! Since tinplate boats that were intended to operate in water were normally hand-soldered and hand-painted, to ensure their waterproof durability, they were generally highly-priced in comparison with toys of other kinds, and although production runs might be long-lasting, they often were not large in number. Thus, a toy boat by a wellknown maker, in good condition, will usually command a high price on the present-day collectors' market.

EARLY MAKERS

As has already been noted in the case of mechanical novelty toys (with which toy boats have in common the fact that styles changed very little over the years),

makers in the USA were earliest into the field of metal mechanical toys. The firm of Ives, Blakeslee and Company, Bridgeport, Conn., was producing clockwork rowing boats—not very much unlike the toy of a considerably later date shown at (12) on *pages 132-133*, in style—by about 1875. Before that date, such firms as Stevens and Brown, Cromwell, Conn., were already producing "carpet toy" boats of pull-/push-along type, often in the cast iron favored by US makers for such toys.

In Europe, the most famous early makers of metal toy boats were Radiguet (from 1889, Radiguet et Massiot) of Paris, France, and Jean Schoenner of Nuremburg, Germany. The fine gunboat shown on this spread is typical of boats made by Radiguet: steam-powered, with a hull of zinc rather than tinplate, with brass fittings and a wooden deck. It is rare to find a boat by Radiguet in good condition—the example shown has undergone some restoration—and rarer still to encounter an early boat by Schoenner, a maker active only from c1875 until c1906, and one whose boats usually bear no trademark. The steam launch shown at (1), *pages 132-133*, typifies the attractive simplicity of Schoenner's boats.

Although production was not large until the first decade of the 20th century, the great German tradition of high-quality metal boats was established from the 1890s. Such makers as Bing, Carette, Marklin, and Plank established themselves in the field in the later 1890s, and were soon to be followed

by Fleischmann, Hess, and Lehmann.

Many collectors would say (and, on the evidence of present-day auction prices, many more would agree) that of all the famous German makers, Marklin is the finest. Gebrüder Marklin's output of the pre-World War I period, especially, includes many of the most splendid examples of the genre; for example, the battleship, HMS *Terrible,* shown at *Inset, pages 124-125.* Dating from no later than 1905, this steam-driven warship may have been produced only in a "limited edition". Although a most impressive representation of a warship of the time, it is given added attraction by its "toy-like" quality, its boats, guns, upper works, and masts (lacking some of the original rigging) all being noticeably "larger than life". Similar boats made by Gebrüder Bing of Nuremburg are usually closer to scale.

Like many earlier boats by Marklin and other makers, HMS *Terrible* is largely hand-painted. Such details as port-holes were usually also hand-painted on earlier models, but applied transfers soon came into use, followed by rubber-stamping. The flags on *Terrible* are fabric, a characteristic feature of Marklin boats of the period: the firm did not fit tinplate flags (usually hand-painted) until after World War I. Like other makers, Marklin would fit the same model with different flags, and furnish it with an appropriate name, for sale in various foreign markets.

Note also the "semi-flat" crew of the *Terrible.* The firm of Heyde produced figures like these to complement boats

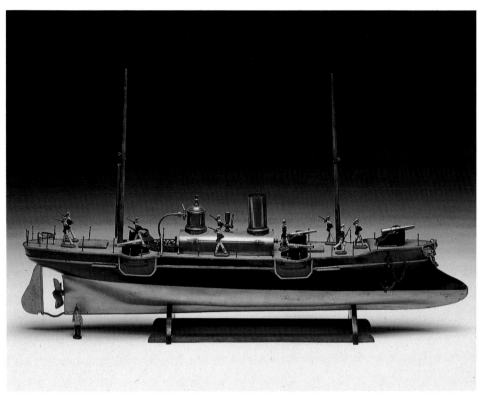

Above: *This steam-powered gunboat by the Parisian firm of Radiguet features a zinc hull, brass boiler, and the wooden deck and masts characteristic of this manufacturer's toys. Possibly dating from as early as 1880, it is on its original stand, though the rigging is missing and some restoration has been carried out.*

by Marklin, Bing, and Carette; but Marklin was the only maker to market its boats complete with such figures, and the only one to incorporate into the decks of its boats small raised tabs beneath which the bases of the figures could be secured.

The fine finish achieved by hand-painting on Marklin's most expensive boats is seen to advantage on the Liner of the pre-World War I period shown at (3), *pages 130-131.* A smaller Marklin liner shown at (5), dates from just after World War I, although, as is also the case with boats by other makers, the style differs very little from an equivalent example dating from the 1910s or even from the 1930s.

OTHER GERMAN MAKERS

Although we have given a good deal of the space available here to the boats of Marklin, as being typical of the best of the genre, the average collector is more likely to encounter good-quality boats by other German makers, notably Gebrüder Bing, a firm perhaps second in importance only to Marklin and one whose pre-World War I products are to be found in much greater number. Bing's very wide range extended from battleships to motorboats—see (6) and (13), *pages 132-133,* and to smaller, "novelty-type" items such as rowing boats (now scarce, since they proved less popular than other types) and the "Swamp Craft" for the US market shown at (2), *pages 132-133.*

Georges Carette, a French national working at Nuremburg until World War I, produced both large boats of fine quality, now rare, like the Paddle Steamer shown at (3), *pages 132-133,* and small, low-priced toys like the Warship at (12), *pages 128-129.* Many of Carette's boats bear no trademark, and attribution depends upon information from contemporary catalogs and on the characteristic style of such details as ships' boats and guns. Carette's hulls are sometimes of zinc, rather than tinplate; the same hull-shapes appear in boats by Fleischmann, since that firm acquired much of Carette's tooling after 1917. Fleischmann's boats of the 1930s reached a high standard—see, for example, the Tanker at (4), *pages 130-131*—and a number of the firm's models, notably a liner made in no less than eleven hull lengths, from 6·3in (16cm) to 31·5in (80cm), appeared in the same form in the years both before and after World War II.

The firm of Hess, Nuremburg, in production until 1930s, is noted for the production of clockwork-powered "carpet toy" boats: a particularly attractive example, a Battleship with a linked flotilla of gunboats, is shown at (1-7), *pages 124-125.* Lehmann, more famous for its "land-based" toys and novelties, also produced notable "carpet toy" ships. Finally, the firm of Arnold deserves special mention because it was, with Fleischmann, about the last to maintain the German tradition of tinplate boats after World War II (see *Inset, pages 130-131),* until the growing dominance of plastic in the 1960s, along with the aggressive marketing of Japanese tin-

plate-toy makers, rendered uneconomical the mass-production of such comparatively expensive toys.

BRITISH AND FRENCH MAKERS

In the 1930s, when "record-breaking" on land, in the air, and on water exerted great popular appeal, toy speedboats became increasingly common. Notable makers of these toys, which often had clockwork motors geared to give high speeds at some expense to the distance attained on one winding, included such companies as Hornby (Meccano Limited) of Great Britain, and Jep (Jouets en Paris) of France.

Hornby's speedboats were constructed on four basic hulls, 8·5in (21·5cm), 9·25in (23·5cm), 12·5in (32cm), and 16·5in (42cm) long: the "limousine" version on the largest hull is shown at (8) on *pages 132-133.* Hornby's boats were available only until World War II, but Jep's speedboats, see (5) and (7) on *pages 132-133,* were made both before and after World War II, the pre-War examples being the more attractive.

A further notable British maker, still in production, is Sutcliffe of Yorkshire. The firm began its production in 1920 with "toc-toc" boats but by the late 1920s was producing clockwork-powered boats, sometimes on the same hulls as the "toc-tocs".

POINTS FOR COLLECTORS

Since toy boats generally saw fairly tough and, as stated at the outset, fairly hazardous service, examples in good condition (especially from the earlier years) are more rarely encountered than is the case with toys of other kinds. Such details as ships' boats, guns, anchors, flags, and especially rigging, are frequently missing or, if present, may be replacement items. Many boats will have been repaired or even completely restored. However, *if* the renovation has been expertly carried out (as is the case with the restored examples among the selection shown in this book), it will not detract too greatly from the appeal to the collector or the market value of the boat.

As with other toys, possession of the original packaging is desirable. However, it may be noted that the finer early models were often marketed in robust but fairly plain boxes of wood or heavy cardboard: colorfully-printed pictorial labels feature more often on the cheaper toys. Unless the collector has great faith in his own ability, the renovation or mechanical repair of such comparatively valuable specimens is best entrusted to professional hands. Ideally, toy boats should be displayed on purpose-made stands, or some similar securing device, in glazed cabinets, at an even temperature, away from damp, and out of direct sunlight.

All the boats shown on this spread were photographed at the London Toy & Model Museum. The warship shown *Inset* is from the collection of Ron McCrindell.

1-7 Carpet Toy Battleship & Flotilla, lightweight tinplate, by Hess, Nuremburg, Germany, c1910. The two-funneled battleship (6), with the White Ensign of the Royal Navy at its masthead, is powered by clockwork. Concealed beneath its hull are three eccentric wheels which give a pitching-and-rolling effect as it moves. It is linked by jointed rods—detached example at (7)—to five gunboats (1-5) of differing types, each with a peg at bow and stern to fit into an aperture on a rod. Note that the rods are provided with several apertures so

that the gunboats may be arranged in varying formations. The battleship and the individual gunboats could be bought as separate items. Lengths: (battleship) 8·25in (21cm), (gunboat) 5·5in (14cm).
8 Carpet Toy Battleship "New York", cast iron with tinplate masts, by Arcade, USA, c1912. This impressive pull-along toy is attractive in its disproportion—note particularly the large figure of the captain on the bridge—for many collectors feel that "toy-like" items like this have greater charm than more faithful models. The ship bristles with guns, although some gun barrels are missing from the sponsoned turrets to both port and starboard. Length: 20·375in (52cm). Limited.

9 Carpet Toy River Boat, cast iron, certainly by an American maker (probably Kenton), c1910. The hand-enameled finish is rather less "play-worn" than that of (8). The central wheels are concealed within the paddle boxes; the beam on the central deck is connected to the cranked axle of the main wheels and rocks as the boat is pulled along. Length: 10in (25cm). Limited.
10 Novelty Boat, tinplate, possibly by a French maker, dating from c1900; an unusual pull-along toy. As the boat is pulled, a striker operating from the cranked axle hits the two bells. Length: 4·75in (12cm). Limited.
11 "Toc-Toc" Boat, tinplate, British-made and dating from around 1900. This toy was

patented by Thomas Pilot in 1898 and was probably the first of its kind: it is propelled by water-jets from a heated coil—see note at (9) on *pages 132-133*—and its name derives from the sound made by its propulsion unit. This example bears a brass tablet impressed: "J. Robinson & Sons, Opticians & Photographers, 172 Regent St."; this London retailer specialized in late 19th century optical and other "scientific" toys. Length: 9·75in (25cm). Scarce.
12 Gunboat "Mikasa", tinplate, by Bing, Germany, dating from c1904 and perhaps inspired by the Russo-Japanese War of that time. Its operation is ingenious: as the clockwork motor runs down it activates a cap-firing mechanism in the gun turret; one gun fires and

5

6

11

12

MIKASA

13

22.

14

15

the boat changes course by 90°; the second gun fires and the course alters a further 90° to return the boat to its launching point. The bridge section hinges back to allow the guns to be loaded. The Japanese battle-flag at the stern is a replacement; the original would have been a smaller tinplate flag. Length: 19·5in (50cm). Scarce.

Battleship, "HMS Terrible", tinplate, by Marklin, Germany; a magnificent toy dating from no later than 1905, probably earlier. Concealed beneath the superstructure is a maker's number "7": the present owner believes that this may indicate very limited production. It is, in any case, extremely rare. Length: 24·5in (62cm).

13 Torpedo by Ernst Plank, Nuremburg, Germany, c1902. An unusual clockwork toy, of soldered tinplate and with an enameled finish, which operated semi-submerged, directed by its adjustable rudder. The hatch amidships is unscrewed to give access to the winder. Note the applied Plank trademark forward of the hatch and patent number aft. Length: 12in (30cm). Rare.

14 Two-Man Racing Motorboat by Bing, Germany, c1910. This tinplate toy is more fully noted at (6) and (13) on *pages 132-133*, where an example with a different pennant number is shown. Length: 8·5in (21·5cm). Limited.

15 Lifeboatman, a diecast figure by Britains, Britain, dating from c1935. Height: 3in (76mm).

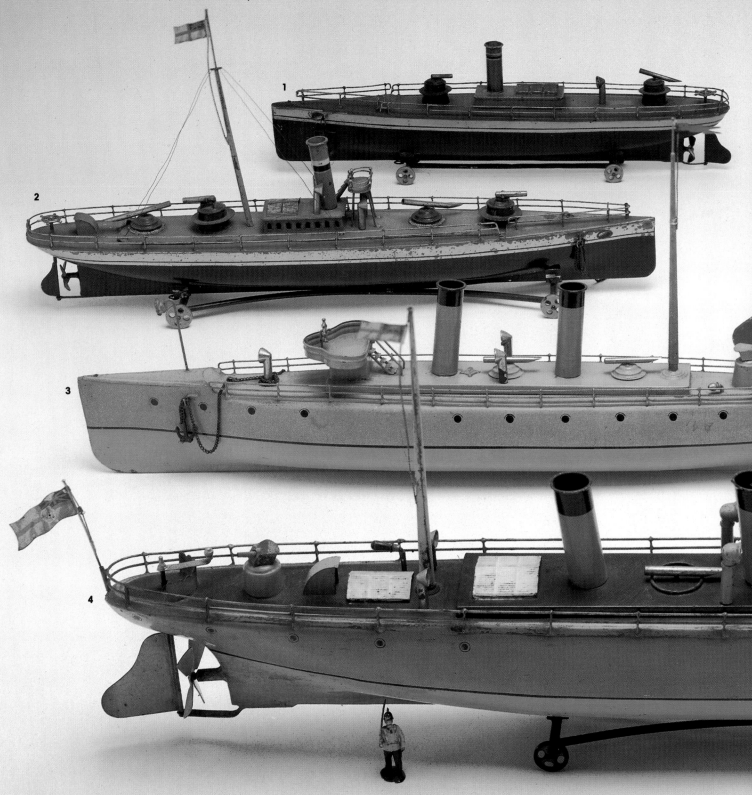

In comparison with toys of other kinds, boats are both fragile and liable to accidental loss during play. Therefore, all tinplate boats of the kind shown here and on the three following spreads—almost all of which are of pre-1939 manufacture and in fine condition—may be properly described, in the terms of the classification system used throughout this book, as "Rare". No classification has, therefore, been applied to most of the items shown.

All the boats shown on this spread are from the collection of Ron McCrindell, London.

1 Torpedo Boat by Gebrüder Bing, Germany; first cataloged in 1902 and offered by the famous store of Gamage's, London, in that year at

a price of 9s 11d (49½p, 70c). This boat is clockwork-powered, running for about five minutes on one winding (winder in funnel), but it was also available in steam and is, indeed, described in Gamage's Catalog as a "Steam Torpedo Boat". It is a pleasing and fairly accurate model and, like all this early series, rare. Note the original cradle, or trolley, 9in (23cm) long; this was supplied with the boat and incorporates a ring through which a cord could be tied temporarily to convert the craft to a pull-along toy. The boat was made in three sizes: 15in (38cm); 20in (50cm), as shown here; and 24in (60cm), as shown at (2).

2 Torpedo Boat by Bing, c1902: the de luxe version, cataloged as a "Steam Torpedo Division Boat", of

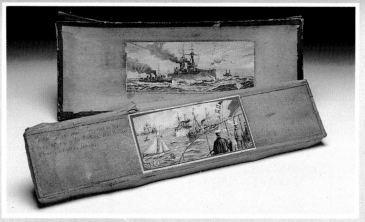

Box lids for Bing boats of the pre-1914 period: (top) for the Dreadnought Battleship shown at (10) on pages 128-129; (bottom) for the Large Torpedo Boat with three funnels shown at (4) on this spread.

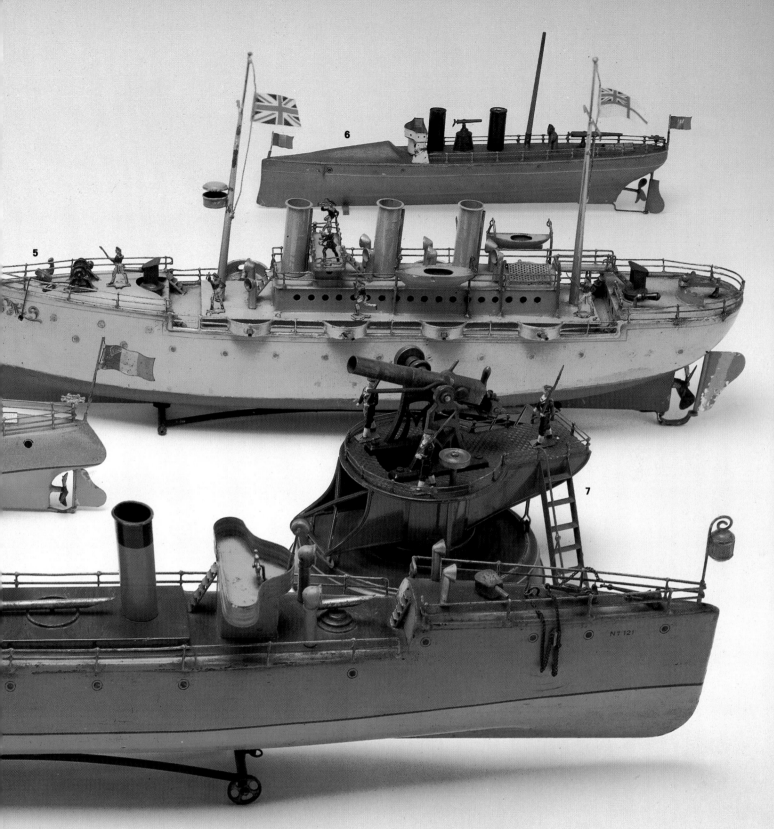

the boat shown at (1). This example is clockwork, it was available also in steam, and was sold in Britain by Gamage's at a price of 15s 0d (75p, $1.07). This example is in excellent original condition, with no restoration. Note the detail, including the original lithographed tinplate flag, wire rigging, anchor and chain, and wheel that turns rudder. It rests on its original 14in (36cm) cradle. Length: 24in (60cm).

3 Torpedo Boat by Bing, dating from *c*1906 and probably available until World War I. A more utilitarian model than those of the 1902 series shown at (1) and (2), this has its original tinplate Italian tricolor at the stern and original tinplate mast. The two-funneled example shown is 27·5in (70cm)

long and is powered by clockwork; it was also available in steam, and was made in a larger, three-funneled version; see (4).

4 Large Torpedo Boat, "No 121", by Bing, cataloged by Gamage's at £1 17s 6d (£1.87½p, $2.66) in 1908. It is powered by clockwork and was also available in steam. It is a later, larger, three-funneled version of the boat shown at (3). Length: 39·5in (100cm).

5 Gunboat *(Canonenboot* in the maker's catalog) by Bing, first cataloged in 1902 and originally named (for the British market) "King Edward". This example is clockwork, the powerful motor giving about ten minutes' run on one winding; it was also available in steam. It has undergone minor restoration: two lifeboats are

missing (it is rare to find a boat of this vintage with all accessories intact), but the masts are the original rolled tinplate. The boat shown is 30in (75cm) long: it was made also in a 24in (60cm) version, with two funnels and this smaller version has only two lifeboats. The sailors are contemporary small "flats" by a Nuremburg maker.

6 Large Coasting Cruiser (maker's catalog description) by Georges Carette, a French maker working until World War I at Nuremburg, Germany. Dating from 1911, when it sold in Britain at 11s 6d (57½p, 82c), this boat was made only in clockwork. The mast of this example is wood: the original would have been tinplate. Note the simple bracket-stand on the hull

forward, a feature later adopted by Bing. The boat shown is 18in (46cm) long; it was also made in 14in (36cm), 20in (50cm), and "fully detailed" 24in (60cm) versions.

7 Coastal Gun, tinplate, by Marklin, Germany, cataloged in 1902. As an explosive cap is fired in the breech, a spring launches a white metal shell from the muzzle. The gun may be elevated, depressed, and fully traversed by means of the control wheels seen in the photograph; note the small flanged wheels of the traversing mechanism running on a track around the base. Base diameter: 10in (25cm); maximum height: 9in (23cm). The sailors are British-made Britains figures of *c*1935.

All the boats shown on this spread are from the collection of Ron McCrindell, London.

1 Warship by Fleischmann, Germany, dating from the mid-1930s. Note the "funnel-smoke" winder for the clockwork, one of several Carette features that appeared on Fleischmann boats following the acquisition of Carette's boat division after 1917. Fleischmann often used Carette hull pressings, but the original Carette products can be identified by the styles of guns and ships' boats. The single mast is missing from this example. Length: 12in (30cm).

2 Submarine by a British maker, dating from the World War I period. Note the balance weight that is moved along a screw thread to adjust the trim. This simple toy dives on launching and surfaces when its clockwork motor runs down. Length: 15in (38cm).

3 Battleship, clockwork, by Bing, Germany, issued before World War I but still cataloged in Britain (as "HMS Neptune") by Bassett-Lowke in the 1920s. This example has undergone some restoration and repainting: the anchors, after tripod mast, and two gun turrets originally sited under the flying bridge are missing. It was available in three sizes: 12in (30cm), without anchors; 20in (50cm), with anchors; and 26in (65cm), as shown here.

4 British Armored Cruiser (Gamage's 1913 Catalog description) by Bing, 1912: an interesting example of a later Bing series. It is clockwork, Bing having almost abandoned steam-propelled boats by this time, and was made in no fewer than seven sizes: the example shown is 22in (55cm) long. Of the five sizes listed in Gamage's Catalog, the largest is 37·5in (95cm). This boat is in very good condition, although the rigging needs attention.

5 Submarine by Marklin, Germany: the largest toy submarine produced commercially. This had a long production run, from c1914 until the late 1920s, but it is rarer than many other Marklin boats—all of which are eagerly sought by collectors. This example is complete and in fine original condition. Note the transfer detail of port-holes and machine-gun positions, and the brass hatch aft the conning tower; the latter forms a waterproof seal over the clockwork mechanism and is unscrewed for winding. The action is realistic: the diving vanes are geared to the clockwork mechanism to make the boat submerge and surface alternately. Length: 31·5in (80cm); also available in smaller sizes.

6 Warship by Arnold, Germany, dating from the mid-1920s. This simple, two-funneled clockwork ship (from which the single mast and flag are missing) was sold in Britain at around 1s 0d (5p, 7c). Length: 9in (23cm).

7 Three-Funneled Destroyer by Bing, probably dating from the early 1920s. It is more attractively colored than many toy boats of its

period. Well detailed, it has tinplate flags; the flag from the after mast is missing. This example is 16·5in (42cm) long—probably the largest size in which this clockwork boat was produced; it was also available in a smaller, two-funneled version.

8 Battleship, clockwork, by Fleischmann, mid-1930s. As its flags show, this was intended for the US market; it was also produced with German and British flags. It is 20·5in (52cm) long: Fleischmann's standard 52cm hull was used for a number of different boats, and although production of the series ended in 1939, it made a brief reappearance in almost identical form in 1955-56.

9 Submarine by Bing: the largest submarine by this maker and a very rare specimen. It was first

cataloged as early as 1902 and was available in the large size shown until 1910, or possibly a little later. A most attractive design, it is simple in operation, diving after launch and surfacing when the clockwork runs down. Note the very large, original, key: the powerful motor is wound through a separate compartment reached by unscrewing the small turret forward of the conning tower. This example has been restored to close to original condition: such restoration is acceptable, especially in the case of such a rare boat. Gamage's, London, listed this toy in three sizes in the 1902 Catalog: the largest, as seen here, 27in (68cm) long, priced at £1 17s 6d (£1.87½p, $2.66); 18in (46cm); and 13·5in (34cm). Only

the two smaller sizes remained in the Catalog in 1913.

10 Battleship by Bing, c1913, modeled on the Royal Navy's revolutionary "all big gun" HMS *Dreadnought*. This is a fairly plain, utilitarian model—the anchors are soldered on and the superstructure cannot be raised to give access to the clockwork—but a solid and pleasing toy. It has triple screws: only the central shaft is driven, but the outer screws revolve as the boat moves through the water. Note the metal plaque with the Bing trademark on the central superstructure. Length: 19·5in (50cm).

11 Submarine by Arnold, dating from soon after World War II (it is stamped "Made in US Zone,

Germany"). A simple clockwork-powered toy, winding through the turret, it is in fully original condition and, despite being relatively recent, is scarce. Length: 12in (30cm).

12 Warship by Carette, dating from c1905 or possibly earlier: an extremely simple boat, with no rudder, which sold in Britain at 0s 6d (2½p, 4c). Note the "funnel smoke" winder—see also (1)—and, even on so basic a design, the readily identifiable Carette guns and, especially, the single-ring stand (just visible beneath the hull forward) which was a feature of almost all Carette boats. The hull is not tinplate but zinc, as found in some other earlier boats, and the paint is now flaking away. This example is complete, apart from a flag aft. Length: 5·75in (15cm).

All the boats shown on this spread are from the collection of Ron McCrindell, London.

1 "Viking" Liner by Arnold, Germany, dating from the 1930s, when this simple clockwork toy sold in Britain for about 0s 7½d (3p, 4c). The lithographed deck fittings—hatchways, ropes, and winches—typical of Arnold boats are just visible; the foremast is missing. Length: 8in (20cm).

2 Liner by Fleischmann, Germany, dating from the 1920s. As in the case of the Battleship at (1) on *pages 128-129,* this boat shows many features adopted from Carette: the hull is a Carette pressing and the masts, the shape of the rudder, and much of the superstructure are of Carette type.

The lifeboats and flags, however, are characteristic of Fleischmann. This is therefore an interesting "borderline" case. Length: 17in (42cm).

3 Liner by Marklin; a very large and grand model—and of surprisingly modern appearance for its date of origin, *c*1910. It was available for some years, making a brief reappearance after World War I. This impressive craft surely pushes the classification of "toy" to an extreme: it sold in Britain for around £25 0s 0d (£25.00, $35.50) at a time when that sum probably represented more than one month's pay for the average worker. The excellent detail is evident: the boats are hand-painted, as is usual on larger models, and the "deck planking" effect is also

the result of hand-painting. The large and powerful two-speed clockwork motor, driving two propellers, gives a running time of 15-20 minutes. This liner is in good order: it took part in a regatta on the Round Pond, London, in 1983. Length: 39·5in (100cm).

4 Tanker by Fleischmann, dating from the mid-1930s. This clockwork boat is based on the maker's favored 52cm hull—a Carette pressing—but is unusual in being one of the few toy tankers. Note the attractive detail; also the Fleischmann trademark, "GFN" in a triangle, in the bows. Length: 20·5in (52cm).

5 Liner by Marklin, Germany, dating from immediately after World War I. A Marklin (Wittenburg) trademark stamped on the rudder is

part-visible. This most attractive boat, well-proportioned, interestingly-detailed, and nicely finished (the port-holes on the hull are "rubber-stamped"), is in excellent original condition, with its large key shown in place. It is a pity that this series, which included both liners and warships, had only a short production run. Length: 14in (36cm).

6 Liner by Arnold. This clockwork boat is not unlike the "Viking" Liner shown at (1); it dates from the same period but is a little larger and has a differently-designed superstructure. Again, the foremast is missing. The Arnold trademark stamped on the deck aft is just visible. Length: 9in (23cm).

7 Liner by Fleischmann, dating from the 1930s and based on the 52cm

6

7

8

Set of Liners by Arnold. The boxes in which these clockwork boats were sold are marked "Made in Germany, US Zone", but the boats are probably of pre-World War II manufacture, re-packaged and tactfully fitted with Swiss flags for sale post-1945. The two larger boats have twin propellers; the two smaller, single propellers. They are of especial interest in being among the last of the "quality" tinplate boats in the great German tradition. Lengths: 18in (46cm); 14·5in (37cm); 12in (30cm); 9in (23cm).

hull favored by this maker. This clockwork boat appeared in the Fleischmann 1936 Catalog, was made until 1939, and made a brief reappearance in 1955-56.

Note particularly the lifeboats: their simple design is a Fleischmann characteristic. Length: 20·5in (52cm).

8 Liner by Bing, Germany, dating from the mid-1920s. Most Bing liners of this later period have black-and-red hulls; this is unusual in having a lower hull of light copper color. The yellow deck is, however, typical of Bing boats of the period, as is the lifeboat pattern. The propeller and after mast are missing from this boat, but note the Bing trademark stamped forward of the fore-funnel. This simple, three-funneled, clockwork boat was made in several sizes: the example shown is 14in (36cm) long; a smaller, two-funneled version was 9in (23cm) long.

All the boats shown on this spread are from the collection of Ron McCrindell, London.

1 Steam Launch by Jean Schoenner, Nuremburg, Germany, c1900; a rare example of the work of a maker who appears to have ceased production around 1906. The simplicity of the design is typical of Schoenner, as is the power unit: a methylated spirit burner firing a vertical boiler with a single oscillating cylinder. The tinplate ensign at the stern is the Stars and Stripes. The graceful hull of the launch has an overall length of 12in (30cm).

2 Swamp Craft by Bing, Germany, mid-1920s. This rare and interesting toy, probably aimed at the American market, is clockwork-driven via a large traction propeller. The winder can be seen just forward of the driver; the rudder is between the floats. Length: 7in (18cm).

3 Paddle Steamer by Carette, Germany, cataloged in 1911 but probably dating from some years earlier. It has been restored to near-original condition and finish, although the fore and aft masts are missing. Note that the winding aperture, with key in position, is very near the waterline: operation in all but a dead calm would be hazardous! This boat was available in several sizes: the example shown was the largest, with a length of 21in (53cm).

4 Speedboat made in the USSR (Moscow) in the late 1940s—and strikingly similar to the Jep speedboat at (5). Although slightly smaller than the more beamy Jep boat, it is definitely a copy, although it is not known whether the design was pirated or whether Jep sold pressings to Eastern Europe. Even the driver (a composition half-figure) is similar, although in this Soviet model he is better-proportioned and protected by a celluloid windscreen. The cockpit cover and the clockwork motor beneath it may be lifted out as one piece for servicing. Length: 14in (36cm).

5 Speedboat, "Ruban Bleu No 1", by Jep (Jouets en Paris), France, mid-1930s. Compare with the Soviet copy at (4) and with the contemporary Hornby "Venture" at (8). Note the large key in winding position: clockwork engines for speedboats have fewer gears than conventional mechanisms, to give "high revs", and it is not advisable to let the clockwork run while the boat is out of water. The central cockpit section lifts out to give access to the mechanism: if a spring broke, a new engine could be purchased and easily fitted. The half-figure of the driver is composition. This example of a boat available in several different sizes and color schemes is 14·5in (37cm) long.

6 Two-Man Racing Motorboat by Bing, c1910. A most attractive clockwork toy, sold in Britain at 2s 3d (11½p, 16c), this example is the middle size of the range, at 8·5in (21·5cm). It was also available at 10·5in (26·5cm) and 7·5in (19cm); see also (13).

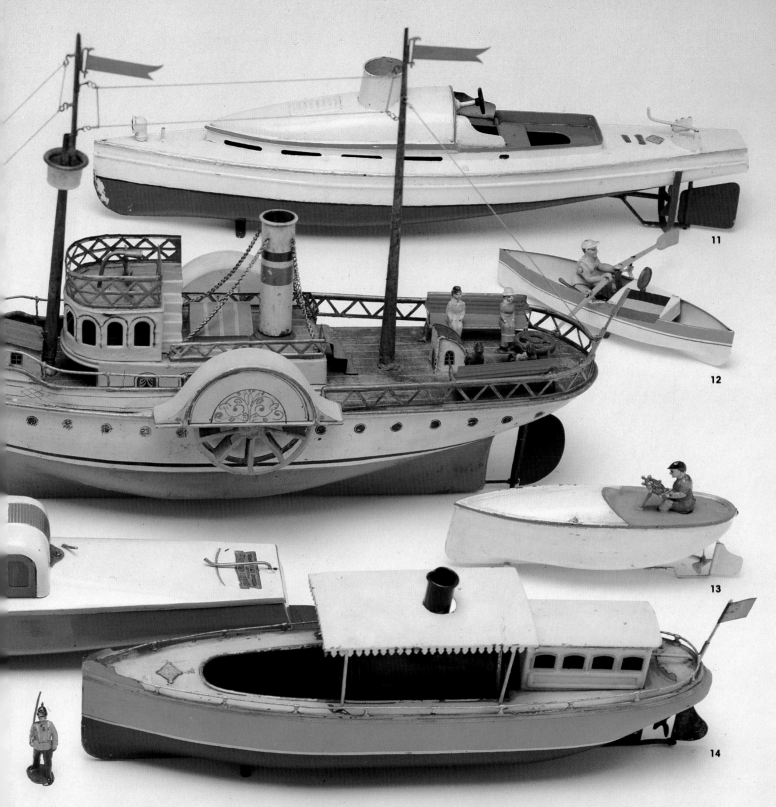

7 Speedboat, "JEP 3", by Jep; a simpler and cheaper toy than the Jep boat at (5), dating from the 1950s. The hull is flat-bottomed and there is no access to the clockwork mechanism (note fixed key) except by removing the tabbed and slotted deck. The composition driver and the windscreen are typically Jep. The boat's name refers to its size: the model was available in other sizes, "JEP 1" being the smallest. Length: 15in (38cm).

8 Limousine Boat No 4, "Venture", a clockwork boat by Hornby, Britain, available from the late 1920s until World War II. This attractive saloon version (note seat and steering wheel) of the Hornby series was available in three different color schemes. Length: 16·5in (42cm).

9 "Toc-Toc" Boat, marked "Made in US Zone, Germany" and thus dating from c1946 or later. This simple toy takes its name from its water-jet propulsion: the two ends of a coil tube protrude from the stern and a candle in the cabin heats the coil until water is sucked into one end of the tube and forced out of the other with a "toc-toc" noise. Length: 5in (13cm).

10 Paddle Steamer by Marklin, Germany, c1910. Paddle steamers of this series are particularly rare, and although this example has undergone some small restoration it is in near-original condition. The composition figures on the benches aft are of the type made for use with contemporary Marklin trains. This splendid clockwork boat is 20in (50cm) long.

11 Steam Motor Racing Boat by Bing, Germany. The early Bing trademark on the stern decking suggests a date of c1908, by which time the simple bracket-stand on the hull forward had replaced the wheeled cradle supplied with earlier models. The superstructure hinges towards the stern to give access to the steam engine, with its brass boiler and brass oscillating cylinder. Provision is made for a peg-in driver, but no such figure is known to have been supplied. The boat was listed by Gamage's, London, in 1913 at 14s 6d (72½p, $1.03) for the 22in (55cm) model, as shown, or 8s 6d (42½p, 60c) for an 18in (46cm) version.

12 Rowing Boat by Arnold, West Germany, dating from after World War II. The oars are tinplate, but the rower is composition, an unusual feature at this period when tin figures were more common. Length: 8in (20cm).

13 One-Man Racing Motorboat by Bing, c1910. This smaller version of the toy shown at (6) has undergone some restoration. Length: 7·5in (19cm).

14 Turbine Steamboat by Bing, c1906. Another rare boat, and a particularly interesting one in that it is driven by a tiny steam turbine, with a boiler fired by methylated spirit. As the canopy, Bing used a stamping for a model railway station, and the cabin aft is, in fact, a Bing Gauge "0" railway carriage, minus wheels. This boat was made in three sizes, one larger and one smaller than the example shown, which is 16in (41cm) long.

Airplanes

Below and below left: *Late 1930s English-made tinplate airplane with clockwork nose propeller and battery-powered lower wing lights. Wartime propaganda photo shows the toy being sacrificed to the war effort.*

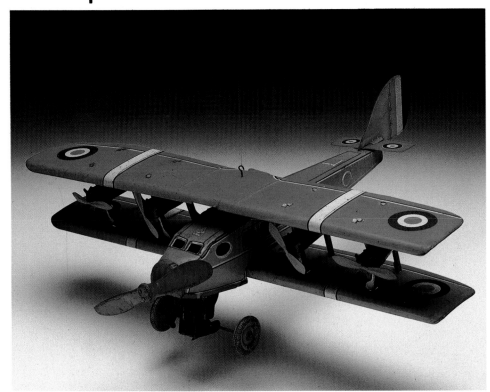

Although toy airplanes did not, of course, engage the interest of manufacturers or buyers until some time after the Wright Brothers' first "heavier-than-air" flights at Kitty Hawk, N.C., in 1903, aeronautical toys based on balloons and dirigibles were in evidence at least as early as the 1890s. Although examples are now very scarce, and none is shown in this book, it may be said that most of these early tinplate aeronautical toys were of the "novelty" type. A fairly typical example was a "balloon" of hollow tinplate, its envelope concealing a clockwork mechanism that powered the antics of the figure of an acrobat slung beneath it.

Rather more common (although scarce and expensive today) in this early period were tinplate representations of Zeppelin-type airships, which were produced by such famous German makers as Lehmann and Marklin from c1908 onward. Most toy Zeppelins, like the early tinplate airplanes described below, had clockwork motors of sufficient power to enable them to "fly" in a circle, with the help of somewhat over-sized propellers, when suspended from a cord.

TINPLATE AIRPLANES

As has been amply demonstrated in other sections of this book, German makers led the field in the production of tinplate toys before World War I. It was, therefore, not until the powers of the Wright biplane had been triumphantly displayed in Europe, in 1908, that

airplanes began to feature at all significantly in the catalogs of such makers as Bing, Günthermann, Marklin, and Plank of Nuremburg.

By 1909, Marklin's catalog listed a tinplate Wright biplane in three sizes, the largest with a wingspan of 17·3in (44cm). The model had a clockwork motor that enabled it to taxi on rubber-tired wheels or, driving a pusher propeller with large, paddle-shaped celluloid blades, to fly along a wire threaded through a top-mounted pulley. The model could also be suspended to fly in a circle, steered by a movable aileron. In the same year, Günthermann produced a toy inspired by another pioneer aviator, Louis Blériot, whose monoplane made the first heavier-than-air crossing of the English Channel in July 1909. Günthermann's toy involved an alternative method of "flight": the clockwork-powered monoplane was mounted at one end of a counter-weighted rod pivoted on a central pillar.

All these early aeronautical toys, including also some small "penny toy" airplanes, are now scarce and valuable, and the average collector's attention is likely to center rather on the tinplate airplanes produced after World War I, when the wartime exploits of air power had considerably stimulated the interest of toymakers and their customers alike—although neither tinplate nor diecast airplanes, it may be noted, were ever as popular with the toy-buying public as the equivalent automotive toys or boats.

AIRLINERS AND RECORD-BREAKERS

From about the mid-1920s (by which time the major German makers had recovered from the setbacks inflicted by World War I), the rapid expansion of commercial avaiation and the great excitement caused by various "record flights" led to the issue of an increasing number of toy airplanes (and, still, some airships). It is from this time, as well as later periods, that the examples of tinplate airplanes shown on *pages 136-137* are taken.

Among the wellknown toymakers that produced tinplate aeronautical items in the 1920s-1930s, the names of Distler, Fleischmann, Günthermann, and Tipp, Germany, Jep of France, and Cardini of Italy are prominent. Representations of flying boats were particularly popular: in real life, these were generally larger than their land-based contemporaries and, since they could also be given more luxurious interior fittings, were used to pioneer the long-range passenger routes. In the selection shown on *pages 136-137*, note particularly the Dornier-type flying boat by Fleischmann (1), a "floating" model as might be expected from a maker noted for toy ships, and the racing seaplane by Jep, with working rudders on its floats. The Japanese-made Lockheed-type monoplane at (4) displays another of the popular features of toy aircraft of this period: pressed-tin figures of the airmen in their cockpits.

Above: *Dinky Toy No 738, the DH 110 Sea Vixen, in the original English-made version and (foreground) as produced under license in India.*

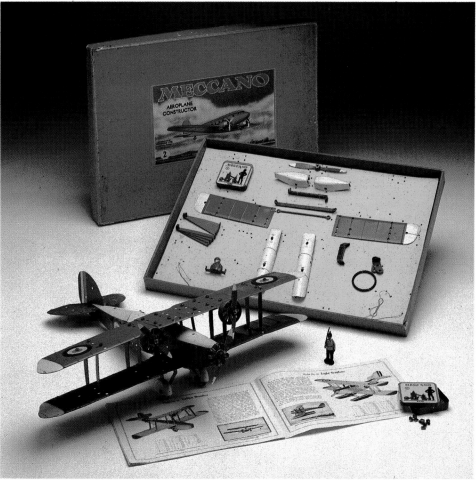

Right: *Meccano's mid-1930s Aeroplane Constructor Set No 2, used to build the tri-motor biplane shown, along with instruction book covering various types.*

In the 1930s, an era of rearmament and rumors of war, toy warplanes became increasingly popular—some incorporating such grim detail as "droppable" bombs and flint-sparking machine guns. On *pages 136-137,* note the Japanese-made bomber at (9), dating from early in the decade, in camouflage finish with a detailed twin-gun turret forward, and the later German-made military monoplane, also in camouflage finish, at (5). At this time, too, the earlier "space" toys appeared in the shape of tinplate rocket-ships, spearheaded by the US maker, Marx, in *c*1934.

After World War II, the "space" category became increasingly popular, although both German and, especially, Japanese makers continued to produce good-quality, detailed airplane models in tinplate (although often with plastic details) of the kind shown on *pages 138-139.* These post-War specimens are likely to become increasingly collectable as the aircraft that they are designed to represent pass out of service.

CONSTRUCTOR KITS

From 1931 onward, Meccano of Great Britain introduced a series of airplane constructor kits (see photograph here) featuring the nut-and-bolt assembly of metal parts. The kits ranged from the "Number 00" outfit, priced at 3s 3d (16½p, 23c) in the mid-1930s, to the "No 2 Special" at £1 2s 6d (£1.12½, $1.60). Very late in the decade, the kits were available with the parts in camouflage

or gray finish as well as in the usual blue-and-white colors seen in the photograph above. From the larger kits, which included the diecast half-figure of a pilot, a number of different types of aircraft could be built, and a clockwork motor specially adapted to power wheels and propeller could be separately purchased. Constructor kits incorporating a greater number of diecast parts, for a more realistic finish, along with composition figures of aircrew, were made in Germany by Gebrüder Marklin during the same period.

DIECAST AIRCRAFT

As in the case of automotive toys, the production of diecast airplane models was pioneered in the later 1920s by Tootsietoy of the USA. Until quite recently, diecast airplanes were generally considered to be of less interest to collectors than diecast vehicles, but they are now increasingly collectable and, as with vehicles, the attention of the average collector is likely to center on the extensive range of airplanes made by Dinky Toys, in both Great Britain and France, from the 1930s onward. A fine collection of these models is shown on *pages 140-143;* note also the Indian-made "Nicky Toys", produced from Dinky dies, shown on this spread and on *pages 142-143.*

The earliest Dinky Toys issues were mainly of civil airplanes and, as in the case of tinplate toys, flying boats were especially popular: note particularly

the Mercury Mayo Composite, now fairly scarce, at (13), *pages 140-141.* Some of the earlier biplanes are also hard to find, as is the early (*c*1934) Cierva Autogiro shown at (16), *pages 140-141.* As war approached, the number of military airplanes issued increased, and by the later 1930s many of these were available in camouflage finish as well as in the silver (aluminum) finish used both pre- and post-War. A number of boxed sets were also issued.

In some models of the 1930s—eg, the "Singapore" flying boat shown at (36), *pages 140-141*—tinplate was used for wings, but metal fatigue, manifested as "wing droop", is all too common on Dinky diecast aircraft and may be seen on some of the examples illustrated. Propellers are a vulnerable point, but replacements are still available if these are found to be missing. In the case of post-World War II issues, as shown on *pages 142-143,* possession of the original box is particularly important to the value—in any case, diecast airplanes are best kept in their boxes and at an even temperature.

A number of the post-War Dinky airplanes are, like pre-War issues, now in short supply, for from the later 1950s onward the increasing popularity of airplane constructor kits in plastic, made by such firms as Airfix (which would eventually take control of the Meccano company), severely limited the sales, and consequently the production runs, of diecast models.

From the very beginning of man's attempts to fly, toy manufacturers have reflected the romance of the conquest of the air, their products ranging from toy balloons and airships to futuristic models like the Flying Car shown at (2) below—and, of course, in more recent times, space vehicles. As may be seen here, most tinplate aircraft (unlike the diecast models shown on *pages 140-141, 142-143)* are only loosely based on the real thing. The collector may find it hard to acquire examples in the generally fine condition seen here—the efforts of children to "fly" such non-flying models may have something to do with this! All the aircraft shown on this spread were photographed at the London Toy & Model Museum.

1 Flying Boat by J. Fleischmann, Nuremburg, Germany, c1937. It is based on a contemporary Dornier type, with a raised tailplane assembly and aerofoil floats that resemble stub wings. It is appropriate that this large and impressive—although plainly finished—tinplate aircraft should be the work of a company best known for its toy boats, for it is designed to float. The six engines with tractor/pusher propellers mounted on the upper wing are unpowered, but the large and rather clumsy propeller at the nose is driven by clockwork (note winding shaft in fuselage just forward of the upper wing) and pulls the model across the water, albeit somewhat slowly. Length: 17·25in (44cm). Limited.

2 Flying Car by Blomer & Schüler, West Germany, dating from c1948-50 and no doubt inspired by reports of immediate post-War attempts by US designers to make such a vehicle a reality. It is clockwork-powered; the wings fold back into the body, springing out when the brake (note lever on boot) is released. Length: 7·5in (19cm). Wingspan: 8in (20cm).

3 Supermarine Spitfire, marked "Empire Made" (possibly in Hong Kong), c1950. Of tinplate construction, with printed "camouflage" and Royal Air Force roundels, it is a "push-and-go" toy, with an axle geared to a heavy flywheel which maintains momentum after an initial push. The propeller is plastic. Note that this is a "clipped wing" Spitfire

of the type once built for low-altitude use during the later stages of World War II. Length: 9·875in (25cm).

4 Lockheed Monoplane by E.T.Co., Japan, dating from the 1930s. In tinplate, with a plated cowl to simulate a radial engine, this representation of an American two-seater has colorful printed detail, including the registration letters "J-BAMC" on wing and fuselage, and is crewed by two pressed-tin aviators. It has a fixed undercarriage with the wheels concealed by fairings. Clockwork-powered, it could be suspended by a cord through the loop just in front of the windscreen and, with the aid of its large plastic propeller (now broken), "flown" in a circle. Wingspan: 14in (35·5cm).

5 Military Monoplane by "PW", Germany, c1938. This twin-engined low-wing airplane is of tinplate construction and has printed "splinter" camouflage and German national markings. Both the wheels and the tin propellors are driven by clockwork; note the suspension loop aft the printed cockpit. Wingspan: 14in (35·5cm). Limited.

6 Airliner by S. Günthermann, Nuremburg, Germany, c1935. Undoubtedly based on the famous civilian and military Junkers Ju 52 transport, this triple-engined tinplate airplane has printed lines to represent the corrugated construction of the real thing; note the wealth of further printed detail, including registration marks. The open cockpit contains two tin

aviators, and a battery-operated headlight is fitted on the nose. Clockwork drives the wheels and the large central propeller; a wire suspension loop is fitted atop the fuselage. Wingspan: 20·25in (52cm). Limited.

7 Racing Seaplane by Jep (Jouets en Paris), France, mid-1930s. This fine tinplate toy is most attractively finished, with detail including French national markings and squadron insignia. A floating toy, it is powered by clockwork (note the large removable key in winding position) driving the four-bladed propeller; the floats have rudders. Wingspan: 19in (48cm). Limited.

8 Airliner by Cardini, Italy, mid-1920s. This biplane has wings of aluminum and a tin fuselage with printed detail (note "Nord-Sud"

legend above cabin). The wings fold to allow storage in its box, which was designed as a hangar. The propeller is clockwork-driven and a raised wire suspension attachment is fitted above the wing. Wingspan: 10in (25·4cm). Limited.

9 Twin-Engined Bomber by "TN" (Nomura Toys Ltd), Tokyo, Japan, c1930. The tinplate body is printed in four-color camouflage with French national markings, and the plane is crewed by tin figures of a gunner (in the nose, behind a revolving gun turret), pilot, and observer, all in open cockpits. The wheels are driven by clockwork. Wingspan: 15·75in (40cm).

10 Racing Seaplane, British-made and dating from c1927. This single-sided, stand-up, pressed-tin

representation of a Supermarine S.5 Seaplane (one of a series of Schneider Trophy winners of the time) was distributed free as a promotional ploy by the British juvenile publication *Modern Boy* (Number 3, 1927). The magazine also distributed similar models of various locomotives and of Segrave's "Sunbeam" world land speed record car of 1927. Length: 5in (13cm).

11 Large-scale hand luggage, probably of German origin (since the basket-work case bears the printed message *Glückliche Reise,* "Lucky Journey") and dating from the 1930s: attractive accessories for the proud owner of a large tinplate aircraft or ship.

Tinplate Airplanes by European and Japanese Makers, 1950s-1970s

The boom in civil aviation since World War II has seen the appearance of long-range airliners of ever-increasing size. Japanese makers have been particularly active in producing toys — latterly often of part-metal part-plastic construction, and usually battery-powered or friction-driven — based on these giant aircraft. Such models are likely to gain in popularity with collectors as the airplanes they depict become a part of aviation history.
All the aircraft shown on this spread were photographed at the London Toy & Model Museum.

1 "Pan American World Airways" Boeing 377 Stratocruiser by a German maker (it is marked only "Made in Western Germany"),

dating from the mid-1950s. The four-engined airliner has a tinplate fuselage and wings with printed detail (it is identified beneath the US flag on the tail fin as a "Strato Clipper") and plastic propellers. It is battery-operated and, as seen here, has a remote-control hand-set that starts the motor and taxies the airplane. Wingspan: 19in (48cm).
2 "Pan Am" Boeing 747, a four-engined Jumbo Jet by "ATC" (Asahi Toy Company), Tokyo, Japan, dating from the 1970s. This tinplate airliner with printed detail is a toy of a kind especially popular in gift shops at major air terminals. Although well-modeled, it may be felt to lack the charm of the earlier aircraft shown on *pages 136-137*. Wingspan: 26in (66cm).

3 Convair (General Dynamics) B-36 Heavy Bomber by "E.T. Co.", Japan, dating from the mid-1950s. This is a fine model of the largest and most powerful airplane of its time. The B-36 had an interesting history. Designed early in World War II, it was intended to be able to bomb European targets from bases in Canada, in case Britain should be occupied by German forces. As this eventuality became increasingly remote, work on the long-range monster slowed and it did not make its first flight until 1946, remaining in service thereafter until early 1959. The six-engined bomber (with twin-jet booster pods beneath the wings, as seen here) has a tinplate fuselage and wings, with printed detail that includes US Air Force

markings. Note the green plastic blister canopy at the nose and the smaller blisters (one missing towards the tail) for identification lights on this battery-powered model. Wingspan: 26in (66cm).

"BOAC" (British Overseas Airways Corporation) Concorde Airliner by a Japanese maker, dating from the 1960s. This is an interesting example of a toymaker's desire to be up-to-date outrunning reality: by the time the real Concorde entered service, BOAC was no longer in existence. This friction-drive model has a tinplate body and wings with printed detail (the wings are detachable; note the plastic turnbuckles), and has its nose permanently fixed in the "up" position. Length: 14in (36cm).

138

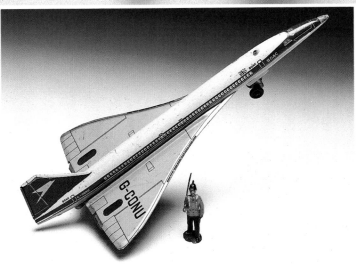

4 "American Airlines" "Electra II" Airliner by "TN" (Nomura Toys Ltd), Tokyo, Japan (with trademark visible just beneath the tailplane), dating from the 1950s. In tinplate with printed detail, and with plastic engine cowlings and propellers, this model is battery-powered. Wingspan: 16·5in (42cm).

5 "B.O.A.C." (British Overseas Airways Corporation) Vickers Viscount Airliner by Schuco (Schreyer and Company), West Germany, dating from the 1950s; note the name of the maker, well known both before and after World War II for mechanical toys of fine quality, prominently printed on the upper wing and tailplane. This battery-powered model has a tinplate fuselage and wings, with printed detail that includes registration markings, and plastic engine nacelles and propellers. A bubble canopy of clear plastic through which the plastic figures of the pilot and co-pilot can be clearly seen is fitted at the nose. Wingspan: 19in (48cm).

6 Delta-Winged Jet Fighter by Joustra, France, dating from the mid-1950s. This friction-driven airplane is of tinplate construction with printed detail that includes French national markings. It incorporates a novelty based on a feature that was being generally fitted to real airplanes of this type at the time of manufacture. When the nose-cone is pressed, a spring-loaded mechanism ejects the pilot, complete with parachute. Wingspan: 7·25in (18cm).

Diecast Airplanes by Dinky Toys, Britain and France, 1930s-1950s

1 Potez 56; French Dinky Toys (FDT) Catalog Number 61B, introduced c1938, deleted 1940. Wingspan: 2·756in (70mm). Limited.

2 As (1), Potez 56, but with tapered tailplane. Limited.

3 Clipper III Flying Boat; Dinky Toys (DT), Great Britain, Catalog Number 60W, introduced 1938, finally diecoted 1949. Wingspan: 6·46in (164mm).

4 Douglas DC-3 Airliner; DT No 60T, introduced 1938, deleted 1941. Wingspan: 5·197in (132mm).

5 DH (De Havilland) "Comet"; DT No 60G, introduced 1935, finally deleted from range in 1949. Wingspan: 3·375in (86mm).

6 Dewoitine 500; FDT No 60E, issued 1935-40. Wingspan: 3·15in (80mm). Limited.

7 Farman F360; FDT No 61C, issued 1938-40. Wingspan: 2·756in (70mm). Limited.

8 Bloch 220; FDT No 64B, introduced 1939, reissued after World War II, and finally deleted in 1948. Wingspan: 4·09in (104mm). Limited.

9 Giant High-Speed Monoplane; DT No 62Y, introduced 1939 – but previously available, c1938, as Junkers Ju 90 Airliner (Cat No 62N) – and deleted in 1949. Wingspan: 6·22in (158mm).

10 Potez 662; FDT No 64D, issued 1939-40. Wingspan: 4·055in (103mm). Limited.

11 Henriot H 180T; FDT No 60C, issued 1935-40. Wingspan: 3·15in (80mm).

12 General "Monospar"; DT No 60E, introduced 1934, deleted 1941. Wingspan: 3·15in (80mm).

13 Mercury Mayo Composite; DT No 63, introduced 1939, deleted 1941. The "pickaback" combination consists of (below) large four-engined "Maia" flying boat, and (above) "Mercury" seaplane; the example shown here has been repainted. For wingspan, see (14) and (15). Limited.

14 "Maia" Flying Boat; DT No 63A, issued as a separate item in 1939-41, and, as such, not as scarce as in (13). Wingspan: 6·18in (157mm).

15 "Mercury" Seaplane; DT No 63B, issued as separate item 1939-41, finally deleted 1954. Wingspan: 3·98in (101mm). Fairly common.

16 Cierva Autogiro; DT No 60F, issued 1934, deleted 1941. Rotor diameter: 2·91in (74mm); length of fuselage: 2·008in (51mm).

Limited.

17 Potez 58; FDT No 60B, issued 1935-40. High-wing monoplane; this example has been repainted and has been re-fitted with a three-bladed propeller. Wingspan: 2·99in (76mm).

18 Four-Engined Airliner; DT No 62R, issued 1945-49, but previously available, 1939-41, as DH 'Albatross' Mail Liner. Wingspan: 5·71in (145mm).

19 Armstrong-Whitworth Airliner; DT No 62P, available c1938-41; this example was issued 1945-49. Wingspan: 6·81in (173mm).

20 Airspeed "Envoy", "King's Aeroplane"; DT No 62K, introduced 1938, deleted 1941. Wingspan: 3·62in (92mm). The model with this finish is limited.

21 Airspeed "Envoy"; DT No 62M,

issued post-War, deleted 1949. The same casting as (20); not limited in this form.

22 Twin-Engined Fighter (modeled on Messerschmitt Bf 110); DT No 70D, introduced 1946, renumbered 731, deleted 1955. Wingspan: 2·95in (75mm). Common.

23 DH "Leopard Moth"; DT No 60B, issued 1934-41. Wingspan: 2·99in (76mm).

24 Low-Wing Monoplane (modeled on Vickers "Jockey"); DT No 60D, issued 1934-41. This example has been repainted. Wingspan: 3·03in (77mm).

25 Bréguet Corsaire; FDT No 60D, issued 1935-40. Wingspan: 3·125in (79mm).

26 Percival "Gull"; DT No 60C, issued 1934-41, re-issued post-War as "Light Tourer" (DT No 60K), finally

deleted 1949. Wingspan: 2·99in (76mm).

27 Dewoitine D338; FDT No 61A, issued 1938-40. Wingspan: 5·275in (134mm). Limited.

28 Vickers-Supermarine Spitfire; DT No 62A. Example of later issue, 1945-49, with later type cockpit; see example at (29). Wingspan: 2·008in (51mm).

29 As (28), but 1940-41 issue, with earlier type cockpit. Also issued in camouflage finish (DT Catalog No 62E). Limited.

30 Hawker Hurricane; DT No 62S, issued 1939-41. This early wartime example — see also (32) — is characterized by its undercarriage and two-blade propeller. It has been repainted. Wingspan: 2·24in (57mm). Limited.

31 Hawker Hurricane; DT No 62H,

issued 1939-41, in camouflage finish. Wingspan: 2·24in (57mm). Limited.

32 As (30), but post-War example, issued 1945-49.

33 Boeing "Flying Fortress" Bomber; DT No 62G. An early example, issued 1939-41, with a square aperture for a "flying" pin — see (4). It was reissued, as Long Range Bomber, 1945-48. Wingspan: 5·67in (144mm). Limited.

34 Amiot 370; FDT No 64A, first issued 1939, finally deleted 1948. Wingspan: 4·09in (104mm).

35 Potez 63; FDT 64C, first issued 1939, finally deleted 1948. Wingspan: 3·54in (90mm).

36 "Singapore" Four-Engined Flying Boat; DT No 60H, introduced 1936, deleted 1941. Wingspan: 4·99in (127mm). Limited.

37 Bristol "Blenheim" Medium Bomber; DT No 62B, first issued 1940-41. A post-War example, issued 1945-49, is shown. It was also issued in camouflage finish (Dinky Toys Cat No 62D). Wingspan: 3·07in (78mm).

38 Fairey "Battle" Bomber; DT No 60S. With camouflage finish, this was issued 1938-41; it was also available in aluminum finish (Cat No 60N). Wingspan: 3·07in (78mm). Limited.

39 Armstrong-Whitworth "Whitley" Bomber; DT No 60V, issued 1937-41, in aluminum finish. Wingspan: 4·21in (107mm). Limited.

40 Armstrong-Whitworth "Whitley" Bomber; DT No 62T, issued 1939-41. As (39), but in camouflage finish. Limited.

Diecast Airplanes by Dinky Toys, Britain, France, and India, 1940s-1960

Among the diecast aircraft by Dinky Toys of Great Britain and France shown on this spread are a number of examples of toys made in India, using Dinky Toys dies, during the 1960s. Further information on *pages 136-137*.

1 Vickers Viscount Airliner; Dinky Toys (DT), Great Britain, Catalog Number 706, issued in 1956-57. In "Air France" finish; wingspan: 5·87in (149mm). Limited.
2 Caravelle SE210; DT No 997, introduced in 1962 and discontinued in 1965. A twin-engined jet airliner in "Air France" finish; compare with the French Dinky Toys version (8). Wingspan: 7·09in (180mm). Limited.
3 Vickers Viking Airliner; DT No 70C, introduced in 1947, later

renumbered 705, and discontinued in 1962. An early-issue example, in gray finish, is shown: later examples are finished in silver. Wingspan: 5·51in (140mm).
4 Lockheed Constellation; French Dinky Toys (FDT), Catalog Number 60C, introduced in 1959, later renumbered 892, and discontinued in 1962. A four-engined airliner in "Air France" finish; wingspan: 7·87in (200mm). Limited.
5 Bristol 173 Helicopter; DT No 715, introduced in 1956 and deleted in 1962. The same Catalog Number was allocated in 1968 to the model of a Beechcraft C55 Baron. Rotor diameter: 2·83in (72mm); fuselage length: 3·425in (87mm).
6 Shetland Flying Boat; DT No 701, introduced in 1947 and deleted in 1949. The example shown has

been repainted and fitted with replacement propellers. Wingspan: 9·25in (235mm). Limited.
7 Avro "York" Airliner; DT No 70A, introduced in 1946, later renumbered 704, and discontinued in 1959. Wingspan: 6·29in (160mm). Fairly common.
8 Caravelle SE 210 Airliner; FDT No 60F, introduced in 1959, later renumbered 891, and deleted in 1968. Again in "Air France" finish, but the arrangement of the registration lettering on this French-made example differs from that of the British-made example shown at (2). Wingspan: 7·09in (180mm).
9 Westland-Sikorsky "Dragonfly" S.51 Helicopter; DT No 716, introduced in 1957 and deleted in 1962. Rotor diameter: 2·83in

(72mm); fuselage length: 2·64in (67mm).
10 DH (De Havilland) Comet Jet Airliner; DT No 702, introduced in 1954, later renumbered 999, and discontinued in 1965. In "B.O.A.C." (British Overseas Airways Corporation) finish; wingspan: 7·24in (184mm).
11 DH (De Havilland) Comet Jet Airliner. This is DT No 999 "type", but is a model made in India, after 1964, using Dinky Toys dies. Compare with (10), and note that it has applied "B.O.A.C." decals and fewer cabin windows. Wingspan: 7·24in (184mm).
12 Vickers Viscount Airliner; DT No 708 "type", made in India during the 1960s. In "B.E.A." (British European Airways) finish; compare with the British Dinky Toys

142

example shown at (13). Wingspan: 5·87in (149mm).

13 Vickers Viscount 800 Airliner; DT No 798, introduced in 1957 and deleted in 1965. An early-issue example is shown; later examples are finished in metallic gray. Again in "B.E.A." finish; but note the considerable difference in finish from the Indian-made example shown at (12), and compare also with the French Dinky Toys example shown at (14). Wingspan: 5·87in (149mm).

14 Vickers Viscount Airliner; FDT No 60E, introduced in 1959, later renumbered 803, and deleted in 1961. In "Air France" finish; compare with the British Dinky Toys example shown at (13) and note the "streamlined" spinners over differently-colored propellers.

Wingspan: 5·87in (149mm). Scarce.

15 Bristol Britannia Airliner; DT No 998, introduced in 1959 and discontinued in 1965. In "Canadian Pacific" finish; wingspan: 8·86in (225mm). Limited.

16 Supermarine Swift; DT No 734, introduced in 1955 and discontinued in 1962. A British jet-propelled fighter aircraft in camouflage finish; wingspan: 1·97in (50mm). Fairly common.

17 DH (De Havilland) 110 Fighter; DT No 738 "type", but made in India from Dinky Toys dies during the 1960s. Compare with the British Dinky Toys example shown at (18). Wingspan: 3·19in (81mm).

18 DH (De Havilland) 110 Naval Fighter; DT No 738, introduced in 1960 and discontinued in 1965.

Note the difference in finish from the Indian-made example shown at (17). Wingspan: 3·19in (81mm).

19 Hawker Hunter Fighter; DT No 736, introduced in 1955 and deleted in 1963. A British fighter in camouflage finish; wingspan: 2·125in (54mm). Fairly common.

20 Gloster Javelin Delta-Wing All-Weather Fighter; DT No 735, introduced in 1956 and deleted in 1966. In camouflage finish; wingspan: 3·25in (83mm). Fairly common.

21 P.1B Lightning Fighter; DT No 737, introduced in 1959 and deleted in 1968. Wingspan: 2·165in (55mm). Fairly common.

22 Gloster Meteor Twin-Engined Jet Fighter; DT No 70E, introduced in 1946, later renumbered 732, and deleted in 1962. This was the first

model of a jet-propelled aircraft to be produced by Dinky Toys, Great Britain. Wingspan: 2·68in (68mm). Common.

23 Hawker Tempest II Fighter; DT No 70B, introduced in 1946, later renumbered 730, and deleted in 1955. Wingspan: 2·46in (62·5mm). Fairly common.

24 Lockheed Shooting Star Jet Fighter; DT No 70F, introduced in 1947, later renumbered 733, and deleted in 1962. With US Air Force markings; wingspan: 2·4in (61mm). Fairly common.

25 SNCAN (Societe Nationale Construction Aéronautique du Nord) Noratlas; FDT No 804, originally issued in c1960. A French military transport aircraft; wingspan: 6·69in (170mm). Limited.

Soldiers and Military Toys

Miniature fighting men have been a significant feature in the upbringing of male children for several thousand years. However, not all model soldiers are toys: the Ancient Egyptians made model armies that were placed in the tombs of their rulers, and the same custom was observed in Imperial China. Genuine toy soldiers survive from classical and medieval times, and in Europe, from the Renaissance onward, jewelers were often commissioned to supply military figures in precious metals for use in the martial education of the sons of princes and noblemen.

The origins of the mass-produced "toy soldier", as we understand the term today, lie with the *Zinnfiguren*, "flat" tin figures, first produced in Germany around 1730. Earlier examples tended to be quite large in comparison with later ones, but the price of metal and the cost of transportation combined to make the production of smaller figures more attractive to the manufacturer.

To make a more sturdy figure, and one more easily painted with the use of fewer colors, German makers in the later 19th century produced the figures known as "semi-flats". While these were still not fully three-dimensional, their deeper relief enabled them to be painted much more quickly, thus saving on labor costs. Examples of figures of this kind exported from Germany to Great Britain are shown on *pages 148-149*. The most common size for "semi-flats" and "flats" is a height of 1·1in (28mm).

SCALE IN SOLDIERS

Scale in toy soldiers is normally quoted as the height of an infantryman —assumed to be 6ft (1·83m) tall in real life—from the soles of his feet to the crown of his head (without a hat), expressed in millimeters. The most popular size is 54mm (2·125in)—the "standard" size, equivalent to model railroad Gauge "1"—and other sizes vary between 70mm (2·755in) and 20mm (0·787in), the latter being equivalent to model railroad Gauge "00".

From the later 18th century, the making of fully-rounded toy soldiers spread downwards from the jewelers to other craftsmen, as the use of base metals to produce solid models increased. The earliest center of large-scale production was Paris, during the Napoleonic era, and by the mid-19th century considerable production was taking place in both France and Germany. In the latter country, in common with the rest of the German toy industry, there grew up a lively export market: from 1870 to 1900, German figures of flat, semi-flat, and solid types were extensively sold in Great Britain and the eastern states of the USA.

In 1893, however, William Britain and his family, then a small but well-established firm of toymakers in London, applied the "hollow casting" process to the manufacture of toy soldiers. Within the next ten years, Britains effectively surplanted German-made toy soldiers in Great Britain and followed this by building up a large export business. The method of making toy soldiers in alloy by the hollow-cast method became widely used, notably in Britain and the USA, and it was by this method that the soldiers most widely collected today were produced.

A further process of toy soldier manufacture, developed in Germany during the early 20th century, must be mentioned. A mixture composed principally of sawdust, plaster, and glue formed a "composition" which could be pressed into a mold around a wire "skeleton" (armature) to form a figure. The process was inexpensive, but the figures were generally of larger size than those produced by the well-established hollow-cast manufacturers of Great Britain, and although the figures were widely successful in Germany, and were exported in some number, they never really became universally popular. These "composition" figures fall outside the scope of this book.

A further major attempt at a new method of manufacture, that of making figures of aluminum in sand-and-oil molds, was developed in France and had considerable success in that country. In Great Britain, the firm of Wend-Al was set up to exploit this technology and, for a few years after World War II, was energetic in promoting the advantages of aluminum figures, notably their greater durability, over hollow-cast models. Aluminum is, however, difficult to cast into fine detail—and

Above: *Dinky Toy No 675, Army Staff Car, carries No 170 on its base, reflecting its origin as the Ford Four-Door Sedan and underlining the crucial importance of the box.*

Left: *Packaging some of the 35,000 lead toys of all kinds that were being produced every day at the Timpo factory at Chiswick, London, in November 1949.*

Far left: *Royal Horse Artillery Gun Teams, as rendered by Crescent Toys in the 1930s (background) and by Britains in their "B" size, c1910.*

further technical developments in toy-making, described below, rendered the aluminum process redundant.

The "death" of the metal toy soldier—although he remains, of course, very much alive among collectors—was signaled when injection-molding with plastic became commercially viable. The first British toys of this type were produced by a firm called Malleable Mouldings, based in Kent, in 1947. Although this particular venture proved unsuccessful, the trend of the future became unmistakable in 1954, when Britains purchased the trademark and models of the plastic-toymaking firm Herald. Britains continued to sell both hollow-cast and plastic soldiers for eleven years thereafter, but since the mid-1960s all production of *toy* soldiers (as opposed to models made for specialist collectors and enthusiasts) has been in plastic—and plastic has become the predominant material in all commercial toy-making.

SOLDIER TYPES

To summarize the brief history given above, the seven major types of commercially-produced toy soldiers may be listed as follows:

Flat:

Two-dimensional, solid-cast figures of tin, with finely-etched detail on both sides, in production from c1730 to the present day, and most popular in Germany, their country of origin.

Semi-Flat:

A halfway stage between the "Flat" and "Solid" figures. Molding was comparatively simple, and less detail was needed in the modeling than in a "Flat" to give a pleasing result. Although fine commercial examples were produced in Germany in the later 19th century (see *pages 148-149*), many molds for non-professional use were sold in Europe from c1890 onward, and many "Semi-Flats" were produced by amateurs for sale at charity bazaars and similar functions. The vast majority of these non-commercial figures are of no value or interest to collectors; however, they may sometimes be encountered offered for sale as "something special" by non-specialist dealers.

Solid:

Fully three-dimensional, solid-cast metal figures, made from lead/tin alloys. As toys, they have been in commercial production from c1790 to the present day, but they are now made for adult enthusiasts rather than for children (as is also the case with "Flats"). Examples are shown on *pages 150-151*.

Hollow-Cast:

Fully three-dimensional, hollow metal figures, made from lead/tin alloys, and produced between 1893 and 1966, principally in Great Britain and the USA. Examples of this category, the most popular with collectors almost everywhere, are shown on *pages 152-175*.

Composition:

Three-dimensional figures of non-metallic molded material, produced by German toymakers from c1910 to 1960. A few composition figures are shown, with the tinplate military vehicles they complement, on *pages 176-177*.

Aluminum:

Three-dimensional figures made by sand-casting, and produced from c1945 to 1960, principally in France.

Plastic:

Three-dimensional figures, solid-cast by injection molding in various petro-chemical-based materials. These are the only "true" toy soldiers of the present day and, although they fall outside the scope of this book, the earlier examples are now becoming collectable.

BRITAINS FIGURES

In the extensive selection of hollow-cast figures shown on *pages 152-175*, most are the product of a single company: Britains Ltd, Great Britain. The reason for this is that the Britain family that founded the firm and, until recently, retained controlling interest in the company which bears their name, invented the hollow-cast method of toy soldier manufacture and probably produced as many figures as the combined production of all their many competitors, who copied the hollow-cast method, all over the world. Britains figures are certainly the most widely collected internationally: the firm maintained first place for quality, variety, and marketing, and, from the collectors' point of view, their range is attractive for other reasons. First, all items in Britains main range are consistently in scale with one another. Second, Britains issued many catalogs describing and numbering their figures, which are, consequently, much easier to collect in a systematic fashion than are those produced by their rivals.

The size of most Britains figures is the so-called "standard" scale of 2·125in (54mm)—that is, 1:32, or model railroad Gauge "1"—and almost all the Britains products shown in this book (*pages 152-153* and *156-175*) are in that scale.

BRITAINS NUMBERING

Britains numbering of sets in its main series was consecutive in order of production: .
Sets with Catalog Numbers 1 to 197 were first issued from 1893 up to the cessation of production in 1916, during World War I.
Sets with Catalog Numbers 198 to 1920 were first issued from the end of World War I up to the second cessation of production in 1941, during World War II.
Sets with Catalog Numbers 2002 to 2189, and from 9104 to 9770, were first issued from 1947 until 1966, when production of metal figures finally ended.

However, there are a number of points regarding the Catalog Numbers of sets that the collector must bear in mind:
Not all Catalog Numbers were applied to sets for general trade distribution; many were used for sets made up for sale through particular outlets, such as Woolworth's stores.
Sometimes (although not often), Catalog Numbers left unused in one year were later used out of sequence.
Catalog Numbers remained the same throughout the entire range of production between 1898 and 1960: thus, the set with Catalog Number 1 may have been manufactured in any year between those dates, and the collector must rely on other evidence than the set number to determine its date.
In 1961, all sets still in production were given new Catalog Numbers in the "9000" series, and these numbers were applied until production ended for good in 1966.
It should be noted also that Catalog Numbers 501 to 1200 in the main series were allocated to Farm, Zoo, and other "civilian" items (see *pages 184-189*); and these were usually numbered as individual pieces rather than as sets. But some "civilian" sets were included

at various points in other parts of the main number sequence.

Reprints have been issued of Britains Catalogs for the years 1915, 1933, 1936, 1939, 1940, 1953, 1958, and 1960. These will provide the collector with a good basis for a full understanding of the numbering system. From these, he will see that, as mentioned above, there were in addition to the main numbering sequence a number of other sequences determined by different sizes of model, figures issued as individual items, figures of "second grade" paint quality, and other variations from the standard run of production.

Although, as stated, sets retained their original Catalog Numbers, whatever their date of issue, the figures themselves were often revised, and part of the fascination of collecting lies in tracing the different versions and variations that each set underwent over the years. The exact date of each change of mold or paint style has not yet been fully researched, but the main trends have been charted, making it possible to ascertain the date of issue of any set to within a few years.

BOXES AND LABELS

The changing style of boxes and labels (see *pages 174-175*) is also most helpful in dating sets. A Britains standard single set usually consisted of eight "infantry" (ie, on foot) figures or five "cavalry" (ie, mounted) figures. The set was packed in a red cardboard box, with an individually printed label for each set. The label ran the length of the box-top and was carried over its end, where the Catalog Number and title of the set were usually printed once more, for easy reference when the boxes were stored on a retailer's shelves. Sets were invariably presented for sale in boxes, and the value of a set to a collector is much enhanced if it is still in its original box.

From c1913 to 1930, Britains labels were designed by the artist Fred Whisstock, whose signature appears on his work. Although new label types were introduced from 1930 onward, Whisstock's labels also appeared until c1952. From 1950 onward, full-color standard labels bearing the title "Regiments of all Nations" were progressively introduced to replace the former labels as stocks ran out. Very early labels were sometimes illustrated, but more often bore intricate patterns of type motifs and lettering. Labels marked "Famous Regiments of the British Army", "Armies of the World", or "Types of the British Army", belong to the period between 1935 and 1952.

CHANGES IN FIGURES

Early Britains figures, produced c1893-96, generally do not have the movable arms that are a feature of most figures made from c1900 onward. But it should be noted that some "firing" figures (ie, showing soldiers with rifles in firing positions) were produced always with fixed arms: until 1939, such infantry figures were usually sold ten to a box rather than eight. Until c1908, most infantry figures had oval bases; later, most had rectangular bases (and are, accordingly, usually called "square-based" by collectors).

The main changes in mold or paint style are normally indicated (as they are in this book) by designating the figures "1st version", "2nd version", and so on. Lesser changes are called "variations". Since each figure was manufactured with the use of several molds, variations in, for example, heads, will be found to be fairly numerous if large numbers of sets are closely examined, as will variation in paint detail.

No dates or identification marks were incorporated into any Britains molds made before 1900. From 1900 to 1912, all newly-designed figures were marked with the date on which the design of the master figure was completed, the "copyright date", which is embossed beneath the base, on infantry figures, or beneath the horse's belly, on cavalry figures. "Dated" figures like these were issued from 1900 to c1925—although "dating" was, in fact, discontinued after 1911, when Britains no longer needed to date toys in order to obtain the protection of the laws regarding copyright. Naturally, the firm continued to use existing molds bearing dates until they wore out, but new or replacement molds made after 1912 no longer incorporated dates. After that date, however, some such wording as "Britains Ltd, Copyright Proprietors" was always to be found incorporated somewhere on each figure.

CONDITION OF FIGURES

Certain conventions are now becoming established among collectors in all countries, to enable them to describe and compare the condition of toy soldiers. The following descriptions apply, of course, to all metal soldiers, not to Britains figures alone.

Mint:

The soldiers have never been removed from their original box, and the box itself has not sustained any external damage.

Excellent:

On a brief examination of the figures, no damage to the paintwork is evident.

Good:

The soldiers have obviously sustained some "playwear", but only a small amount of chipping or scratching is evident.

Fair:

The soldiers have obviously been much used, but approximately 75 per cent of the original paint finish remains.

Poor:

This classification covers any condition worse than "Fair": most collectors, unless they are specialists in restoration, would think seriously before adding "Poor" figures to their toy armies.

Above: *Dinky Toy No 693, 7·2in Howitzer, introduced in 1958. The later version (right) has a plastic elevating wheel and directional tires.*

Right: *Early (left) and late versions of Dinky Toy No 621, 3-ton Army Wagon. The bronze-green finish was not consistent; later version has a driver.*

Left: *A selection of Dinky Toys and Supertoys representing French military vehicles produced at Bobigny in France. The high quality of the finish makes these items particularly popular.*

DEGREES OF RARITY

In the captions describing the figures shown on the photographic spreads in this section *(pages 148-175)*, the same indications of rarity as are used throughout this book have been added wherever it is meaningful to do so. In the case of military figures, however, it is possible to be a little more specific as to the implications of these terms.

Rare:

An item that will probably appear on the market less often than once a year.

Scarce:

An item that may be expected to be available perhaps once in a year.

Limited:

An item likely to appear for sale on about two occasions in a year.

Common:

An item that will be generally available at all times. The qualification "Fairly Common" is used for an item that should be found for sale within a few weeks.

This scale assumes a collector who subscribes to major auction catalogs and keeps in regular contact with specialist dealers. He is likely to be a member of one of the many model soldiers collectors' societies.

It must be remembered, also, that while the post-World War II version of a set may be common, the same set in a pre-World War I version may be rare or scarce. An effort has been made in the captions to indicate the different degrees of rarity of different versions of some

sets. Finally, remember that while single figures can often be very easily found, the desire for a boxed set will often lift the particular item in question one degree up the "rarity scale".

MILITARY VEHICLES

Both tinplate and diecast military vehicles are shown in this section on *pages 176-183*, and, of course, many of the remarks made in the section devoted to "Automotive Toys" *(pages 62-113)* will apply equally to the military vehicles and accessories shown here.

Not very many military vehicles in tinplate were produced before the 1930s. Some tanks of World-War-I type appeared, but generally in forms that qualify them as "novelties" rather than military toys: see, for example, the "Doughboy Tank" at (8), *pages 18-19*, a later US-made version of a German toy of the 1920s. The collector is likely to find most interest in the tinplate "war toys" produced in Germany in the 1930s by such makers as Tipp, Arnold, and, especially, Hausser and Lineol. Very many large, detailed models of *Wehrmacht* equipment were issued, along with a wide range of composition figures, notably produced by Hausser under the "Elastolin" tradename, to supplement them. Examples of these, and of some post-World War II military models in tinplate by East and West German and British makers are shown on *pages 176-177*.

From an early date in its activities Britains produced diecast vehicles to complement its range of soldiers. These

were made both in the "standard" 2·125in (54mm) scale and, in the "Lilliput" series, in Gauge "00"/"H0" size. The earlier models are of horse-drawn vehicles —for example, the Royal Army Medical Corps Ambulance Wagon shown at (30), *pages 172-173*—with a change to motorized transport, and the addition of armored fighting vehicles (AFVs), in the 1920s-1930s. Non-vehicular models, including searchlights—see (8), *pages 178-179*—and anti-aircraft artillery, were usually designed in such a way that they could be mounted on vehicles, and were often marketed thus in sets. Britains diecast vehicles are, generally, not so eagerly sought after by collectors as the firm's soldiers, although certain models, notably the Armored Car (Cat No 1321; 1933-34), Staff Car (Cat No 1448; 1936-37), and the Balloon Unit (Cat No 1757; 1939)—see also (11), *pages 178-179*—are scarce and highly prized in consequence.

DINKY AND SOLIDO

One of the first six "Modelled Miniatures" announced by Meccano Limited in 1933, launching the Dinky Toys range of diecast vehicles, was the Tank shown at (13), *pages 180-181*, and during the later 1930s Dinky produced a fair number of military models. After World War II, the military range recommenced with the Jeep shown at (29), *pages 180-181*. By the 1950s-1960s, it had become far more comprehensive than the pre-War range, including such complex models as the "Corporal" Missile unit shown at (3), *pages 180-181*. Rather less sophisticated diecast military models were produced in Britain by such makers as Crescent and Lone Star; see examples on *pages 178-179*.

At the same time as the British parent company, the Dinky Toys subsidiary at Bobigny, France, was also producing a range of military vehicles: a selection is shown on *pages 182-183*. These French-made models are very popular with collectors, since it is generally felt that their finish and detail—some came with such refinements as cargo items, camouflage nets, and decals—is superior to that of the British-made models.

Finally, mention must be made of the finely-detailed diecast models, notably of tanks and other AFVs, produced since World War II by Solido, France: see (12) and (18), *pages 178-179*. Solido tanks feature tracks with cast links (British Dinky Toys used chain links on pre-War models; rubber or plastic on post-War models) that produce a realistic sound when the toy is pushed along. Although of comparatively recent date, the attention to detail and the high quality of the finish applied mean that diecast models by Solido are now thought to be most collectable.

"Semi-Flat" Military Figures by German Makers, late 19th Century

"Semi-flat" figures of the kind shown here were generally made of lead or pewter in heights between 0·79in (20mm) and 1·57in (40mm). Nuremburg was a major production center and noted makers were Allgeyer, Ammon, Haffner, Heinrich, and Spenküch. Small sizes generally precluded the incorporation of makers' marks, but all the figures shown here are believed to be of German origin, dating from the later 19th century. Although they cannot be classified as "Common", they can be found at reasonable prices.

1-4 Military Bandsmen; possibly by Allgeyer, Fürth, Germany, dating from c1870-90, in the standard "small flat" scale with a height of 1·10in (28mm).

5-7 Military Bandsmen, in a slightly different style to the figures shown at (1-4). Height: 1·10in (28mm).
8-9 Officers; at (8) in a commanding pose; at (9), stooping, and perhaps intended to be shown with some item of military equipment. Height: 1·34in (34mm).
10 Infantryman; in standing firing position and wearing uniform typical of continental armies of the period. Height: 1·34in (34mm).
11-13 Native Warriors (apparently North American Indians); armed with rifles and in various color finishes. Height: 1·10in (28mm).
14-19 British Infantrymen; at (14) with folded arms; (15) carrying buckets; (16) with a rifle, using a ramrod or cleaning rod; (17) holding aloft a drinking glass; (18-19) officers with swords. Note that (14-24) and

(37), (38), (41), (44), and (50), are typical of a popular set entitled "Camp of Aldershott" (sic), made by Haffner, Heyde, and (probably) other Germany makers. Height: 1·10in (28mm).
20-23 Soldiers in Camp or Barracks: (20) beating dust from tunic; (21) cooking; (22) drinking a toast; (23) pumping water. Height: 1·10in (28mm).
24 Barrels. Height: 1·06in (27mm).
25-26 Infantrymen: (25) officer carrying colors; (26) soldier advancing with bayonet fixed. Height: 1·46in (37mm).
27 Piled Arms. Height: 1·46in (37mm).
28 British Guardsman; in marching order. Height: 1·65in (42mm).
29-31 Infantrymen: (29) marching at the slope; (30) bugler; (31) officer. Height: 1·496in (38mm).

32 Officer with Flag. Height: 1·10in (28mm).
33 North African Cavalry Bugler; a one-piece casting. Height: 1·73in (44mm).
34 Cavalryman; a one-piece casting. Height: 1·85in (47mm).
35 North African Lancer on Camel; a two-piece casting, with detachable figure. Height: 1·496in (38mm).
36 Cavalry Bugler; a two-piece casting. Height: 1·34in (34mm).
37-38 Camp Scenes: (37) shaking

(Front) Field Ambulance with Two-Horse Team and Driver, by a German maker, late 19th century; in similar scale to the semi-flat figures shown above. (Rear) Cannon, German-made, c1890; in differing scales, but again intended for use with semi-flats.

32　33　34　35　36

37　38　39　40　41　42　43

44　45　46　47　48

49　50　51　52

53　54　55　56　57

out tunic; (38) splitting kindling. Height: 1·10in (28mm).

39 Soldiers Drinking a Toast; a one-piece casting. Height: 1·38in (35mm).

40 Guards Officer; holding aloft a tankard. Height: 1·26in (32mm).

41 Kneeling Soldier; possibly a farrier. Height: 0·94in (24mm).

42 Standard Bearer. Height: 1·10in (28mm).

43 Side Drummer. Height: 1·38in (35mm).

44 Sentry and Sentry Box; a one-piece casting. Height: 1·10in (28mm).

45 Medical Officer and Orderly with Wounded Man. Height: 1·10in (28mm).

46-47 Infantrymen: (46) officer with sword; (47) soldier marching with rifle (somewhat oversized) at the slope. Height: 1·26in (32mm).

48 Stretcher Bearers with Casualty. Height: 1·26in (32mm).

49 Infantryman; in lying firing position on grassy mound—note "muzzle flash". Height: 0·71in (18mm).

50 Camp Cooking; kneeling soldier, with camp kettle suspended over fire. Height (figure): 0·71in (18mm).

51-52 Wounded Soldiers: (51) on stretcher; (52) "fallen in action". Length: 1·18in (30mm).

53 Cavalryman. Height: 1·38in (35mm).

54 Cavalryman; compare casting of horse with (53). Height: 1·42in (36mm).

55 Cavalry Bugler; a one-piece casting. Height: 1·38in (35mm).

56 Cavalryman; on "small" horse. Height: 1·26in (32mm).

57 British Army Camel Corps Trooper. Height: 1·42in (36mm).

Military Figures by German and French Makers, 1890-1900

1   2   3   4   5   6

7   8   9

10   11   12   13   14

Three-dimensional figures with a more realistic appearance than the "flats" shown on *pages 148-149* were introduced around the middle of the 19th century. They were solid-cast in lead, the heads often cast separately. Such accouterments as swords and rifles were frequently made of tin, and are thus often found now in bent or otherwise damaged condition. During the early period of production, German makers remained dominant, the most successful being Heyde (*fl* 1840-1944). Heyde's range was comprehensive, although quality varied—as did the scale of the figures produced—and the company established an international reputation, although increasingly faced by competition

from Mignot of France and Britains of Great Britain.
Mignot began production towards the end of the 19th century, at first in competition with Lucotte. The two firms amalgamated in the early 20th century: Mignot remains active, but Lucotte figures did not appear separately after 1940. Mignot's figures are generally in the 2·125in (54mm) size—the "standard" size of 1:32 scale, corresponding to Gauge "1" railway models—and span a wide range, including such historical series as Greeks, Romans, and Napoleonic troops. Again, quality is variable. Mignot appears to have established a more successful export market in North America than in Great Britain, and Mignot figures are now more easily found

in the USA than in the UK.
It is worth noting that makers on the European continent faced tough competition from such manufacturers as Hausser of Germany, producer of the famous "Elastolin" figures which, being "composition" figures of compressed sawdust and glue, fall outside the scope of this book.

1-6 British Soldiers by Heyde, Germany, *c*1890. These solid-cast

The box in which the French Hussars by Mignot, France—see (7-9) above—were marketed in c1905 bears a colorful label incorporating prize medals and scenes of French Army life. On the inside of the lid is a list of Mignot's then current range.

150

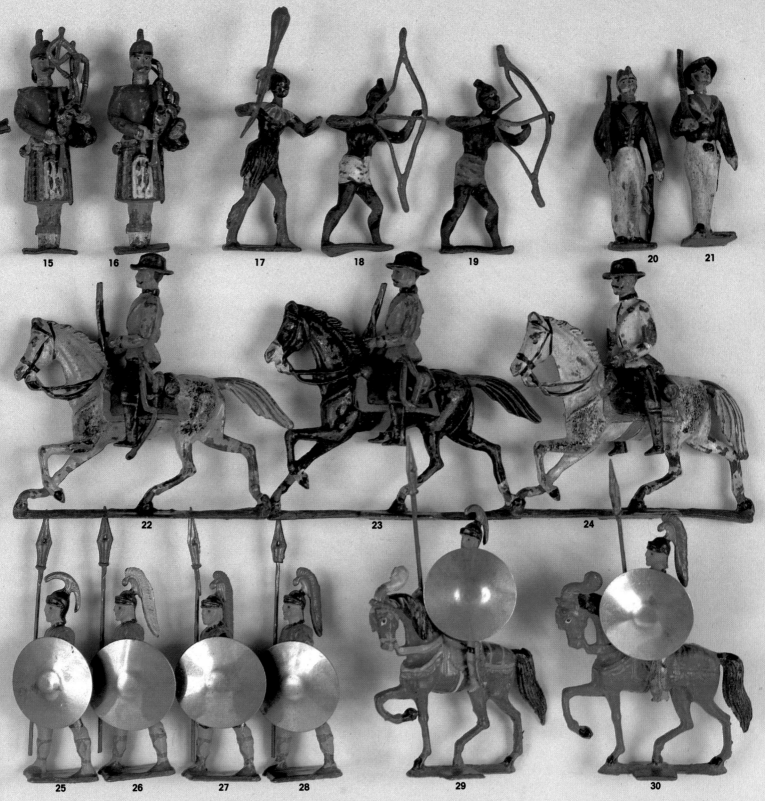

15 **16** **17** **18** **19** **20** **21**

22 **23** **24**

25 **26** **27** **28** **29** **30**

figures with removable "plug-in" heads are in 1·7in (43mm) size. They show British soldiers in the uniforms of the mid-18th century, armed with swords and muskets of tin. Shown here are: (1) infantryman in the standing firing position; (2) kneeling infantryman with fixed bayonet; (3) infantry officer, or standard bearer, armed with a sword and holding the Union Jack on a color staff; (4) drummer; (5) infantry officer with raised sword; (6) kneeling artilleryman holding rammer for loading.

7-9 French Hussars by Mignot, France; Catalog Number 214, c1900. These are figures of fine quality from Mignot's extensive range of French infantry and cavalry, and are in the "standard" 2·125in (54mm) size—the total

height of the mounted figures being 2·95in (75mm). The hussars may be removed from their horses, but their heads are not removable. Shown here are: (7) hussar armed with carbine; (8) reverse side of the figure shown at (7), with gray horse; (9) hussar with bugle.

10-13 British Guardsmen by Heyde; part of a display set made around 1890. The 1·97in (50mm) solid-cast figures have "plug-in" heads. Shown here are: (10) Guards officer with sword; (11) Guards bugler; (12-13) Guardsmen marching with bayoneted rifles at the slope.

14 Mounted Bandsman by Heyde, c1890. The figure, with an overall height of 2·44in (62mm), has a "plug-in" head and may be

removed from the horse.

15-16 Highland Pipers by Heyde, c1890. These 2·165in (55mm) solid-cast figures have "plug-in" heads; their bagpipes are tin (and reinforce the pont made in the introductory remarks, that this material is easily bent or damaged).

17-19 African Natives by Heyde, c1890. These 1·85in (47mm) solid-cast figures have non-removable heads. Shown here are: (17) native armed with club; (18-19) natives armed with bows.

20 Naval Officer by Heyde, c1890: a solid-cast 1·85in (47mm) figure with a "plug-in" head, carrying a sword. This was presumably part of the same set as (21).

21 Naval Rating by Heyde, c1890; as (20), but marching with a rifle at the slope.

22-24 Mounted Infantry of the Boer War period, c1900, by a German maker (possibly Heyde). These solid-cast figures—overall height 2·677in (68mm)—may be removed from their horses. Mounted men with rifles are shown at (22-23) and an officer at (24).

25-28 Infantrymen of Ancient Greece by Heyde, dating from around 1900 and issued as part of a display set that also included (29-30). These solid-cast 1·93in (49mm) figures have non-removable heads; note the variations in the style of the helmet plumes.

29-30 Cavalrymen of Ancient Greece by Heyde; see (25-28). These figures, with an overall height of 2·48in (63mm), may be removed from their horses.

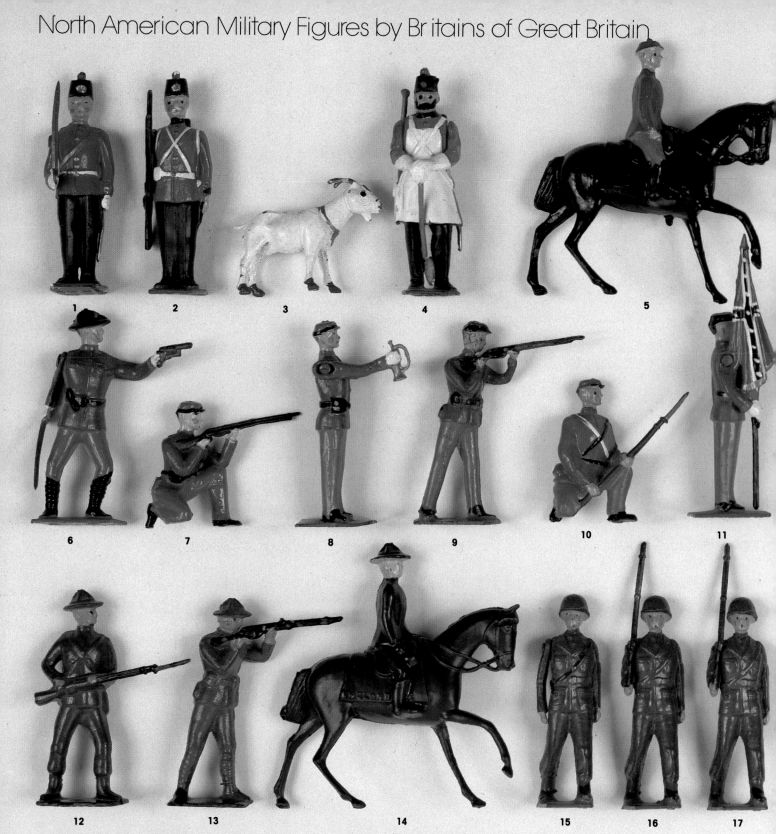

Both before and after World War II, Britains offered a wide range of US and Canadian military figures: the company's 1940 Catalog listed more than forty different sets of US servicemen. Britains US Civil War figures, introduced in the 1950s, are common, but they are now becoming increasingly sought after by collectors.

All the Britains figures shown on this spread are of the "standard" 2·125in (54mm) size.

1-3 Fort Henry Guard; Britains Catalog Number 9158. These figures are from a seven-piece set issued in 1958, consisting of an officer with a sword (1), five enlisted men in the shoulder arms position (2), and a goat mascot (3). All wear uniforms of the mid-19th century. Fairly common.
4 Fort Henry Guard Pioneer; Britains Cat No 2182. The pioneer, with an ax in movable arms, was issued as a single figure in 1959. Limited.
5 US Civil War Confederate Cavalry Officer; a Britains second-grade figure with fixed arms. Compare with the figure of standard finish shown at (18). Scarce.
6-9 US Civil War Confederate Infantry; Cat No 2060. These figures are from a set issued in 1951-66, consisting of an officer with a sword in a movable arm and a pistol in a fixed arm (6); another officer (not shown); four soldiers, including a kneeling firing figure (7) and a standing firing figure (9); a bugler with a movable arm (8); and a standard bearer with a movable arm (11). Common.

10 US Civil War Confederate Infantryman; Cat No 1242B (the "B" indicating issue as a single figure in a "Picture Pack"). This kneeling "on guard" figure was also included in set No 2060—see (6-9)—until 1960, when the set was reduced to six figures. Common.
11 See notes at (6-9).
12-14 US Soldiers of pre-World War II type; Britains second-quality figures. Shown here are: infantryman standing on guard (12); infantryman standing firing (13); cavalry officer, with fixed arms (14). Limited.
15-17 US Infantry; Cat No 2033. These figures are from a set issued in 1949-65. The officer (15) has a movable arm. Common.
18 Officer, US Civil War Union Cavalry; Cat No 2056. This officer,

with a sword in a movable arm, was issued in c1950-54 in a set that also included a bugler and two troopers with carbines. Common.
19-20 US West Point Cadets. These figures were available in Winter Dress, as shown here, in set Cat No 226, issued 1927-41; and in Summer Dress, with white trousers, in set Cat No 299, issued 1929-66. However, the two figures shown here come from a three-row combination set, Cat No 232, available 1927-66. This large boxed set was the only way in which cadets in Winter Dress could be obtained after 1941. Limited.
21-23 US Infantry; Cat No 227. The "Doughboys" marching with rifles at the slope are from an eight-piece set consisting of seven enlisted men and an officer—the officer at

18   19   20   21   22   23

24   25   26   27   28   29

30   31   32   33   34   35

(23) is a second-quality figure—first issued in 1927 and available until 1948, when it was superseded by the figures shown at (15-17).

24-29 US Civil War Union Infantry; Cat No 2059. First issued as a seven-piece set in 1951, this was listed in the 1966 Catalog as the six figures shown: bugler with movable arm (24); man standing firing (25); officer with sword in movable arm and pistol in fixed arm (26); man standing "on guard" (27); man kneeling "on guard" (28); standard bearer with colors in a movable arm (29).

30 Officer, US Army Air Corps; Cat No 330. One of an eight-piece set, all pieces identical, issued in 1929 (when Britains issued nine sets of US Army Air Corps figures).

31 Aviator, US Army Air Corps; Cat

No 332. Like (30), a figure from an eight-piece set issued in 1929.

32-34 US Air Corps; Cat No 2044. The eight- (later seven-) piece set was issued 1950-65. It consisted of a marching officer with movable arm (32) and airmen marching with slung rifles (33-34).

35 Officer, US Marines; Cat No 228. The eight-piece set first issued in 1927 remained in production until 1966. It consisted of a marching officer with movable arm, as shown, and seven Marines marching with rifles at the slope.

Fort Henry Guard, 49th Foot, 1812; Britains Cat No 9155, 1960s. This set, comprising six figures of the type shown, was sold only at the Fort Henry Souvenir Shop, Canada; but is fairly common.

1
2
3
4
5

11 12 13 14 15 16 17 18

26 27 28 29 30 31

Although internationally pre-eminent, Britains had a number of rivals in the field of military figures; notably Hill & Company (Johillco), Timpo, and Crescent, in Great Britain, and Barclay, Manoil, and Marx in the USA. The better-quality hollow-cast figures of some British makers are shown here alongside Britains figures.

All the figures shown on this spread are near the "standard" 2·125in (54mm) size.

1-10 Combat Soldiers of the US Army in World War II, by Timpo, Great Britain, dating from c1950-55. Timpo began production of hollow-cast figures in 1947. Its output included acceptable series of Knights in Armor and Farm Animals; the US soldiers shown

here were particularly successful in their degree of realism. Timpo was one of the companies that survived the transition to injection molding in plastic in the 1950s, and later re-issued some of these figures in that material. The hollow-cast figures shown here are: (1) Military Policeman, with white helmet and feggins; (2) Infantryman carrying equipment, with shouldered Garand rifle; (3) Infantryman charging with bayonet fixed; (4) Negro Infantryman in standing firing position; (5) Infantryman squatting, with mess-kit; (6) Officer with pistol, leading assault; (7) Infantryman in kneeling firing position; (8) Infantryman seated with bucket washing; (9) Infantryman with rifle, in "at ease" position; (10) Wounded

Infantryman, with bandaged arm and head. Common.

11-14 US Sailors (Whitejackets); Britains Catalog Number 1253. An eight-piece set consisting of US sailors marching at the slope (rifle in movable arm), with officer—see (21), was first issued in 1933 and remained available until 1966. The figures at (11-12) are pre-1939 examples, with dark-colored leggins, belts, and collars; those at (13-14) are post-War issue, with light-colored details. Common.

15-16 US Sailors (Bluejackets); Britains Cat No 230. These figures of US sailors marching with rifles (movable arm) at the slope come from a set issued between 1927 and 1941. Limited.

17-18 US Sailors (Bluejackets); Britains "New Crown Range", Cat

No 92P, c1956. These second-quality figures, with fixed arms and less detailed finish, were marketed as single items. Limited.

19-20 US Sailors (Whitejackets). These figures bear no maker's name (their plain bases are visible in the photograph). They were possibly made by Cherilea, Great Britain, in the late 1950s. Compare with the Britains examples shown at (11-14). Scarce.

21 US Sailors (Whitejackets); Britains Cat No 1253. The officer of the set shown at (11-14); this figure is a post-War example, like the figures at (13-14). Common.

22-23 US Marine Corps Officer (22) and Marine with rifle, standing at ease (23); by Crescent, Great Britain, and dating from the late 1950s. Limited.

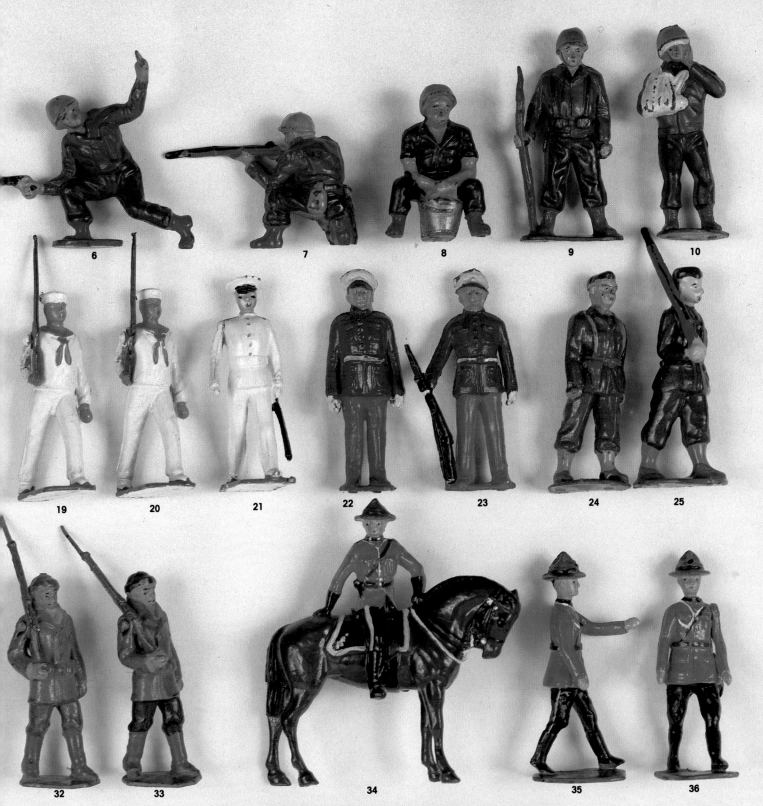

6

7

8

9

10

19

20

21

22

23

24

25

32

33

34

35

36

24-25 US Infantry Officer (24) and Infantryman, marching at the slope (25); by Timpo, dating from the mid-1950s. Like all Timpo figures, these US soldiers have fixed arms. Common.

26-31 West Point Cadets; by Timpo, dating from the late 1950s. These figures, in summer dress, are: (26-27) Cadets with rifles, in "at ease" position (front and rear views); (28-30) Cadet Bandsmen, with trombone (28), with drum (29), and with double bass horn (30); (31) Cadet Bugler with bugle. Common.

32-33 Royal Canadian Mounted Police; Britains Cat No 214. The eight-piece set of men of the RCMP in winter dress, marching with rifles at the slope, was first issued in 1924 and remained in

production until 1941, re-appearing when marketed as a "picture pack" in 1954-59. Scarce.

34-36 Royal Canadian Mounted Police; Britains Cat No 1554. This set was first issued in 1937 and consisted of eight dismounted figures in full dress. The examples shown at (35-36), with movable left arms, date from c1960. The mounted officer (34) was substituted for two of the dismounted men in the set in 1953; he was also available separately. Common.

Governor General's Horse Guards of Canada; Britains Cat No 1631, from a five-piece set issued in 1938 and still listed (but as a four-piece set) in the 1966 Catalog. (Left) Officer; (right) Trooper.

British Cavalry Figures by Britains, Great Britain

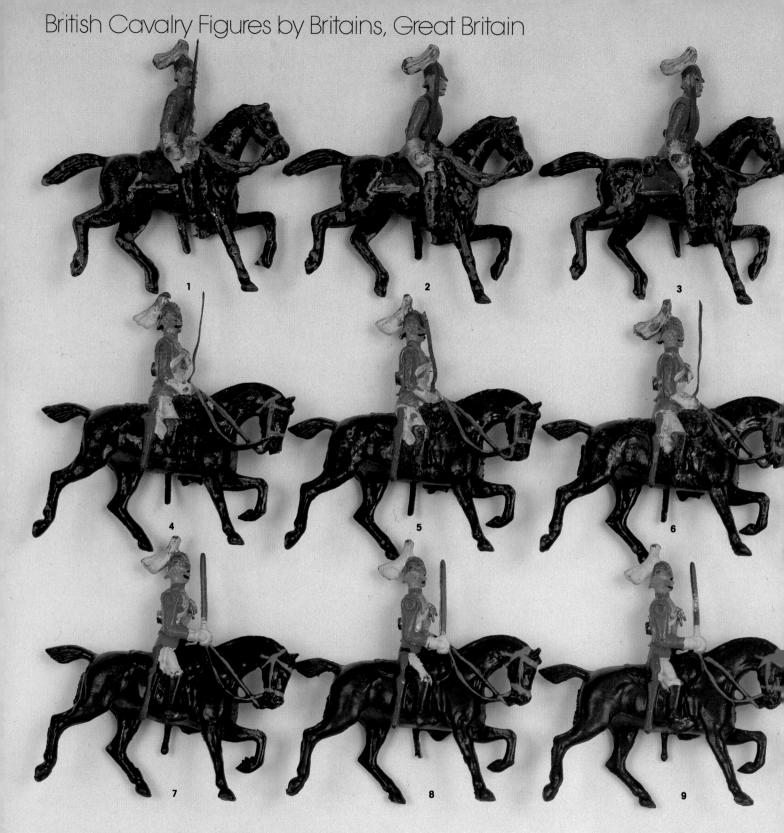

1   2   3

4   5   6

7   8   9

Probably the best known of all makers of toy soldiers is the aptly-named British firm of William Britain Limited — universally called "Britains". Its production of metal soldiers, hollow figures made by a then innovatory process known as "hollow-casting" (most earlier soldiers being of solid construction), began in 1893 and continued, interrupted only by two World Wars, until the completion of the changeover to plastic figures in the later 1960s.

With the exception of numbers (1-3), which are slightly smaller, all the Britains figures shown on this spread are in the "standard" 2·125in (54mm) size; ie, the scale is 1:32.

1-3 1st Life Guards; Britains Catalog

Number 1. It was fitting that this famous regiment of the Household Cavalry, tracing its foundation back to 1659, should be the subject of Britains first set, which remained in production, through five versions, for 74 years. These troopers are of the 1st version, issued 1893-97. The original boxed set consisted of five of these "Germanic" style troopers on walking horses; in c1895, an officer on a prancing horse (see *Inset*) relaced one of the troopers. To aid in identifying figures of the 1st version, compare with the later versions shown at (4-6) and (7-9), and note particularly the size and pose of the horse, the detail of the shabraque (saddle blanket), and the broad-bladed tin sword held in the fixed arm of the 1st version.

This version is scarce.

4-6 1st Life Guards; Britains Catalog Number 1, 2nd version, issued 1897-1902. The figure of the trooper is improved, with a more realistic helmet and added aiguillettes (corded ornaments worn around the shoulder); the figure still has a fixed arm, but the blade of the tin sword is thinner. A bearskin covers the saddle, to which a carbine in a "bucket" has been added at the rear. The horse has a bowed head and a shorter tail, with a more pronounced "hook" to the front hoof. Limited.

7-9 1st Life Guards; Britains Catalog Number 1, 3rd version, issued 1902-25. Trooper and horse resemble the 2nd version (4-6), but a movable arm with a cast sword has been introduced. (For

10

11

12

13

14

15

16

17

officer, 3rd version, see *Inset, pages 158-159*). A variation in which the troopers had no aiguillettes was introduced *c*1912. In the 4th version the horse's head was better detailed; eg, the ears were cast separately instead of together. In the 5th version, issued post-1953, the troopers had differently-shaped plumes and were mounted on walking horses, while the officer was on a trotting

1st Life Guards; Britains Cat No 1: the officer of the 1st version, 1893-98—see (1-3) above—on a prancing horse, with a broad-bladed tin sword in a fixed arm. Compare detail of saddle blanket with the 3rd version figure (Inset, pages 158-159), and note also that the horse has no throat plume.

horse with a rounded shabraque. The 3rd, 4th and 5th versions of this set are common.

10-12 9th Queens' Royal Lancers; Britains Catalog Number 24, 1st version, issued 1894-1903 (after which a new figure with a movable arm was used for the troopers; see (15-17) below). This regiment was one of several Dragoon units raised by King George I in 1715. Its equipment as a Lancer regiment was ordered in 1816 and its "Royal" title was take in honor of Queen Adelaide, consort of King William IV, in 1830. The trooper has a fixed arm holding a lance vertically; later versions have movable arms holding wire lances. The horse, with detailed harness, is shown at the halt, with back hoof lifted. The officer was half-turned

in the saddle and held a tin sword.
13-14 2nd Life Guards; Britains Catalog Number 43, introduced in 1896. Shown here is the 2nd version, *c*1902, the set consisting of a trumpeter (13) and four troopers with carbines, as (14). In 1904 the trumpeter was provided with a new, trotting horse. The 1st and 2nd Life Guards were, in reality, amalgamated into one regiment in 1922, but Britains continued to issue set Number 43 as a separate item from Set 1, using a 3rd version figure similar to the 2nd version, but with a two-eared horse and longer carbine.
15-17 5th Royal Irish Lancers; Britains Catalog Number 23. The first version was issued in 1894 and the 2nd version (shown here) in 1903; both had the same officer (not

shown), half-turned in the saddle and holding a tin sword. The troopers, whose horses are at the halt, have movable arms and hold wire lances. The horse harness is simplified, and on the horse's belly is the date "18.8.1903". Seen from the side shown in the photograph, the uniforms of the 9th Lancers (10-12) and the 5th Lancers (shown here) are indistinguishable from each other. Britains used the same figures for each set, the only distinction being a black-and-white plume for the 9th Lancers and a green plume for the 5th Lancers. Note that 1st version figures are shown at (10-12) and 2nd version figures here. Note also that the lance heads are missing from (15) and (17): a common breakage that much reduces the value.

British Cavalry Figures by Britains, Great Britain

All the Britains figures shown on this spread are of the "standard" 2·125in (54mm) size.

1-3 Band of the Life Guards; Britains Catalog Number 101. These three figures are of the 1st version, dating from 1899, when the 12-piece boxed set was first issued. Note that they have slot-in arms: later, post-1911, versions have movable arms. The tip of the sword scabbard is visible below the horse's belly: in the post-1953 version, the sword is absent. The price of a box of 12 figures in 1913 was 5s 6d (27½p, 39c); in 1938 it was 9s 0d (45p, 63c). The figures with slot-in arms, as shown here, are scarce; but later versions, with the figures in red-and-gold uniforms, are fairly common.

4-6 Imperial Yeomanry; Britains Catalog Number 105. As might be expected, this set was introduced during the Boer War, the 1st version (shown here) dating from 1900. As will be apparent elsewhere in this section, Britains quickly capitalized on current military events by issuing relevant figures. This set consisted in all of five figures, in foreign service dress and mounted on trotting horses. The slouch-hatted troopers, with their officer (5) distinguished only by his white horse, are armed with carbines (in "buckets" to the rear of the saddle) and have fixed arms. The horse's belly bears the date "1.6.1900". The 2nd version figures are similar, but with the horse's belly undated. These figures are scarce.

7-9 South African Mounted Infantry; Britains Catalog Number 38. This set of five figures was originally introduced in c1896 as "Dr Jameson and the South African Mounted Police", marking the ill-fated raid on the Boer Republic of the Transvaal led by Dr Leander Starr Jameson on 29 December 1895. Although the raid, intended to provoke an anti-Boer uprising in Johannesburg, was a total failure, Jameson, in spite of rather half-hearted official condemnation by the British government, became a popular hero in Britain. The set was renamed in 1897 (the box bearing the "Jameson" name is thus extremely rare), but the figures remained the same until a movable-arm version was introduced in 1927. The same

figures were used for a set showing the Royal Canadian Mounted Police. Of the three figures shown here, the troopers are armed with rifles and the officer (originally Dr Jameson) with a revolver. All have fixed arms. The same castings, with different finish, were used for a set of Boer Cavalry (Catalog Number 6, issued 1896). The set was still available in the 1941 Catalog, but it is now scarce.

10-12 The Royal Scots Greys (2nd Dragoons); Britains Catalog Number 32, introduced 1895. These 1st version figures have headgear more appropriate to the Foot Guards than the Scots Greys: this mistake was very soon corrected, making the figures shown a rare variation. The figures shown have fixed arms and carry

158

10 11 12

13 14

15 16 17 18

1st Life Guards; Britains Cat No 1: the officer of the 3rd version—see (7-9), pages 156-157, and compare with 1st version officer shown at Inset there. In comparison with the 1st version, this is a larger figure, with sword outstretched and a more detailed saddle blanket.

tin swords; the gold facings and crossbelt on (12) indicate the officer (the chevrons on his arm have been added by a later owner!). This set, issued as a box of five, was in production for many years: later versions have movable arms, the officer with sword outstretched, and are common.

13-14 4th Queen's Own Hussars; Britains Catalog Number 8, introduced as a five-piece set in 1896. The figures shown here have movable arms and date from c1930; earlier versions had squared cap lines. Note the red plume and yellow busby bag. These features distinguish the various Hussar regiments; eg, the 3rd King's Own Hussars have a white plume and a blue busby bag. These figures are fairly common.

15 16th Lancers; Britains Catalog Number 33. The figures of the 1st version, issued in 1895, were the same model as those of the 9th Lancers shown at (10-12) on pages 156-157. The figure shown is of the 2nd version, dating from 1903, and is the same model as that used for the 5th Lancers, shown at (15-17) on pages 156-157. Formed as Light Dragoons in 1759 and converted to Lancers in 1816, the 16th Lancers amalgamated in 1922 with the 5th Royal Irish Lancers to form the 16th/5th Lancers.

16-18 11th (Prince Albert's Own) Hussars; Britains Catalog Number 182. As seen from the figures shown here, not all Britains soldiers conform to the types of mounted cavalry and "foot-slogging" infantry. These dismounted cavalry troopers of the famous "Cherry Pickers"—note the crimson breeches—with a standing horse come from an eight-piece set first issued in 1914, consisting of three troopers and one officer, all dismounted and with movable right arms, and four horses. Note that the trooper at (16) lacks his busby plume. These figures are fairly common.

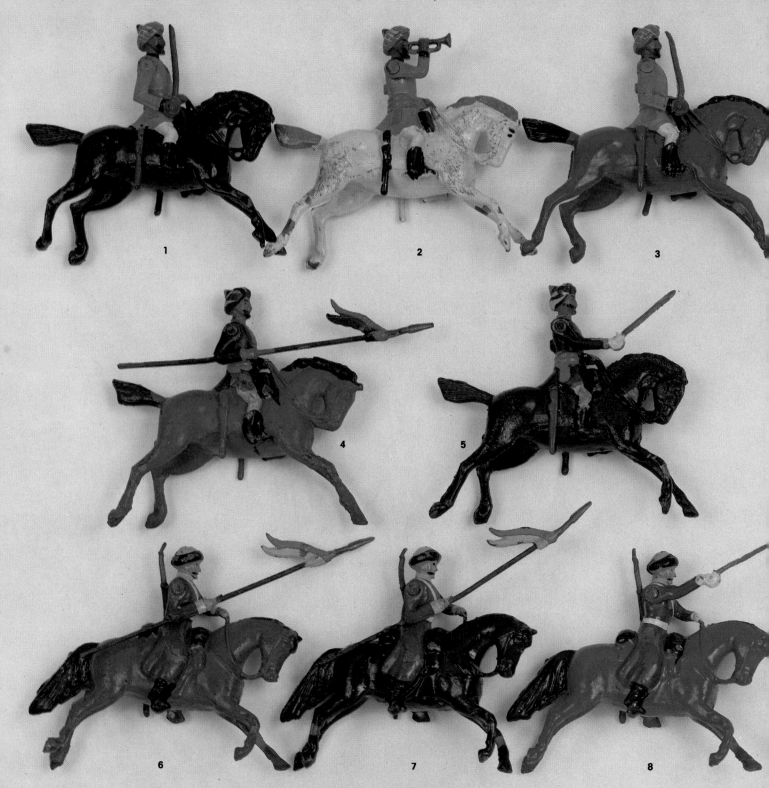

All the Britains figures shown on this spread are of the "standard" 2·125in (54mm) size.

1-3 1st Bengal Native Cavalry; Britains Catalog Number 47. This set in Britains Indian Army series, comprising in all four sowars (troopers) armed with sabers, as shown at (1) and (3), and a trumpeter (2), was first issued in 1896. It was still listed in Britains 1966 Catalog, but by that time the set had undergone a title change and, in 1962, had been renumbered 9261. The title change, to Skinner's Horse (1st Duke of York's Own Cavalry), took place in c1936, when the color of the troopers' uniforms was changed to bright yellow and they were given lances instead of

sabers. This set is much rarer in the early uniform color, as shown here, than in the later yellow.

4-5 10th Bengal Lancers; Britains Catalog Number 46. Another of Britains Indian Army series, this was issued as a set of five figures—consisting of four sowars with lances, as (4), and a native officer armed with a sword, as (5)—in 1896. In later sets, the officer was usually replaced by a trumpeter. As·is also the case with (1-3), there is no date on the

West India Regiment; Britains Cat No 19. This mounted officer was added to the set of nine marching figures issued in 1894—see (1-7), pages 162-163—in 1895. The figure is a one-piece casting with a fixed arm.

9

10

11

12

13

14

15

16

horse's belly. This item remained in the Catalog until 1941, but from c1936 the title was changed to Hodson's Horse (4th Duke of Cambridge's Own Lancers).
6-8 Russian Cavalry; Britains Catalog Number 136. These figures, issued as a set of five—four Cossacks armed with lances, as at (6-7), and an officer with a sword (8), all on charging horses—provide a further example of the way in which Britains issued sets that reflected current military events: the copyright date on the horse's belly is "7.3.1904", indicating that the set appeared on the market very soon after the outbreak of the Russo-Japanese War (February 1904). Although the figures shown here bear the copyright date of the 1st version,

they are, in fact, from a later set of c1910: the very earliest figures have greatcoats in a lighter shade of green. Note, therefore, that a copyright date on a Britains figure does not necessarily mean that it was made on that date, merely that it was issued between that date and the date when that particular figure ceased to be issued with a date stamped on it (which may be as late as 1925). The later versions of the Cossack figures are common, but those in the light green, dated, variation are scarce.
9-11 Chasseurs a Cheval; Britains Catalog Number 139, issued in 1905. The horse's belly bears the dates "12.12.1902" and "9.5.1905", the latter marking the conversion of the horse copyrighted 1902 to service as a

chasseur's mount. The five-piece set consisted of four troopers with carbines, as shown here, and an officer armed with a sword. Note that several variations may be encountered; notably, a longer carbine from c1915. This was one of a number of sets depicting French soldiers issued at this time: the others were French Cuirassiers (Cat No 138), French Dragoons (Cat No 140), French Infanterie de Ligne (Cat No 141), French Zouaves (Cat No 142), and French Navy Matelots (Cat No 143). Boxes of assorted French cavalry were later issued.
12-13 Egyptian Cavalry; Britains Catalog Number 115. The set consisted of five figures: four troopers armed with lances, as (12), and an officer with a sword

(13), all on trotting horses. The figures shown bear on the horse's belly the date of the 2nd version, "12.2.1903". The set was still listed in Britains 1966 Catalog, but by that time had been reduced from five pieces to four. Fairly common.
14-16 Arabs; Britains Catalog Number 164. Britains series of "Native Warriors" included these Bedouin Arabs: the boxed set of five figures consisted of three Arabs with scimitars, as shown, and two with jezails (matchlock muskets), all on galloping horses. This set was first issued in 1911—the horse's belly bears the date "17.7.1911"—and was still available, although reduced to four pieces, in 1966. Although now thought to be highly collectable, these figures are common.

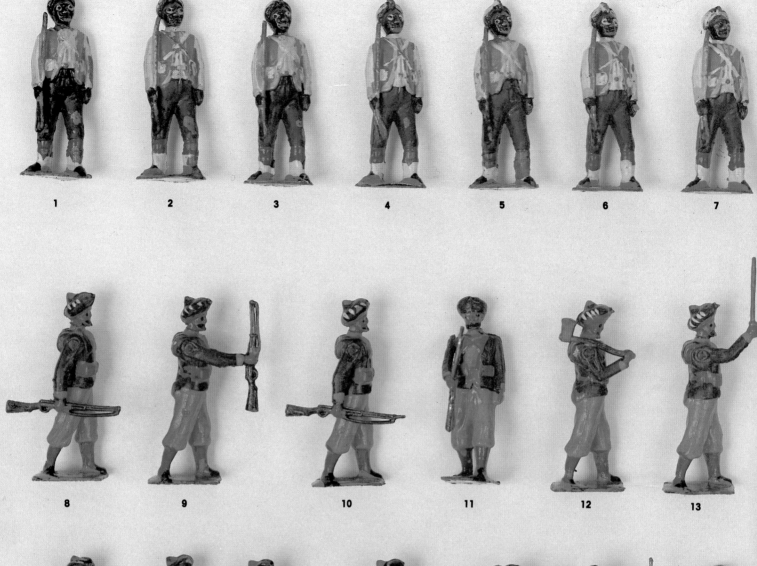

All the Britains figures shown on this spread are of the "standard" 2·125in (54mm) size.

1-7 West India Regiment; Britains Catalog Number 19. These figures were first issued in 1894 as part of a ten-piece set consisting of nine marching enlisted men with fixed arms, with rifles at the "shoulder arms" position (as shown here), and a marching British officer (not shown); all on oval bases. In 1895, the set was reduced to nine pieces: the marching officer and one of the men were replaced by the figure of an officer mounted on a walking horse (see *Inset* on *pages 160-161*). The figures of the 2nd version, with square bases, were introduced *c*1930 — a very late

date in comparison with that of Britains usual change from an oval to a square base, *c*1909. The figure of the officer on horseback underwent the same changes as those detailed for the officer of the Mountain Battery Royal Artillery; see (1-8) on *pages 172-173*. In 1939-41, the set was reduced to seven figures, consisting of six marching men and the mounted officer; it is, however, sometimes found as an eight-piece set of marching men only.

8-13 2nd Bombay Native Infantry; Britains Catalog Number 68. These figures were first issued in 1896 and were part of an eight-piece set consisting of six sepoys marching with their rifles at the trail, as seen at (8-11), a further sepoy as a pioneer, carrying an ax

(12), and a native officer with a sword (13). Note that the examples shown have square bases, marking them as the 2nd version; figures of the 1st version had oval bases. In *c*1926, a new sepoy figure, without a pack and with a rifle at the slope, replaced the figures shown here: no pioneer or officer was then included.

14-16 1st Madras Native Infantry; Britains Catalog Number 67. These figures were first issued in 1896 in a set made up in the same way as Number 68, (8-13).

17-20 1st Madras Native Infantry; as (14-16), but figures of the 2nd version, introduced in 1918, with square bases. Britains sometimes had a change of mind on the uniform detail to be used for a regiment, and these figures have

white puttees rather than the brown ones shown on the earlier figures (14-16). Some sets of both 1st and 2nd versions of Number 67 did not contain a pioneer figure. In *c*1926, the figures were changed to men marching with their arms at the slope, and the title was changed to Corps of Madras Pioneers in *c*1935. The Indian Army sets shown here and at (8-13) are fairly scarce; paticularly in the square-based version showing men with rifles at the trail.

21-26 Royal Navy Bluejackets; Britains Catalog Number 78. These figures were first issued in 1897 and were part of an eight-piece set — priced at 1s 0d (5p, 7c) before World War I — consisting of seven sailors running with Long Lee-Enfield

21 22 23 24 25 26

27 28 29 30 31 32

33 34 35 36 37 38

rifles at the trail (21-25) and a bearded petty officer with a sword (26). The figures shown are the square-based variation of the 1st version; the 1st version figures are also found with oval bases, as in (27-32). Fairly common.

27-32 Royal Navy Whitejackets; Britains Catalog Number 80. These figures were first issued in 1897, using the same casting — but with a different movable arm — as (21-26), and were part of an eight-piece set containing seven sailors running "at the double" with Long Lee-Enfield rifles (note Pattern 88 bayonets fixed) at the slope (27-31), and a petty officer with a sword (32). The figures shown are of the 1st version, with oval bases; later variations have figures with rifles

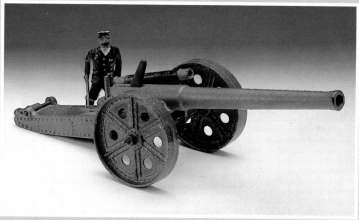

4·7-inch Naval Gun; Britains (no Cat No), c1912. The breech-firing mechanism is actuated by a flat spring. A 1932 version, with a gun shield and cap-firing breech with coiled-spring action, was Cat No 1264.

carried at the trail, and late versions have rather larger heads. Limited.

33-38 French Navy Matelots; Britains Catalog Number 143. These figures were first issued in 1905 as part of an eight-piece boxed set that consisted of eight sailors running with their rifles at the slope; changed very soon to the variation shown, with rifles at the trail position. Note that the rifles here are Long Lee-Enfields, as in the sets of British sailors shown above: the first figures issued, with rifles at the slope, were shown, accurately, with Lebel rifles, but when the position was changed to the trail the British rifle was used. The oval bases show that these are 1st version figures. Very scarce.

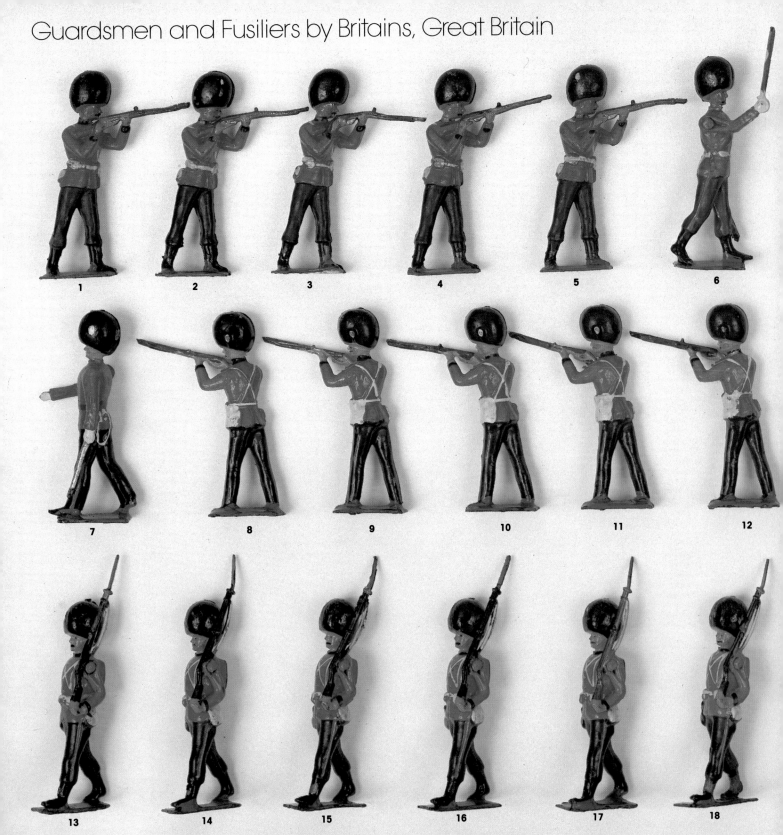

All the Britains figures shown on this spread are of the "standard" 2·125in (54mm) size.

1-5 Grenadier Guards; Britains Catalog Number 34. This set was first issued in 1895, but the figures shown are of the 3rd version, with the copyright date "1.7.1901" embossed on their square bases. Note that the rear sights of their rifles are fully raised, indicating a long-range aim also apparent from the angle at which the rifles are held: this feature does not appear in the 1st version, dating from before 1901. See also (8-12).

6 Officer, Grenadier Guards; Britains Catalog Number 34. This figure, square-based and with a movable arm holding a sword, was added to the set shown at (1-5) in c1908; the

officer of that set had previously been oval-based and, before 1905, of the "be-medalled" type.

7 Officer, Grenadier Guards; Britains Catalog Number 34. This is a figure of a later date than that shown at (6); the change occurring in 1934. The movable arm no longer holds a sword and no gaiters are worn. Note the white plume on the bearskin headdress, the distinguishing mark of the Grenadier Guards.

8-12 Grenadier Guards; Britains Catalog Number 34. These are figures of the 4th version: compare with the 3rd version figures shown at (1-5). After 1934, gaiters are no longer worn and the rear sights are less prominent. Fairly common.

13-18 Scots Guards; Britains Catalog Number 75. These figures were

issued in 1893-1910 as an eight-piece set consisting of six guardsmen (as shown here), an officer (not shown; but exactly the same as (6), although without a white plume), and a piper (see *Inset*). The examples shown here are of the 3rd version. Limited in the version shown.

19-25 Colors and Pioneers of the Scots Guards; Britains Catalog Number 82. These figures were issued in 1893-1910 as an eight-piece set consisting of seven pioneers with axes (as shown) and a color bearer (see *Inset* on *pages 170-171*). The figures shown here in front (19), rear (20), and side (21-25) views are of the 4th version: they have square bases, trousers without gaiters, and no equipment; ax held in a movable arm. Common.

26-28 Coldstream Guards; Britains Catalog Number 120. The kneeling officer with field glasses (26) and the guardsmen in the kneeling firing position (27-28) are figures of the 1st version (with a long production period, 1901-1934) of a ten-piece set consisting of nine guardsmen and one officer. The set was reduced to nine pieces in 1939, to eight in 1940, and to seven pieces in 1960; production ended in 1966. Very common.

29-31 Irish Guards; Britains Catalog Number 124. These figures are from a ten-piece set first issued in 1901 and current until 1941 (by which time it consisted of eight pieces). The examples shown are of the 3rd version. The kneeling officer (29), with field glasses held in movable arms, is the same as

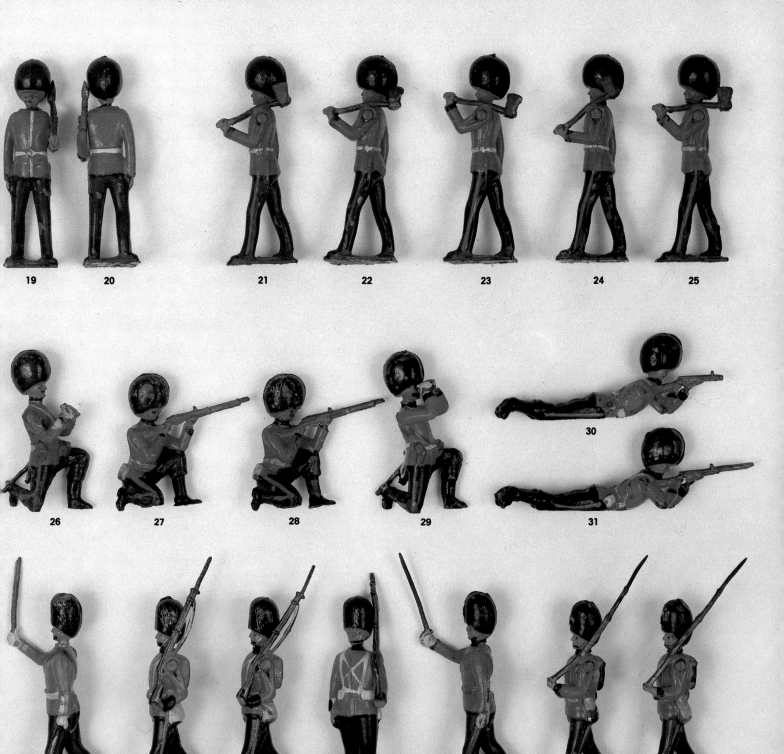

19 20 21 22 23 24 25

26 27 28 29 30 31

32 33 34 35 36 37 38

the Coldstream Guards officer at (26), but should originally have had the distinctive blue plume of the Irish Guards—as seen at (30-31)—on his bearskin, from which much of the paint has flaked away. However, Britains made a habit of painting the Irish Guards plume in dark green, which is difficult to distingish on the black bearskin even when the paint is not worn. Fairly common.

Piper, The Gordon Highlanders; Britains Catalog Number 77. This oval-based version of the Piper formed part of the set of marching Highlanders issued in 1897-1902. (Later sets are shown at (28-35) on pages 166-167.) After 1902, the figure shown was replaced by an improved, taller Piper.

32-35 Royal Welch Fusiliers; Britains Catalog Number 74. These are figures of the 3rd version from an eight-piece set consisting of six fusiliers, as (33-35), and an officer (32) with the regiment's Goat Mascot (shown at *Inset, pages 168-169*). All the figures have a movable arm, wear gaiters, and march in a "heel and toe" position; the officer with a sword and the fusiliers with their rifles (with fixed bayonets and loose slings) at the slope. Note the box packs of the fusiliers and the further details of equipment revealed by the front view at (35). The officer's square base bears the copyright date "16.11.1905"; the square bases of the fusiliers have the date "1.8.1905". Common.

36-38 7th Royal Fusiliers; Britains

Catalog Number 7. This set was originally issued in 1897 with eight pieces: an officer (36) and seven fusiliers (as 37-38). The set underwent changes in detail and finish in 1905 and 1908; the examples shown are of the 4th version, with square bases, which was introduced in 1934. All have a movable arm, the officer holding a sword and the men marching with bayoneted rifles at the slope (note also their box packs). None wears gaiters. There is no difference in casting or painting between the figures of this set and Number 74 (32-35), and the only way to distinguish between them is by possession of the original box or by the presence or absence of the Goat Mascot with Number 74. Fairly common.

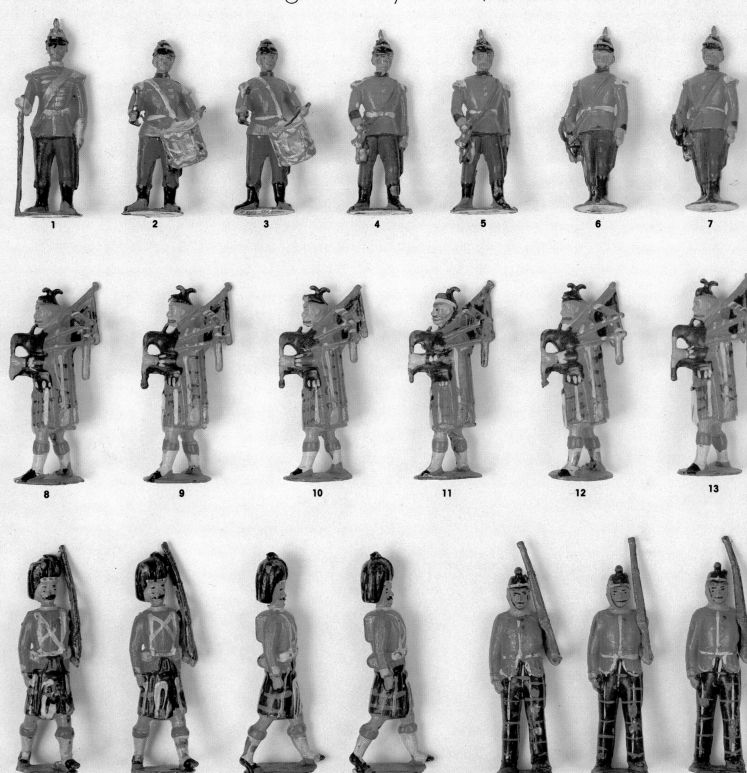

1   2   3   4   5   6   7

8   9   10   11   12   13

14   15   16   17   18   19   20

All the Britains figures shown on this spread are of the "standard" 2·125in (54mm) size.

1-7 Drums and Bugles of the Line; Britains Catalog Number 30. This set was first issued in 1895, and the examples shown are of the 1st version. The drum major (1) holds his mace (the top missing from this example) in a fixed arm and has an oval base. The side drummers (2-3) and buglers (4-7) also have fixed arms and oval bases. The distinguishing feature of the 1st version figures is the way in which the right foot of the drummer is splayed out to the right, as opposed to the "heel and toe" marching action of the 2nd version, introduced c1902. The buglers and drum major remained in the form

seen here until the introduction of the 3rd version in 1908. Figures of the 1st version are scarce; but note that the spikes are missing from the tops of the drummers' helmets in the examples shown, reducing their value.

8-13 Pipers of the the Scots Guards; Britains Catalog Number 69. The 1st version of this set, issued in 1896, consisted of seven figures with oval bases. New versions of the piper (a figure used, with finishes in different tartans, in

Bass Drummer, Drums and Bugles of the Line; Britains Catalog Number 30. This oval-based figure, dating from c1900, formed one of the set shown at (1-7) above. This set was still available in 1960, but by then was reduced to five figures.

various "Highlanders" sets) were brought out in 1912, c1934, and c1938. From 1934, the piper wore a feather bonnet rather than the glengarry seen here. By 1940, the set had been reduced to six pieces. Common.

14-17 Seaforth Highlanders; Britains Catalog Number 112. These Highlanders have a movable arm and march with their rifles (with loose slings) at the slope. The set consisted of eight marching men, as shown. The examples shown here are of the 1st version. Note particularly their bases: these figures were made before the general introduction of square bases, and have square bases with the corners somewhat rounded. The bases bear the embossed copyright date

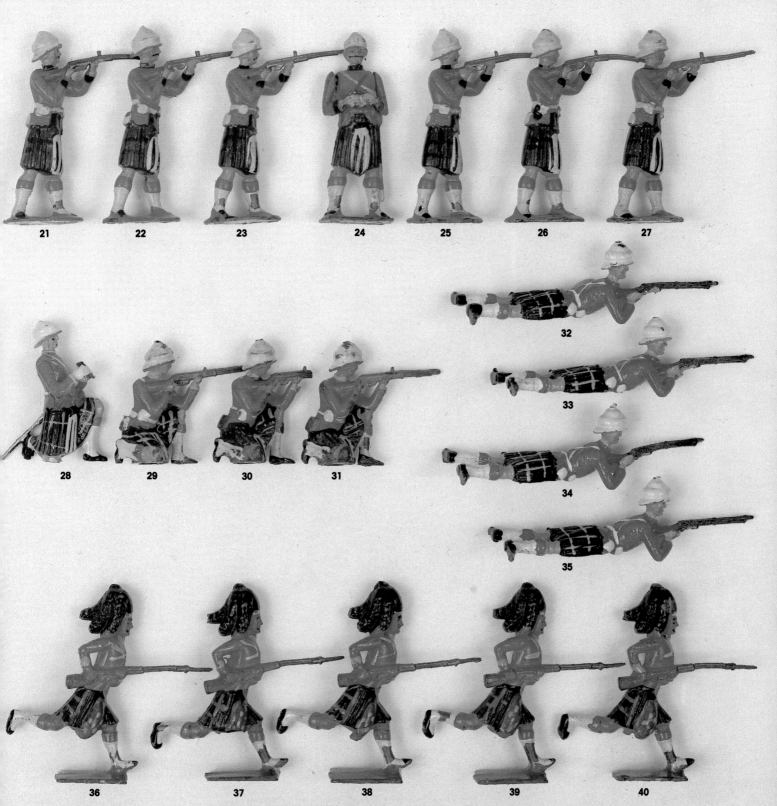

21   22   23   24   25   26   27

32

33

34

35

28   29   30   31

36   37   38   39   40

"20.1.1901". A new version, showing men without packs, was introduced c1913. Figures of the 1st version are scarce.

18-20 Highland Light Infantry; Britains Catalog Number 213. Issued in 1924-41, this set consisted of eight figures of the type shown, marching with rifles (held in a movable arm) at the slope. The Highlanders wear shakoes (round caps) with a plume and, as seen, belong to one of the Scottish regiments that wore tartan trews rather than kilts. Limited.

21-27 The Black Watch (Royal Highlanders); Britains Catalog Number 122. Shown here are seven figures from a ten-piece set that consisted of nine private soldiers—as seen at (21-23) and (25-27)—and an officer (24).

The figures of the men, with oval bases, are certainly of the 1st version, copyrighted 1 July 1901, but the officer has a square base. The officer of the 1st version had a round base—but since the painting of the figures shown is well matched, they may all be from the same set, dating from c1908 when Britains was in the process of changing molds from oval to square bases. The combination of base shapes is unusual, and should normally make the collector suspect that the "set" has been put together from various sources. Fairly common.

28 Officer, The Gordon Highlanders; Britains Catalog Number 118. This kneeling officer, with field glasses held in movable arms, is one of a ten-piece set that included

the lying firing figures which are shown at (32-35).

29-31 The Gordon Highlanders; Britains Catalog Number 157. These figures in the kneeling firing position (with the rear sights of their rifles raised, indicating a long-range aim) are from a set issued in 1907. It consisted of ten figures: three kneeling firing men, as shown; four standing firing figures, similar to (25-27); and three lying firing figures, similar to (32-35). There was no officer. Fairly common.

32-35 The Gordon Highlanders; Britains Catalog Number 118. Nine figures like these completed a ten-piece set, originally issued in 1901, with the officer shown at (28). The soldiers are in the lying firing position: in early issues the

figures are shown with their feet together, but the examples shown here are of the 2nd version, dating from after 1934, and have their legs apart. Fairly common.

36-40 Argyll and Sutherland Highlanders; Britains Catalog Number 15. The five square-based figures of Highlanders charging, with bayonets fixed and feather bonnets blowing back, are from the 3rd version of a set of eight. Britains sometimes painted one of the figures with gold facings to represent an officer. The 1st version contained seven figures: six Highlanders with "plug handed" rifles and an officer with a sword; and in contrast with the charging figures, introduced in 1903, the "plug handed" figure had a rifle at the trail. Fairly common.

All the Britains figures shown on this spread are of the "standard" 2·125in (54mm) size.

1-3 Egyptian Infantry; Britains Catalog Number 117. These figures were first issued in an eight-piece set in 1901. The examples shown are of the 2nd version, with square bases bearing the embossed copyright date "20.1.1901". The figures were also produced with dark blue tunics, in an early, round-based, variation of the 1st version. The 3rd version, produced from 1957-59, included a figure of an officer firing a pistol. Limited.

4-6 Japanese Infantry; Britains Catalog Number 134. These figures were first issued in 1904 in a set that contained eight soldiers charging with rifles. The examples

shown are of the 2nd version, issued c1906, with oval bases bearing the embossed copyright date "16.1.1904". The figures of the 1st version wore a small kepi rather than the cap of the figures shown here. Both 1st and 2nd version figures are to be found either with paper labels or embossed dates, and it may well be that Britains distributed figures from both molds at the same time. The 1st version was not produced after World War I, but the 2nd version, retaining its oval bases, continued in production until 1941. In a late variation, a few sets were produced with dark blue coats: these are extremely rare. The set had no officer. Limited.

7-10 Zulus of Africa; Britains Catalog Number 147. These figures were

first issued, with oval bases, in 1906: the set consisted of eight running Zulus armed with spears and knobkerries, as seen here. The examples shown are of the 2nd version, with square bases bearing the embossed date "23.5.1906". The fame of the martial Zulus, dating from the British Army's campaigns against them in the 19th century, appears to have ensured the popularity of these figures, which are common. In 1914, Britains produced a set entitled Zulu Kraal (Catalog Number 188), containing six running Zulus like those shown here, two "beehive" huts, coconut and date palms (available separately and cataloged as Numbers 919 and 920 respectively), and a printed scenic

background which fitted into the interior of the set's box. A further set of a similar nature, Catalog Number 1299, was produced for a short period only in c1934. Again with a printed scenic background, it features Zulus attacking an RAF monoplane (available separately, Catalog Number 433). This set Number 1299 is extremely rare; indeed, there is no known example in existence in its original box.

11-13 Argentine Cadet Military School; Britains Catalog Number 219. These figures were issued in 1925 in an eight-piece boxed set consisting of eight cadets—note the frogged jackets and white helmet plumes—marching with rifles at the slope. Scarce.

14-17 North American Indians; Britains Catalog Number 150. These

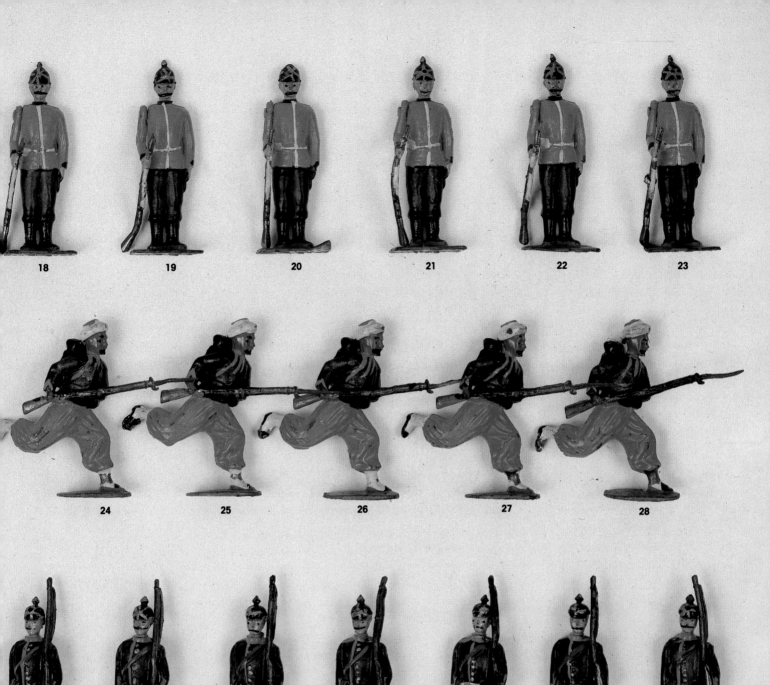

18 19 20 21 22 23

24 25 26 27 28

29 30 31 32 33 34 35

Officer with Goat Mascot, Royal Welsh Fusiliers; Britains Catalog Number 74. A figure from a very popular set issued in various versions from 1897 to 1965.

figures were first issued in 1908 in an eight-piece set consisting of six braves with rifles in the "on guard" position (14-16) and two chiefs (17). Although these figures are less popular than "proper" soldiers among collectors, they were extremely successful toys and the set had a long production life with relatively few changes. Common.

18-23 East Yorkshire Regiment; Britains Catalog Number 114. These figures from a set of eight soldiers at attention, with rifles in movable right arms, are of the 2nd version, issued c1908, with square

bases bearing the original copyright date "20.1.1901". Note that the examples shown have trousers tucked into gaiters (leggins); the version issued after 1925 omits this feature. A second set depicting the East Yorkshire Regiment was brought out in 1937 (Catalog Number 1557); it contained seven marching men with their rifles at the slope, with an officer. Scarce.

24-28 French Zouaves; Britains Catalog Number 142. These are figures of the 1st version, issued in 1905 as a set of seven charging soldiers, as seen, and a walking officer. The officer was soon dropped in favor of another charging figure, and when the set appeared in its 3rd version, in 1949, a mounted officer replaced two of the charging men. The

figures shown have oval bases bearing the copyright date "9.5.1905". Britains used the same casting for an eight-piece set of French Turcos (Catalog Number 191) issued in 1915. The figures of the 1st version, as shown, are limited; otherwise the set of Zouaves is fairly common.

29-35 Prussian Infantry of the Line; Britains Catalog Number 154. These figures were first issued in 1908 in a set of eight, consisting of seven soldiers marching with rifles at the slope, as seen here, and an officer with a sword (not shown). Note that these figures of the 1st version are positioned diagonally on their bases, which bear the copyright date "16.2.1908"; in the 2nd version, the figures march square to the base. Limited.

Infantry and Gunners by Britains, Great Britain

1   2   3   4   5   6   7

8   9   10   11   12   13

14   15   16   17   18   19   20

All the Britains figures shown on this spread are of the "standard" 2·125in (54mm) size.

1-7 Boer Infantry; Britains Catalog Number 26. These figures are from a set first issued in 1899, consisting of eight black-hatted soldiers marching with their rifles, held in a movable arm, at the slope. The examples shown are of the 2nd version, with rifles at the shoulder arms position and square bases bearing the copyright date "15.6.1906". The 1st version used the same casting as the early US Infantry (Catalog Number 91) and wore a "Montana" hat rather than a "slouch" hat. Figures of the 2nd and 3rd versions wear "slouch" hats, like those of the US Army figures. Under the Catalog Number

26, Britains also produced eight-piece sets showing Boer Infantry standing with rifles in the "on guard" position in the 3rd version, which appears to have been available at the same time as the 2nd version shown here. All Britains Boer figures, which also include Boer Cavalry (Catalog Number 6), are eagerly sought after by collectors: the 2nd (shown here) and 3rd versions of the Boer Infantry set are extremely scarce; the 1st version sold far more sets.

8-13 Gloucestershire Regiment; Britains Catalog Number 119. These figures are from a set of ten first issued in 1901, showing enlisted men in khaki service dress, with overseas helmets, in the standing firing position. The examples shown are of the 2nd

version, with square bases bearing the copyright date "1.7.1901".

14-16 Queen's Own Cameron Highlanders; Britains Catalog Number 114. These figures are from a set of eight first issued in 1901; the examples shown are of the 2nd version—compare with the 3rd version at (17-20)—with square bases bearing the embossed copyright date "20.1.1901". Scarce.

17-20 Queen's Own Cameron Highlanders; Britains Catalog Number 114. As (14-16), but figures of the 3rd version, dating from 1913-35. Fairly common.

21-23 Devonshire Regiment; Britains Catalog Number 110. These figures are from a boxed set of eight first issued in 1901, showing soldiers marching with rifles, in a

movable arm, at the trail. The soldiers wear Slade Wallace equipment. Their rifles have loose slings and their helmets have a pronounced puggaree molded into them. (The puggaree was a piece of cloth that was wound around the helmet on foreign service: it could be fastened to the tunic to form a neck flap—like the neck cloths seen in conventional portrayals of the French Foreign Legion—when the wearer was in a tropical sun.) The examples shown are of the 3rd version: compare with the figures of a later version at (24-26). Scarce.

24-26 Devonshire Regiment; Britains Catalog Number 110. As (21-23), but these figures are of a later version, with an altered helmet, equipment of 1908 Pattern, and

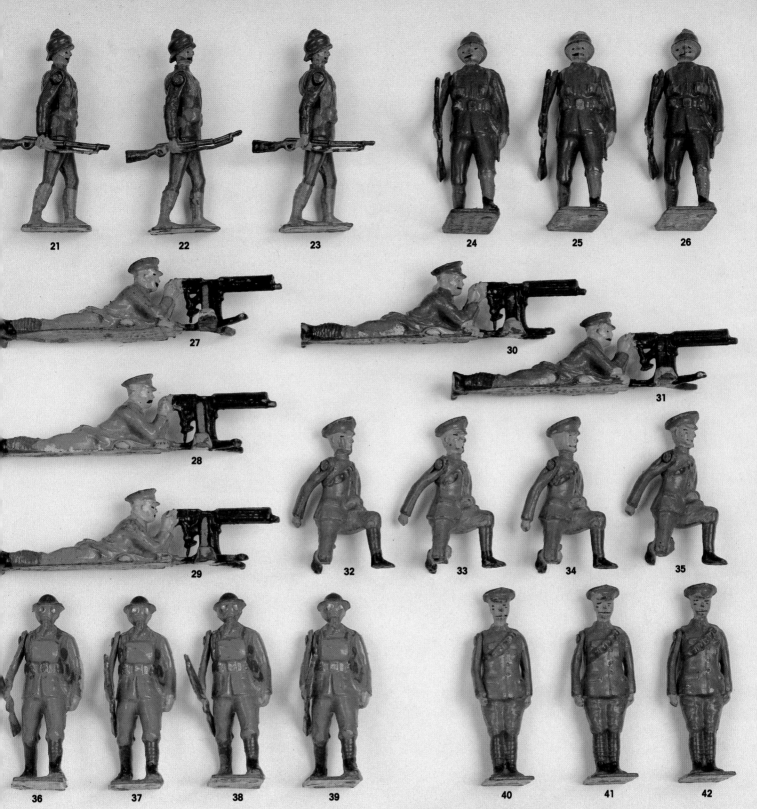

21   22   23   24   25   26

27   30

28   31

29   32   33   34   35

36   37   38   39   40   41   42

black instead of brown boots. Fairly common.

27-29 British Army Machine-Gun Section; Britains Catalog Number 194. These figures are from a boxed set issued in 1916-41, consisting of six soldiers in khaki service dress with peaked caps, shown in the lying position with tripod-mounted Vickers machine guns. The examples shown are of a fairly early date: compare with the figures from a version of a later date shown at (30-31).

30-31 British Army Machine-Gun Section; Britains Catalog Number 194. As (27-29), but these figures are of a later date. Note the change in khaki coloring. Britains used so many different shades of khaki at various times that it is difficult to assign any one color to any one

version. Thus,although the figures shown here and at (27-29) are exactly the same casting, the khaki of the later, 1930s, version tends to a darker shade. A set with the same title (Catalog Number 1318) featured machine-gunners wearing steel helmets in its 2nd version, first issued around c1939.

32-35 Modern Army Team of Gunners; Britains Catalog Number 313. These figures are from a boxed set of eight issued 1929-41. It consisted of four kneeling gunners (Royal Artillery), as

This figure of a Color Bearer, carrying a tin Union flag, is of the type issued as part of a set entitled Color Party of the Scots Guards (Britains Catalog Number 460), available from 1933 until 1941.

shown here, and four standing gunners (40-42). These figures of the 1st version have a movable arm and wear bandoliers and peaked caps of World-War-I type; the 2nd version showed gunners with steel helmets.

36-39 Modern Army British Infantry; Britains Catalog Number 258. These figures are from a boxed set of eight issued in 1928. The infantrymen are shown marching in full equipment, wearing gasmasks, steel helmets, and puttees, with rifles (in a movable arm) at the trail.

40-42 Modern Army Team of Gunners; Britains Catalog Number 313. As (32-35); these are the standing figures of gunners of the Royal Artillery from the set issued between 1929 and 1941.

All the Britains figures shown on this spread are of the "standard" 2·125in (54mm) size.

1-16 Mountain Battery Royal Artillery; Britains Catalog Number 28. This set, first issued in 1895, contained six gunners (1-6), a mounted officer (7-8), four mules (9-12), and a gun (16) that could be broken down into three section (13-15) and loaded onto the mules (*Inset*). Six pieces of ammunition, made of thick wire, were loaded onto the fourth mule. Further information is given in the individual notes that follow.

1-6 Gunners; these figures are of the 1st version, with round bases, and probably date from around 1903.

7 Officer; this officer of the 1st version is mounted on a horse with

a bowed head and raised foreleg.

8 Officer; of the 2nd version, dating from c1915, mounted on a horse with its head in a "normal" position and all four hoofs on the ground.

9-12 Mules; these are of the earlier type, with a raised foreleg. In the 3rd and 4th versions, the mules have all four hoofs on the ground. The mules at (9) and (12) have saddles cut down for carriage of the disassembled gun. Those at (10) and (11) have saddles with raised sections fore and aft to allow for carriage of the gun's trail and its wire projectiles.

13-15 Disassembled Gun. On the barrel (13), note the vertical prongs that are used to secure the barrel to the trail and hold the axle in place. The trail (14) incorporates the firing mechanism, actuated

Mountain Battery Royal Artillery, Britains Cat No 28—see (1-15) above: three mules bear the gun parts (a fourth carried ammunition). The set was available, in various versions, from 1895 to 1966.

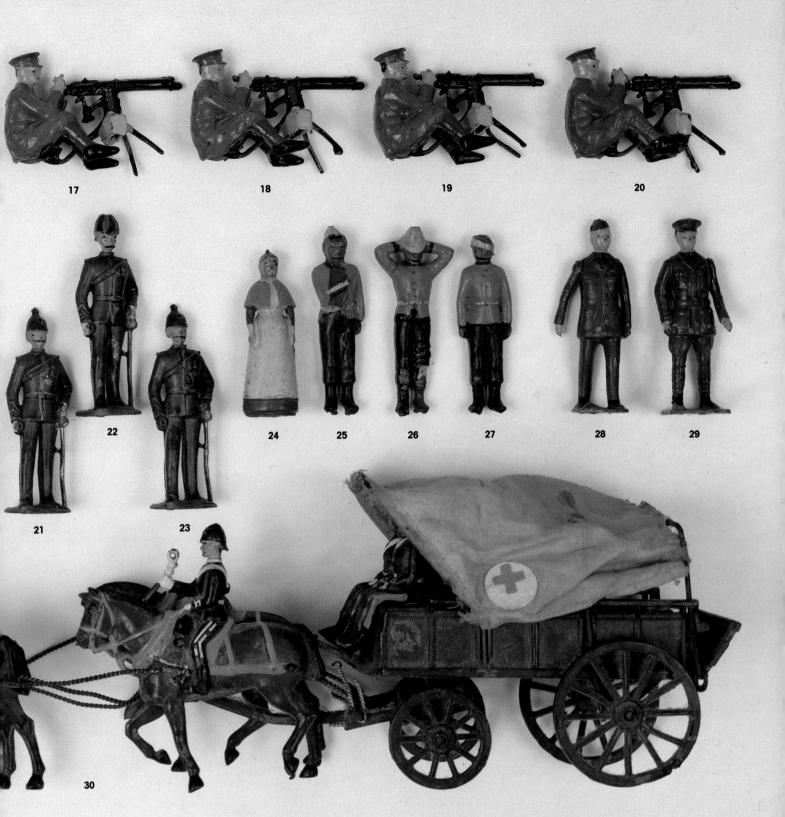

17   18   19   20

21   22   23   24   25   26   27   28   29

30

by a flat spring. Wheels and axle
are shown at (15).

16 Assembled Gun; a later version is
shown: note the color variation
from the 1st version gun shown
disassembled at (13-15).

17-20 Machine-Gun Section; Britains
Catalog Number 198. These
figures are from a four-piece set
(gunner and gun counting as one
piece) issued in 1920-41. In the
later 1930s the set was increased
to six pieces. Color variants of
guns may be found, and the scarce
1st version of this set features
unpainted Maxim guns. The
gunner at (20) has an incomplete
paint finish: this indicates that he is
not from the same set as his
companions, but is a second-
grade-painted figure intended for
separate sale at a lower price.

21-27 Army Medical Service (Royal
Army Medical Corps); Britains
Catalog Number 137. These
figures (individually annotated
below) are from a 24-piece set
containing a senior medical officer
(22), two doctors (21) and (23),
four nurses (24), eight wounded
men (25-27), and six stretcher
bearers with three stretchers
(not shown). The set had a long
production life, with a number of
variations, from 1905 to 1941.

21 & 23 Doctors; on round bases, they
are shown in review order, with
balltopped helmets and swords.

22 Senior Medical Officer; on a round
base, the figure uses the same
casting as (21) and (23), but with a
new head and a feathered hat.

24 Nurse; a figure of an early version,
with full-length skirt. In later

versions the nurse has a shorter
skirt that exposes the ankles!

25-27 Wounded Soldiers; three lying
figures: at (25) a soldier with an
arm wound, his helmet tilted back;
at (26) a soldier with a leg wound,
lying in a sleeping position with his
helmet tilted forward over his eyes;
at (27) a soldier with a head
wound. The figure at (27) was
shown in a khaki uniform when it
was later issued as part of a set that
included a motor ambulance.

28 Officer; RAF Personnel; a Britains
second-grade-painted figure,
issued as a wholesale line, for
separate sale.

29 Officer; RAF Personnel: another
second-grade figure, but an earlier
type than (28), with a movable left
arm and wearing a peaked cap,
puttees, and a high-collared tunic.

30 Royal Army Medical Corps
Ambulance Wagon; Britains
Catalog Number 145. This set,
shown here complete in the 1st
version, consists of four horses
with collar harness and twisted
wire traces, the horse's belly
bearing the copyright date
"14.3.1906"; two drivers, each
with a movable arm holding a
whip, dressed in review order with
double white stripes on their
breeches to denote that they are
men of the Army Service Corps
(but note that the balls that
should adorn the tops of their
helmets are missing); two
seated RAMC figures, also in
review order; and a gray-painted
ambulance wagon with a cotton
canopy bearing an applied paper
Red Cross emblem.

173

The possession of the original box always enhances the value of a set of toy soldiers, particularly so in the case of early sets. Britains did not begin to number its sets until 1898; thus, early boxes carry no Catalog Numbers, while on later boxes the numbers are usually, but not invariably, on the sides of the lids. The design of the earlier labels generally consisted of decorative motifs around the lettering. Around 1913, Britains employed Fred Whisstock, until then a freelance artist, to design labels. Whisstock, whose name appears on many labels of the period c1906-1930, produced many attractive designs, some of which remained in use into the 1950s. Standardization of label design became noticeable from 1935 onward.

1 South African Mounted Infantry; Britains Catalog Number 38. The box has an early label, c1911, with the Cat No (here obscured by the mounted figure) on the front.
2 Chasseurs à Cheval; Cat No 139. The early box label, c1906, for these French Army figures incorporates floral motifs in the art nouveau style.
3 Machine Gun Section; Cat No 198. The box, with an illustration and descriptive text, dates from c1939 and has the Cat No printed on the side of the lid.
4 Zulus; Cat No 147. The box dates from c1920 and has the Cat No on the side of the lid. When the set was illustrated in the 1940 Catalog the label was almost identical: only the name "Wm. Britain, Junr." had been removed.

5 Prussian Infantry; Cat No 154. The box dates from c1914; the Cat No is on the side of the lid. The label, designed by Fred Whisstock (whose name appears below the illustration on the left), features a line drawing of soldiers and the Prussian arms. Note the "A.W. Gamage, Ltd." label in the top left corner: Gamage's sold all kinds of toys in its department store in Holborn, London, and by mail order through its illustrated catalogs. Some of these have been republished in facsimile and they are an extremely useful source of reference for toys marketed during the early 20th century.
6 The Black Watch (Royal Highlanders); Cat No 11. The box, with Cat No on the side of the lid, dates from c1925. The label,

designed by Whisstock (name beneath badge on right) incorporates a drawing of a Highlander, the regiment's badge, and a list of its battle honors.
7 State Landau; Cat No 2094. The box for this "Historical Series" model is of standard post-World War II type, with a knight in armor on the label. The three "Beefeaters" shown below it are from the Attendants to the State Coach (Cat No 1475), a set issued by Britains from 1937 to 1965.
8 Arabs; Cat No 164. The box, with a Whisstock-designed label, dates from c1913: an identical design was illustrated in the 1940 Catalog. Shown to the right is a 1st version figure from the set; the horse's belly bearing the original copyright date "17.7.1911".

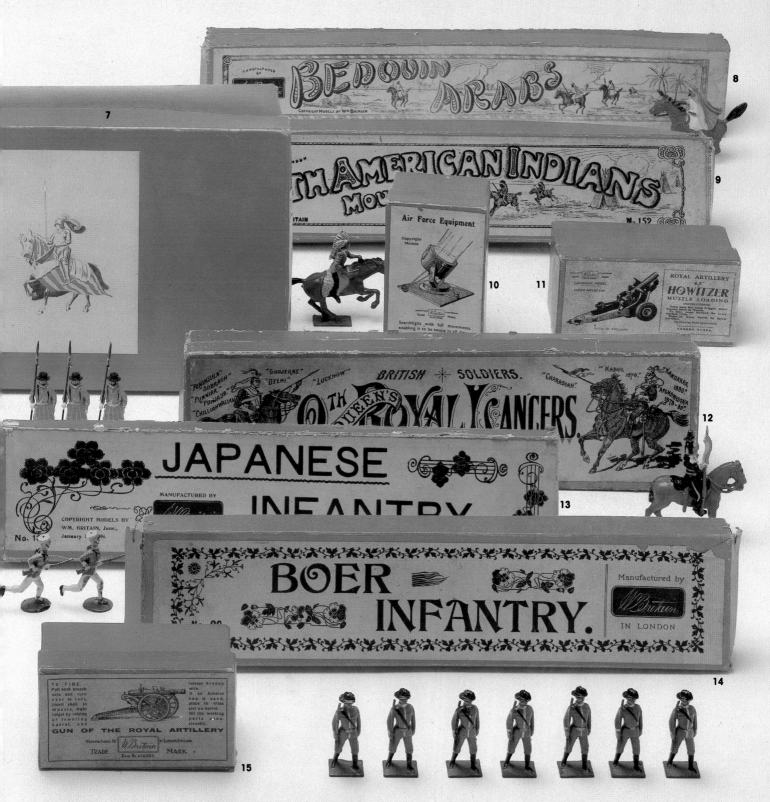

9 North American Indians; Cat No 152. The box dates from c1914 — note Cat No on lower right front — and has a Whisstock-designed label.

10 Air Force Equipment (Searchlight); Cat No 1640. The label, dating from the late 1930s, bears an illustration of the battery-powered toy and descriptive text.

11 Royal Artillery 4·5″ Howitzer; Cat No 1725. Another simple label of late 1930s type, with descriptive text and illustration.

12 9th Queen's Royal Lancers; Cat No 24. A fine early label, featuring

(Left) Trooper and (center) Officer, Royal Canadian Mounted Police, Britain Cat No 1349; issued 1934. (Right) RCMP Trooper on standing horse, John Hill & Co, 1950s.

Lancers and their battle honors, for a set first issued in 1894.

13 Japanese Infantry; Cat No 134. The label for this box of c1904-06 features *art nouveau* floral motifs, with the Cat No in the lower left corner and the copyright date "January 16 1904".

14 Boer Infantry; Cat No 26. Floral motifs and a linked floral border surround the lettering on this box lid dating from c1907. Seven soldiers marching with rifles at the shoulder arms position are shown here; the original boxed set consisted of eight figures.

15 Gun of the Royal Artillery; Cat No 1292. The label, dating from the 1930s-40s, incorporates an illustration of the model and instructions for its operation and its maintenance.

The 1930s brought a new dimension to tinplate vehicles in the shape of "war toys" like these. The larger German-made examples, in particular, achieve an almost alarming realism.

1 Military Truck with Trailer (with other towed accessories) by VEB, East Germany, c1947-50. The truck and trailer are of lightweight tinplate with printed detail; the truck has a detachable tin canopy and a tipping body. Also shown are two "towing" accessories in tinplate, by VEB: a field kitchen (towed behind trailer) and a field gun (in foreground). Lengths: (truck) 3·94in (10cm); (trailer) 3·35in (8·5cm); (kitchen) 3·15in (8cm); (gun) 3·54in (9cm).

2 Volkswagen Automobiles by an unidentified German maker. These small push-along models in tinplate are believed to date from pre-1939: they show autos with the early-type "split" rear window. Length: 3·15in (8cm). Limited.

3 Military Ambulance (based on the contemporary Phanomen Granit ambulance) by an unidentified German maker, c1935. This large tinplate vehicle is clockwork-powered and features headlights (battery-powered), opening doors, opaque celluloid windows, a hinge-down rear step, and a baggage rack. The Red Cross flags are tinplate. Length: 11·4in (29cm). Scarce.

4 Wounded Soldiers on Stretchers; one-piece composition figures (basically sawdust and glue, compression molded on a wire

armature), possibly by Lineol, Germany, mid-1930s.

5 Military Motorcyclists probably German, mid-1930s. Clockwork mechanism is concealed within the sidecars: note winder hole, and also machine gun, in sidecar at the right. Length: 3·35in (8·5cm).

6 Horse-Drawn Field Kitchen by an unidentified German maker, c1935. This is a most pleasing tinplate model with printed camouflage finish, featuring a pressed-tin crew and a hinged chimney and opening lid on the

Probably by Heyde, c1890, this volunteer cyclist is shown mounted on an early military cycle. Note the Martini rifle carried, and the pack attached to the handlebars. Height: 2·83in (7·2cm).

cooker unit. Overall length: 7·09in (18cm).

7 German Army Half-Track by a German maker, probably Tipp and Company, c1935. Clockwork-powered, with rear-wheel drive via chain tracks, it features operating steering, two rear-mounted spare wheels, and a detachable windshield (missing here). Note the provision of holes for "peg-in" figures of a driver and eight passengers. Length: 8·46in (21·5cm). Scarce.

8 US Military Policemen; German-made composition figures, c1950.

9 US Military Police Jeep by Arnold, West Germany, c1950. This example—see also (10)—is shown complete with remote-control handset. Length: 6·69in (17cm).

10 As (9), but here shown with a full

crew of composition figures. Note the fold-down windshield, heavy-treaded rubber tires, driving mirror, and rear-mounted spare and jerrycan. It is clockwork-powered (rear-wheel drive).

11 Jeep by an unidentified maker, probably British, c1948-50. Of heavy-gauge tinplate, with the Allied "Invasion Star" printed on the hood, it is clockwork-powered (front-wheel drive) and has wheels and tires of solid molded plastic. Length: 7·28in (18·5cm).

12 Volkswagen (finished in "Luftwaffe blue") by an unidentified German maker, c1938-39. A push-along toy, with printed detail, and applied tin headlamps and bumper bars front and rear. length: 5·22in 13·25cm). Scarce.

13 Willys Jeep by Minic (Lines

Brothers Limited), Great Britain, c1950—the maker's "No 2" model; a smaller "No 1" version was also made. Clockwork-powered (rear—wheel drive), it has simple steering and features a fold-down windshield and rear-mounted spare wheel and detachable jerrycan. Length: 6·3in (16cm).

14 German Army Kubelwagen (ie, utility vehicle) with Field Kitchen, by a German maker, probably Tipp and Company, late 1930s. Clockwork-powered (rear-wheel drive) and in camouflage finish, it has an open, doorless body and tinplate wheels and tires. A composition driver and passenger are shown; note provision for "peg-in" passengers at the rear. The kitchen unit features a hinged

lid and a fold-down chimney. Lengths: (Kübelwagen) 6·69in (17cm); (field kitchen) 4·33in (11cm).

15 German Police Motorcyclist by Tipp and Company, late 1930s. In tinplate, with printed detail—including "Pol" (= Polizei) on the rear of the sidecar—it has clockwork mechanism in the sidecar: note control lever at rear. Length: 3·35in (8·5cm).

16 Volkswagen Kübelwagen by an unidentified maker, perhaps made for display. It is unpowered and features a folding windshield, opening doors and rear hatch, and rubber tires. A composition driver is shown, and provision is made for "peg-in" passengers. Length: 8·07in (20·5cm).

177

1 **Coastal Gun Battery** by Minic (Lines Brothers Ltd), Great Britain, post-World War II. The turret, with a four-gun battery that fires in salvos, is diecast; the scenic base is molded rubber. Limited.

2 **German Army Hanomag Tank Destroyer;** Dinky Toys, Great Britain, Cat No 694, introduced in 1975 and still in production at the time of the Meccano factory's closure in 1980. The three-quarter-tracked vehicle, with German Army markings, has an elevating, traversing gun with a spring-actuated mechanism to fire plastic projectiles. Length: 6·73in (171mm). Common.

3 **US Army 155mm Mobile Gun;** Dinky Toys No 654, introduced in 1973 and in production until 1980. This model of a self-propelled gun

has a spring-actuated mechanism to fire plastic projectiles (shown beside the model, on plastic sprue). Length: 5·94in (151mm). Common.

4 **Germany Army Leopard Tank;** Dinky Toys No 692, introduced in 1974 and in production until 1980. This model has a revolving turret and its top-loading, elevating gun is fired by turning the hatch on the turret, thus triggering the spring-actuated mechanism. Length: 7·795in (198mm). Common.

5 **Military Ambulance** (based on a Fordson vehicle of the 1950s); Lesney Matchbox Series No 63, Great Britain, issued c1959. Note that other military vehicles in this series are shown on *pages 96-97*. Length: 2·625in (67mm). Common.

6 **Austin Champ;** Britains Cat No 2102, Great Britain, issued 1956-68. The model has a detachable metal canopy and plastic wheels and tires. The example shown has been repainted, and lacks the "snorkel" from the right-hand side of the hood. Length: 4·625in (117mm). Common.

7 **Saladin 6x6 Armored Car;** Crescent Toys, Great Britain, issued c1962. The vehicle has plastic wheels and tires; the gun has a spring-actuated firing mechanism. Common.

8 **Searchlight;** Britains Cat No 1640. An early example of a toy first issued in 1938, with the dark-green finish typical of Britains pre-World War II models. Powered by a 3-volt battery, it is fully adjustable and is designed to be carried on a Heavy Duty Underslung Army Lorry

(Britains Cat No 1642). Height: 2·5in (63·5mm).

9 **25-Pounder Gun;** Britains Cat No 2026, issued 1948-75. This example dates from c1955. The non-elevating howitzer has a simple spring-actuated firing mechanism. Length: 4in (102mm). Common.

10 **Bren Gun Carrier;** Britains Cat No 1876, produced before and after World War II, this example dating from c1955. It has a crew of three half-figures: driver, gunner (with Bren gun), and guard. Length: 3·5in (89mm). Fairly common.

11 **Balloon Unit;** Britains Cat No 1855, produced just before and after World War II. The winch truck and hollow-cast barrage balloon are in Gauge "00": a larger (and now scarcer) version (Cat No 1757).

featured a low-loader truck and a rubber balloon (now usually found in perished condition). Length of balloon: 3in (76mm). Limited.

12 Panther Tank by Solido, France; Cat No 236, introduced 1973. This German Army AFV of World War II, in sand finish, is from Solido's extensive range of tanks and other vehicles of World War II and after—a series with good potential for collectors. It is characteristic of the series in featuring realistic metal-link tracks, a revolving turret, and an elevatable, non-firing gun; some detail is plastic. See also (18). Length: 6·89in (175mm).

13 D.U.K.W. by Lone Star, Great Britain; a model in this maker's "Modern Army Series". This representation of a 6x6 amphibious cargo vehicle (this example

lacking the rocket or anti-aircraft gun that should be mounted at the rear) was issued c1958. Scarce.

14 Bren Gun Carrier; Lone Star "Modern Army Series", issued in the late 1950s-1960s. It was originally available with a crew; compare with the Britains model at (10). Common.

15 British Army Chieftain Tank; Dinky Toys No 683, introduced in 1972 and in production until 1980. Length: 8·54in (217mm).

16 Military Radio Truck; Lesney Matchbox Series No 68, issued in the 1960s. Length: 2·52in (64mm).

17 Alvis "Striker" Anti-Tank Vehicle; Dinky Toys No 691, issued c1978-80. The model features a "pop-up" missile launching bay. Length: 4·8in (122mm).

18 JagD Panther Tank Destroyer by

Solido, France; Cat No 228, introduced in 1971. The excellent detail that characterizes this French series—see also (12)—is evident in this sand-finish model of a German Army AFV. Length: 7·68in (195mm).

19 German Army Leopard Recovery Vehicle; Dinky Toys No 699, issued c1975-77. It features a rotatable jib and a front-mounted bulldozer-type blade. Length: 5·79in (147mm).

20 Gun of the Royal Artillery; Britains Cat No 1292. This model first appeared in 1933-34; the example shown dates from the 1950s. It has a cap-firing breech and a spring-actuated mechanism for firing projectiles. See also (23). Length: 4·75in (121mm). Fairly common.

21 25-Pounder Howitzer by Crescent

Toys, Great Britain, dating from the 1960s—when it was sometimes sold together with the Armored Car shown at (7). The elevatable gun has a spring-actuated firing mechanism. Although common, this gun, with its authentic wheel traverse, is much admired by collectors of military toys.

22 4.5-inch Howitzer; Britains Cat No 1725, first issued in 1939 and also produced after World War II. It features full elevating mechanism (note brass screw), spring-actuated firing of projectiles, and a cap-firing breech. Length: 5in (127mm).

23 Royal Artillery 18-pounder Gun; Britains Cat No 1201. Issued 1932-1967, this is the earliest and largest of Britains three Royal Artillery field gun models. Length: 5in (127mm). Fairly common.

Diecast Military Vehicles by Dinky Toys, Britain, 1930s–1960s

1 Military Ambulance (based on a
3-ton Ford Thames 4x4
ambulance); Dinky Toys Number
626, introduced 1956. The plastic
windows of this example indicate
that it is a later issue. Length:
4·33in (110mm).

2 "Honest John" Missile Launcher;
No 655, introduced 1964. The
spring-launched missile is plastic.
Length overall: 7·4in (188mm).

3 Missile Erector Vehicle with
"Corporal" Missile and
Launching Platform; No 666,
introduced in 1959 and in
production until 1964. A fairly
fragile model: complete and
undamaged examples are much
sought after. Lengths: (Vehicle)
9·56in (243mm); (Missile) 9in
(229mm); (Launching Platform)
3·5in (89mm).

4 Six-Wheeled Army Transport
Wagon (No 151B), shown here
with Water Tank Trailer (No
151D), both introduced in 1938
and shown here in their
pre-World War II forms. Length:
(Wagon) 3·9in (99mm); (Trailer)
2in (52mm).

5 Centurion Tank; No 651,
vetroduced 1954 and with a
long production life. Length:
5·87in (149mm). Fairly common.

6 Thorneycroft Mighty Antar Tank
Transporter; No 660, introduced
1956. With hinged ramps at the
rear, it was intended for use with
the Centurion Tank shown at (5).
Length: 13·2in (335mm).

7 Anti-Aircraft Gun on Trailer; No
161B, introduced 1939 and
produced both pre- and post-War.
Note holes for peg-in figures; one

is shown in place here. Length:
4·53in (115mm).

8 Searchlight on Lorry; No 161A,
introduced 1939 and produced
pre-War only. Length: 3·9in
(99mm). Scarce.

9 Cooker Trailer with Stand; No
151C, introduced 1938—a post-
War example is shown. This was
intended to be towed by the
Wagon shown at (10). Length:
2·375in (60mm).

10 Six-Wheeled Transport Wagon; as
(6), but here shown without the tin
canopy, exposing "seating" for
peg-in personnel. A post-War
example is shown.

11 Armored Car (based on a
Daimler of the 1940s-50s); No
670, introduced 1954 and with a
long production life. Length:
2·875in (73mm).

12 Light Dragon Motor Tractor (No
162A), Trailer (Limber) (No 162B),
and 18-Pounder Gun (No 162C).
These were produced both before
and after World War II and before
the War were sold as a set. Lengths:
(Tractor) 2·56in (65mm);
(Trailer) 2·125in (54mm);
(Gun) 3·07in (78mm).

13 Tank (based on British Medium
Tank Mk III); No 22F, announced
in December 1933 and included in
the first Dinky Toys issue. This
model was produced until the early
years of World War II. Length:
3·43in (87mm).

14 Medium Tank; No 151A,
introduced 1937, and marking
Dinky's change to chain tracks.
Note squadron markings and
radio antenna on turret. Length:
3·62in (92mm).

15 Light Tank; No 152A, introduced 1937 and produced pre- and post-War. A post-War example is shown; note aerial on turret. Length: 2·68in (68mm).

16 Searchlight Lorry; No 22S, based on No 22C (Motor Truck) and produced only in the early part of World War II. Length: 3·31in (84mm). Rare.

17 Reconnaissance Car (based on 6x4 Morris Commercial); No 152B, announced February 1938 and made both pre- and post-War. Length: 3·5in (89mm).

18 Austin Seven Car; No 152C, a pre-War model (wire windscreen missing from this example), shown here with post-War driver. Length: 2in (51mm).

19 Royal Corps of Signals Despatch Rider; No 37C, introduced 1938

and not issued post-War. This example has been repainted. Length: 1·81in (46mm). Scarce.

20 5·5in Medium Gun (with split trail); No 692, introduced 1955. Length: 5·16in (131mm).

21 Missile Servicing Platform Vehicle; No 667, introduced 1960 and available for only four years. Length overall: 7·76in (197mm). Scarce.

22 RAF Pressure Refueller (AEC); No 642, introduced 1957. Length: 5·59in (142mm).

23 Recovery Tractor (Scammell Explorer); No 661, introduced 1957. With working jib. Length: 5·28in (134mm).

24 Medium Artillery Tractor (Leyland Martian); No 689, introduced 1957. Length: 5·51in (140mm).

25 7·2in Howitzer; No 693,

introduced 1958. Length: 5·12in (130mm).

26 Armored Personnel Carrier (Alvis Saracen); No 676, introduced 1955. Length: 3·23in (82mm). Fairly common.

27 Field Artillery Tractor (No 688), Trailer (Limber) (No 687), and 25-Pounder Field Gun (No 686), introduced in 1957 and available either as separate items or as a set. Lengths: (Tractor) 3·125in (79mm); (Trailer) 2·81in (71mm); (Gun) 3·5in (89mm).

28 Armored Command Vehicle (AEC); No 677, introduced 1957. Length: 5·28in (134mm). Fairly common.

29 Jeep; No 153A, announced in 1946 and one of the first post-War issues. Note the Allied Invasion Star on the hood. Early models

have a non-voided steering wheel and smooth road wheels. Length: 2·72in (69mm).

30 Austin Champ; No 674, introduced 1954. Length: 2·72in (69mm).

31 Army 1-Ton Cargo Truck (Humber); No 641, introduced 1954. The canopy is detachable. Length: 3·125in (79mm).

32 Army Water Tanker (Austin); No 643, introduced 1958. Length: 3·5in (89mm).

33 Scout Car (Daimler Dingo); No 673, introduced 1953, and shown here with a fixed driver: also available without driver. Length: 2·68in (68mm).

34 Army Covered Wagon (Bedford QL); No 623, introduced 1954. The tin canopy is detachable. Length: 4·13in (105mm).

It is generally felt that the wide range of Dinky Toys military vehicles produced in the Meccano factory at Bobigny, France, with which such "extras" as camouflage nets and decals were often provided, is of even greater interest to the collector than the British-made range shown on *pages 180-181*.

1 Brockway Bridge Layer; French Dinky Toys Number 884, introduced in 1961. This well-detailed model is shown with its full load of bridge sections and two inflatable pontoons; it was supplied with an instruction sheet that had a scenic "river" setting printed on the reverse. Length (loaded as shown): 7·09in (180mm). Scarce.

2 Berliet "Cross Country"; No 818. This model of a gun tractor (note towing hook) was introduced in 1959. Length: 5·75in (146mm).

3-4 GMC Wrecker; No 808. The model in Sahara sand finish (3) was introduced in 1972; the model in khaki finish (4), otherwise identical, was introduced in 1974. Note the front-mounted winch and the detachable plastic canopy on the cab. The underside bears cast detail of the transmission. Length: 7·09in (180mm).

5 155mm Gun; No 802. Featuring a split trail, this model was introduced in 1974. Length: 5·83in (148mm).

6 D.U.K.W. *Amphibie;* No 825, introduced in 1963. The model of the famous amphibian transport based on a GMC 2½-ton chassis is shown complete with driver and load of cast barrels and plastic crates. Length: 6·69in (170mm).

7 Berliet Tank Transporter; No 890, introduced in 1959. This model is the counterpart of the British-made Thorneycroft Mighty Antar shown at (6) on *pages 180-181*. It is shown here with its hinged rear ramps in the raised position. Overall length (as shown): 11·26in (286mm).

8 AMX Char 15-tonne Tank; No 80C, introduced in 1958 and later renumbered 817. Length: 4·25in (108mm).

9 Mercedes Unimog; No 821, introduced in 1960. This model of a high-ground-clearance vehicle, with a detachable plastic canopy, is shown here with the Field Kitchen (No 823; introduced 1962). Lengths; (vehicle) 3·66in (93mm); (trailer) 2·56in (65mm).

10 EBR Panhard FL10 Armored Car; No 827, introduced in 1964. Only the front and rear pairs of the vehicle's eight wheels are fitted with tires: in the real vehicle, the larger central wheels are used only for cross-country operation. This model (shown here in rear view) uses the same chassis as the Armored Car shown at (11). This example is fitted with a 90mm gun in a rotatable turret. Length (including gun): 4·72in (120mm).

11 EBR Panhard Armored Car; No 80A, introduced in 1958 and later renumbered 815. It has much in common with the later Panhard model shown at (10), but note the first-pattern turret. Length: 4·055in (103mm).

12 AML Armored Panhard; No 814, introduced in 1963. This light armored car has a rotatable turret. Length: 2·83in (72mm).

13 Self-Propelled 155mm ABS Gun; No 813, introduced in 1974. This model, with plastic tracks, features an elevating gun and has hinged anti-recoil spades (in plastic) fitted at the rear. Length: 3·78in (96mm).

14 Camouflage Net; this accessory was provided with several of the models shown on this spread, as were decals of various kinds.

15 GMC Covered 6x6 Truck; No 809, introduced in 1970. A well-detailed model of a US Army truck, with appropriate markings, this features a driver and a detachable plastic canopy. Length: 6·22in (158mm).

16 Berliet Wrecker; No 806, introduced in 1973. This model features an extending jib; note figure of operator. Length: 5·2in (132mm).

17 M3 Half-Track; No 822, introduced in 1960. This model of a US vehicle with French Army markings features a gun ring with (on post-1963 examples, as seen here) a plastic machine gun mounted in place. Length: 4·65in (118mm).

18 AMX Bridge Layer; No 883, introduced in 1964. Note the complex sleeve-valve mechanism for lowering into place the plastic bridge (shown here part-lowered). Length (with bridge loaded onto vehicle): 3·78in (96mm).

19 Berliet Gazelle 6x6 Truck; No 824, introduced in 1963. It is fitted with a detachable plastic canopy. Length: 5·275in (134mm).

20 GMC Military Tanker; No 823, introduced in 1969. This is based on the same chassis as the GMC

trucks shown at (3-4) and (15). The tank section is plastic. Length: 6·22in (158mm).

21 Jeep 106SR; No 829, introduced in 1964. The designation "106SR" is for a Jeep carrying a 105mm recoilless gun, but some catalogs refer to the weapon as a 106mm gun. The gun is plastic. Length: 2·68in (68mm).

22 Jeep SS10 Missile Carrier; No 828, introduced in 1964. Like (21), this is the basic Jeep model, with folding windscreen and detachable driver; in this case, with a detachable missile platform of plastic mounted in rear. Length: 2·64in (67mm).

23 Hotchkiss Willys Jeep; No 80B, introduced in 1958. This model has a non-folding windscreen of tinplate, wheels of the early

type and is not fitted with a towing hook. The driver shown here is not the figure originally supplied. Length: 2·598in (66mm).

24 Renault 1000 Carrier Ambulance; No 80F, introduced in 1959 and renumbered 820 in the same year. Length: 3·35in (85mm). Limited.

25 SINPAR Renault 4x4 Field Car; No 800, introduced in 1974. The model has a detachable plastic canopy and has a plastic radio installation (note whip antenna) at the rear. Length: 3·27in (83mm).

26 Dodge Command Car; No 810, introduced in 1972. This well-detailed model of a vehicle very popular among military enthusiasts has a detachable plastic canopy, a plastic whip antenna, and a windscreen that folds flat. Length: 3·54in (90mm).

Farms and Animals

Although metal soldiers of the kind shown on *pages 148-175,* which were primarily toys for boys, were by far the most common toy figures, manufacturers added "civilian" items to their ranges from the beginning of commercial production in the 19th century. The German makers of "flat" figures produced many imaginative sets, ranging from hunting scenes to skating parties on the Bavarian lakes, and by 1900 German children (for the civilian figures appealed equally to girls) were able to possess almost any real-life scene reduced to miniature scale.

In the United Kingdom, the firm of William Britain, famous for its hollow-cast toy soldiers, introduced few civilian figures (Football Teams being a notable exception) before the death of the elder Britain in 1906. His son, however, produced such civilian figures as the Salvation Army, Boy Scouts, and Railway Figures, before World War I, although no attempt was then made to produce non-military hollow-cast figures in large numbers.

ANTI-WAR FEELING

World War I was responsible for a sharp change of emphasis in Britains production. The horrors and hardships of the War produced so much revulsion among the populace against toys with military associations that, as soon as the War ended and toy production began again, Britains prepared the new molds necessary to launch the Model Home Farm series, which it did at the beginning of 1923.

From the time onward, Britains and its competitors rapidly expanded their non-military ranges. Britains continually added animals and buildings to the Farm series, and introduced figures showing other aspects of civilian life: the 1940 Catalog, covering the figures of the inter-War years, lists, as well as the items already mentioned, Zoo, Garden, Police, Circus, and Hunting figures, as well as Ambulances, Trucks, Mail Vans, Road Signs, and Racing Colors (ie, racehorses and jockeys). Although the most popular toy railroads of the time were reducing in size to Gauge "0" and then Gauge "00", the buildings and vehicles suitable for use with them were all made by Britains in the "standard" 2·125in (54mm) scale (1:32) of the military figures. It was not until after World War II that Britains produced the "Lilliput" series in "00" scale to complement the most popular railroad sets. Export to the USA was considerable, since few US makers were producing non-military figures.

MODEL HOME FARM

Britains Model Home Farm series was just what was wanted in the anti-war atmosphere of the 1920s. The range appealed to both boys and girls, and a new factory had to be built to keep up with demand. Numerous competitors arose also and, as in the earlier days of its hollow-cast soldiers, Britains had to take action in the courts to prevent flagrant copying of its designs.

By 1940, Britains Catalog listed 62 different animals in the Farm series, many of them available in various colors, while the Zoo series then contained 59 different animals. This quantity of model animals in production could be multiplied several times by including other makers' designs. However, Britains models remained by far the best: the quality of the animals made by such a prominent competitor as John Hill and Company (Johillco), for example, was decidedly patchy.

Even more numerous than the animals were the figures of farm people and accessories. It is worth noting also, although the models fall outside the scope of this book, that Britains produced ten different wooden farm buildings and six Zoo buildings: these were issued only for about two years, around the beginning of World War II, and are now extremely rare.

In 1926 Britains introduced the Hunting series, and these figures proved immediately popular—both as toys for children and as ornaments for the home. The two basic sets were "The Meet" (Cat No 1446), with standing and mounted figures of huntsmen and women, and hounds, and "Full Cry" (Cat No 1447), with hunters on galloping horses, running hounds, and a fox. Figures from both sets (all were also available as separate items) are shown on *pages 186-187.* The Hunting series underwent several variations, but the figures remained available until 1966, a production run of 40 years. Britains Circus series was introduced in 1936 and its basic sets were also available after World War II, until 1961. However, two sets much sought-after by collectors—Fair Roundabout (Cat No 1439) and Flying Trapeze (Cat No 1441)—were issued only from 1936 to 1939.

MINIATURE GARDEN

To complement the various animal models, Britains and other makers issued many scenic items, such as fences, trees, gates, hedges, stiles, bushes, and signposts. Perhaps the highest point of miniature toymaking was reached, how-

ever, by Britains Gardening series, issued in metal (as shown on this spread) in 1935-39 and reissued, with new molds, in plastic in the 1960s. The miniature garden set came complete with 27 different kinds of flowers, which were "planted" in metal flower beds. The stems and leaves of the plants were made of a lead alloy softer than that normally used, so that they could be twisted realistically in all directions. Apart from the figures of gardeners, with lawn mowers and rollers, accessories included a rockery, lily pond, trellis fencing, stone walls, sundial, cold-frame greenhouse, seed trays, plant pots, crazy paving, balustrading, pergola garden seat, garden shelter, hose-reel, and wheelbarrow. Obviously, a large number of duplicate items is necessary if the collector wishes to display a miniature garden (or, indeed, a farm) to the best advantage, but the scenic items were made in such enormous quantity that the collector should have no difficulty in acquiring them.

Another favorite subject for collectors of non-military models is farm equipment, particularly horse-drawn vehicles. Britains produced a fine series, comprising a tumbrel cart, two-horse farm wagon, two-horse plow, horse rake, horse roller, timber carriage, farmer's gig, light farm cart, and milk float. Britains competitors, notably the British maker Charbens, were more adventurous, producing such models as brewer's drays, gypsy caravans, and horse-drawn railroad company delivery carts.

These models of the 1930s were the predecessors of such ranges as Dinky Toys (see *pages 62-65,* and the section on "Automotive Toys" in general), that appeared in the same decade, with the development of die-casting in zinc alloy. In the case of vehicles, most companies already producing farm models tended to make vehicles in the same scale: Britains kept their large scale for their earlier motorized vehicles. Taylor and Barrett, however, although in production with many "standard" 2·125in (54mm) farm models, produced series of smaller figures to scale with Gauge "0" railroads, and motorized vehicles, including fire engines, in an even smaller scale. Later, after World War II, many companies attempted to produce ranges of military and non-military figures in lead alloy, and the newer models in zinc alloy. The results were often poor, and as a result some ranges were in production only for very short periods.

POST-WORLD WAR II MODELS

Britains swiftly re-introduced farm and other non-military items after World War II, although not in such a wide range as had existed in 1940. However, by 1953 the plastic injection molding process was perfected, and Britains began the change-over to plastic production with the magnificent "Herald" series of farm animals. Farm equipment, on the other hand, continued to be made in metal, and die-casting in zinc alloy was introduced to make carts and wheels that were formerly of lead. Metal farm animals were finally discontinued by Britains late in 1959, and other British companies, such as F.G. Taylor, Cherilea, Crescent, and Charbens, followed suit.

Even before World War II, Britains had probably been producing more non-military than military items. After 1945 this trend accelerated until, by 1970, military items accounted for only about 10 per cent of production. At the same time, the company's range of metal diecast items was expanding, with finely-made mechanized farm equipment still produced in the 1:32 scale of the original soldiers. The first of the model tractors, the Fordson Major (Cat No 127F; with spiked or tired wheels) was produced in 1948, and since that time so many tractor models have been issued, with variants, that some collectors specialize in these alone. Britains 1984 Catalog lists 10 different tractors, 32 tractor-driven accessories, three combine harvesters, various trucks, and even a crop-spraying helicopter; a horse-drawn tumbrel cart has also been re-introduced—but with a plastic horse. Many of the leading British die-cast toy makers, notably Dinky, Corgi, and Matchbox, have also produced models of farm equipment, but in this field Britains has always remained ahead of the rest.

EASY TO COLLECT

The great attraction of collecting non-military models, as opposed to military figures, lies in the former's greater diversity of subject and greater individuality of models. Compared with the stolid sets of soldiers, which often consist of eight or more identical figures, farm sets are marvels of variety—and from that point of view give the collector more for his money. Since all the non-military items were available separately, as well as in sets, the collector of civilian models is not faced with the same difficulty in completing sets as the collector of soldiers. Finally, the delightful Edwardian dress of the earlier civilian figures, and the changes in their dress over some 60 years in production, is at least as attractive and interesting as the changes in the uniforms of toy soldiers.

Like many of its competitors (see *pages 188-189*) Britains produced a series of "peacetime" figures as an extension to its range of model soldiers. The most popular of these were the "Home Farm" figures, introduced in 1923. Along with the "Zoo" series (see *pages 184-185*) these had a production life that continued until 1959. Similar products that were manufactured by Britains include the "Miniature Garden" series (see *pages 184-185*), some circus figures, and a number of "novelty" items. Most of the items shown here were available either individually or in boxed sets. Like the Britains soldiers shown earlier, the figures shown here are in the "standard" 2·125in (54mm) size, to a scale of 1:32.

1 Huntsman; Britains Catalog Number 610. Dressed in hunting pink, the top-hatted horseman holds a whip in a movable arm and is mounted on a galloping horse.
2 Huntswoman; Cat No 611. Again with a whip in a movable arm, the huntswoman rides side-saddle on a galloping horse. A model showing a standing horse (Cat No 609) was also available.
3 Hounds; Cat No 615. The Cat No refers to a single figure.
4 Fox; Cat No 616.
5 Scarecrow; Cat No 551. The figure had a removable hat (not shown).
6 Farmer; Cat No 501. The standing figure wears a derby hat and should carry a stick in a movable arm (missing from this example).
7 Four-Furrow Tractor Plow; Cat No 138F. The arms near the wheels

can be used to adjust the angle of the plow's blades to three different positions. Length: 7in (178mm).
8 Farm Trailer; Cat No 130F. The rubber-tired trailer, with detachable racks, a tipping body, and a hinged tailgate, is intended to be towed by a tractor like the model shown at (41). Length: 4·5in (114mm).
9 Hedge; Cat No 526.
10 Country Clergyman; Cat No 593.
11 Garden Seat; Cat No 568.
12 Mounted Huntsman; Cat No 608. The huntsman, wearing a riding cap and with a whip in a movable arm, is mounted on a walking horse.
13 Huntswoman, Cat No 613, and Huntsman; Cat No 604; both standing figures, with a whip in a movable arm.
14 Hounds; Cat No 614 (refers to

two-piece set). These standing hounds were available either with raised heads or sniffing the ground.
15 Seesaw Log & Seated Girl; Cat No 618—see complete model at (9) on *pages 188-189*.
16 Angry Gander; Cat No 519.
17 Milkmaid; Cat No 531. She carries her milk pail on top of her head—see also (19).
18 Young Lady; Cat No 559, issued 1930. Dressed in the style of the late 1920s, she carries a handbag in a movable arm.
19 Milkmaid; Cat No 532. She carries her milk pail in a fixed arm—compare this with (17).
20 Land Girl; Cat No 535. This figure of the early 1930s, with a movable arm, was replaced in 1948 by a Women's Land Army (wartime

35

36

4

40

37

41

33

42

27

28

29

30

38

39

44

31

32

46

45

auxiliary service) figure — see (46) on *pages 188-189*.

21-22 Farmer's Wife with Basket; Cat No 502, issued c1930. Two examples are shown to illustrate color variation in these figures.

23 Goat; Cat No 540, introduced 1930.

24 Fowls; Cat No 518. Shown here is one figure from a two-piece set of cock and hen (both of which were finished in yellow).

25 Milk Churns; Cat No 588, issued as a two-piece set.

26 Bull; Cat No 573, available also in other colors — see (31).

27 Jersey Cow; Cat No 599.

One of the first six "Modelled Miniatures" introduced in 1933, this Fordson Tractor later became Dinky Toys Number 22E.

28 Cow; Cat No 508; this was available also in other colors.

29-30 Calf; Cat No 534. Two figures are shown to give color variation.

31 Bull; Cat No 573; this is a color variation of (26).

32 Cow; Cat No 538.

33 Trees: (background) Oak Trees, Cat No 521; (foreground) Elm Tree, Cat No 523. Britains also produced a Cedar Tree (Cat No 522) and a Fir Tree (Cat No 524).

34 Dove Cote; Cat No 575.

35 Timber Carriage with Log; Cat No 12F. Issued as part of a five-piece set, with two Horses and a Farm Hand. The log is real wood; the chassis is adjustable.

36 Cob; Cat No 550.

37 Shire Horse; Cat No 506.

38 Horse; Cat No 543.

39 Shire Colt; Cat No 507.

40 Field Haystack (hay rack); Cat No 566.

41 Fordson Tractor; Cat No 128F, issued 1948. Shown complete with driver, this has later-type balloon-tired front wheels. A variant with spudded metal wheels is shown at *Inset* on *pages 188-189*.

42 Man for Lawn Mower; Cat No 679. Issued to complement Lawn Mower (Cat No 673); the movable arm of this figure is a replacement, not the original one.

43 Wheat Sheaves; Cat No 542.

44 Fencing; Cat No 586.

45 Shepherd; Cat No 577. In traditional smock, with crook held in movable arm. A variation (Cat No 594) shows a shepherd carrying a lamb under his arm.

46 Lamb; Cat No 512.

Farm Figures by British Makers, 1923 onward

Among the farm figures shown here are a number of unmarked items. Fortunately, both Hill & Co and F.G. Taylor & Sons trademarked most of their output.

1 Poultry Feeders; unmarked, c1930.
2 Fencing; unmarked, 1930s-40s.
3 Stile; unmarked, 1930s-40s.
4 Rustic Stile; Britains Cat No 581, issued c1930.
5 Foot Bridge (section); Hill & Co, 1930s.
6 Bridge; F.G. Taylor & Sons, 1930s.
7 Log Seat; Britains Cat No 567, issued after 1923.
8 Man with Wheel Barrow; Britains Cat No 547. A two-piece set, 1930.
9 See-Saw with Boy and Girl; Britains Cat No 618; four-piece set, 1930.
10 Fallen Tree; Britains Cat No 525, 1930s.

11 Tree; unmarked, c1930-50.
12 Tree; unmarked, probably 1930s.
13 Shrub; unmarked, probably 1930s.
14 Shrub in Tub; unmarked, probably dating from the 1930s.
15 Blacksmith's Forge; Hill & Co, 1930s.
16 Blacksmith; Hill & Co, c1930-40.
17 Fencing; unmarked, 1930s. Note that it is four-barred: Britains fencing is typically five-barred.
18 Goat; Britains Cat No 540, 1930.
19 Hutch; F.G. Taylor & Sons, 1930s.
20 Running Rabbit; Cherilea. Note the large size of this in comparison with Britains rabbits (23-25).
21-22 Rabbits; unmarked, 1930s.
23-24 Rabbits; Britains Cat No 603 (refers to single figure), 1930s.
25 Rabbit; Britains Cat No 636, 1930.
26 & 29 Swan with Cygnets; Britains Cat No 622. Issued in 1930 as a

six-piece set, of five cygnets, as (26), and one swan (29).
27-28 Swans; unmarked, probably dating from the 1930s.
29 Swan; see (26).
30-35 Cattle Troughs; 1930s-1940s.
36 Pig; unmarked, c1940.
37 Berkshire Sow with Litter; Britains Cat No 746; one-piece, 1930.
38 Berkshire Pig; Britains, 1930s.
39 Berkshire Pigs; Britains Cat No 596. Set of Boar and Sow, 1930.
40 Pigs; Britains, 1930s; these were available in a variety of colors.
41 Turkey Cocks; Britains Cat No 515 (refers to single figure), c1930.
42 Farm Girl with Pitchfork; Timpo, Great Britain, issued c1949-55.
43 Carter; Britains Cat No 504, c1930-40. The figure has a movable left arm but does not carry a whip; see (54).

Two examples of Fordson Major Tractor: the larger one is by Britains, Cat No 127F; the smaller is from Britains "Lilliput" series, with the Catalog No 604.

44 Girl with Feeding Bucket; Britains Cat No 747, issued 1948-59 only; two versions of the fixed-arm figure are shown.

45 Farm Hand; Britains Cat No 744, introduced 1939. The "sower" carries a seed basket in a movable arm.

46 Women's Land Army; Britains Cat No 745 (refers to single figure). Introduced 1948 to replace Land Girl shown at (20) on *pages 186-187*.

47 Milkmaid; Britains Cat No 537, 1930.

48 Cow; Hill & Co, c1940.

49 Jersey Cow; Britains Cat No 599. Designated "Champion", issued 1930.

50 Bull; Timpo, c1949-55.

51 Cow; Hill & Co, c1940.

52 Kittens; F.G. Taylor & Sons.

53 Cats; Britains Cat No 604 (refers to single figure), c1930-40.

54 Carter; Britains Cat No 505. With whip in movable arm; see also (43) and (79).

55 Shepherd; Hill & Co.

56 Sheep; Britains Cat No 511, 1930.

57 Ram; Cherilea, Great Britain.

58-59 Sheep; Hornby, Great Britain.

60 Lambs; Britains Cat No 512 (refers to single figure).

61 Sheep; Britains Cat No 530, c1930.

62 Sheep and Lamb; Britains Cat No 536. A one-piece casting, c1930.

63 Chicken Coop; F.G. Taylor & Sons, dating from c1952.

64 Chicken Coop; unmarked, c1950.

65 Hen; Britains. This and most of the following Britains figures were available only as separate items.

66 Cockerel; Cherilea.

67 Cockerel; Britains.

68 Fowl; Britains.

69 Hen; Britains.

70-71 Ducklings; Britains.

72 Chickens; unidentified maker.

73 Ducklings; unidentified maker.

74-75 Haystacks; F.G. Taylor, c1940.

76 Tree; unidentified maker.

77 Grass; unidentified maker.

78 Dove Cote; Hill & Co. Compare with the Dove Cote by Britains, shown at (34), *pages 186-187*.

79 Farm Wagon; Britains Cat No 5F, c1931. This two-horse wagon with tailgate made up a four-piece set with the Carter shown at (54). Length: 9in (229mm).

80 Farmer's Gig; Britains Cat No 20F, 1930s-40s. With seated figure of farmer. Length: 5.5in (140mm).

81 Horse-Drawn Cart; Britains Cat No 126F. With rubber tires, this was issued in the 1950s with a plastic horse (not shown here).

82 Sacks; Hill & Co.

83 Donkey; Britains Cat No 552, 1930.

84 Donkey; possibly by Taylor & Barrett.

85 Pony; Cherilea, c1950.

86-87 Horses; probably Hill & Co.

88 Boy on Shetland Pony; Britains Cat No 600, introduced c1930.

89-94 Dogs; by Britains and other British makers, dating c1930-1950s. Britains in particular produced a wide range of dogs, including figures of Collies and St Bernards and Greyhounds.

95 Dog Kennel; Hill & Co.

96 Dog Kennel; Britains Cat No 569, introduced c1930.

The catalogs issued by toy makers, wholesalers, and retailers, are of great value to the collector as a source of information, particularly for correct dating—as well as being attractive and collectable items in their own right. As well as illustrations, which are of particular charm in the earlier examples, catalogs usually list the sizes and original prices of toys, often with further information on mechanical capabilities. It is not surprising, therefore, that items that were once given away to promote sales, or sold for a few pence or cents, are now often of considerable value.

1 Catalog for the 1923-24 sales season, issued by the Manufacturers Accessories Company Limited (MAC), Great Britain, a firm of factors (wholesalers). From the 45-page listing of toys and games, a spread of "Mechanical Toys" is shown: the items include tinplate automobiles of German manufacture, locomotives, and ships. Note that the prices quoted are wholesale and usually refer to dozens rather than single items. Limited.

2 Catalog for Autumn 1929, issued by the East London Rubber Company (ELRCo), Great Britain. This spread from a retailer's catalog illustrates a fine selection of toy railroad items: most of the locomotives are identifiable as the work of Gebrüder Bing, Nuremburg, Germany. See (4) for a later ELRCo catalog.

3 Catalog issued c1903 by Gebrüder Marklin and Company, Germany.

Consisting of 32 illustrated pages, with text in German, French, and English (see cover illustration at *Inset*), this lists railroad accessories of all kinds and includes suggestions for track layouts. Note that all the items shown are for Gauge "2" railroads. As a relatively early catalog issued by one of the most famous makers of toy railroads, this is rare.

4 Catalog for 1939-40, issued by the East London Rubber Company (ELRCo), Great Britain: see also (2). This catalog issued at the beginning of World War II is particularly interesting in that it lists, as shown, toys made by Schuco (Schreyer and Company) and other German manufacturers—including a German Army half-track vehicle towing an

anti-aircraft gun. A sticker on the front of the catalog advises that because of the outbreak of hostilities in September 1939, "a number of listed products"—ie the German-made military toys—"have been withdrawn". The catalog also lists cast models by Britains, Great Britain, and tinplate vehicles by Kingsbury, USA.

5 Catalog issued in the late 1930s by Bassett-Lowke Limited, London and Northampton, Great Britain. The 110-page catalog lists only the nautical toys made by this famous company, including marine engines (as shown here), waterline models, and steam-, electric-, and clockwork-propelled ships.

6 Catalog (cover shown) for the 1914-15 season, issued by J.R. Smith, London, Great Britain. As

the cover illustration suggests, pedal cars feature largely in this 24-page catalog, along with large, pull-along wooden toys and dolls' baby carriages. Limited.

7 Catalog issued c1920 by W. Butcher and Sons Limited (trading as "Primus"), Great Britain. Primus is now best known for the vehicle construction kit illustrated here, but the 32-page catalog also lists other construction kits, stationary steam engines, and building blocks.

8 Catalog issued in 1937 by Bassett-Lowke Limited, Great

Front Cover of the Catalog—see (3) above—issued by Gebrüder Marklin, Germany, c1903, showing Gauge "2" items then available. Note, text is in three languages.

Britain. The 138-page catalog, photographically illustrated, was originally priced at 0s 6d (2½p, 4c), and lists the maker's model railroad products, including both locomotives and (as shown here) rolling stock.

9 "Scale Models" Catalog (cover shown) issued in October 1923 by Bassett-Lowke Limited, Great Britain. This well-produced 148-page booklet—originally priced at 1s 0d (5p, 7c)—lists not only the British firm's own railroad models but also the many items made for sale in Britain, through Bassett-Lowke, by Gebrüder Bing, Germany, and other continental makers. It includes also informative notes on the contemporary reorganization of the British railroad system.

10 Catalog issued in November 1912 by Bassett-Lowke Limited: a fairly early example of a catalog from this famous British maker; see also (11). Note the wealth of information in this 124-page listing—originally priced at 0s 3d (1½p, 2c)—of both the British company's own railroad items and those made for it by such continental makers as Bing, Carette, and Marklin. Limited.

11 Catalog for 1905-06 by Bassett-Lowke Limited, Great Britain. Although the bulk of the 140-page catalog lists railroad items, it includes tinplate ships (as shown here), as well as tinplate automobiles, steam-driven fire engines, and stationary steam engines, made both by Bassett-Lowke and by its continental associates. Scarce.

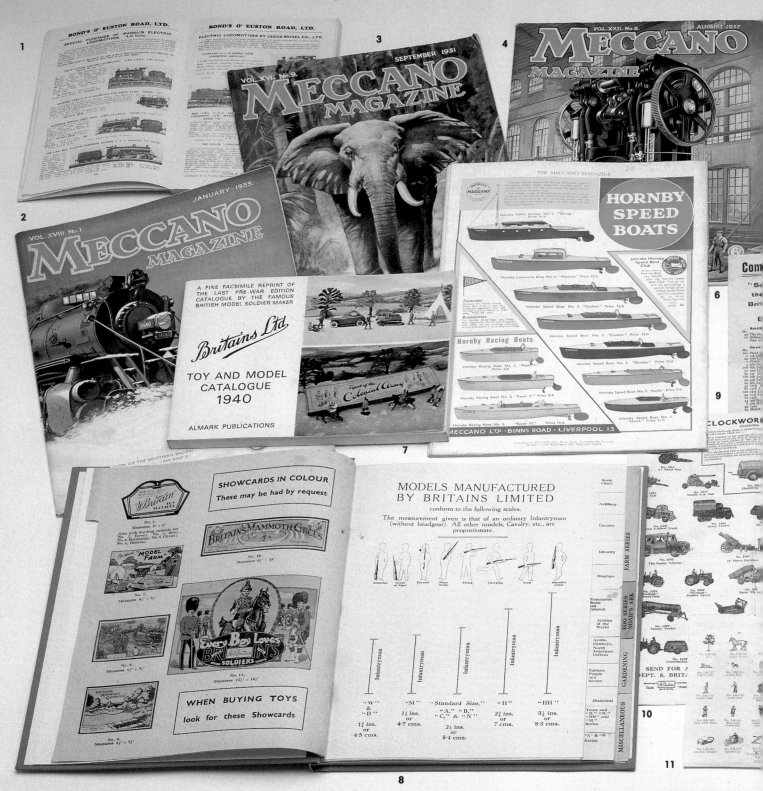

A selection of catalogs, advertising material, and magazines produced by British toy makers and retailers.

1 Catalog for 1934-35, issued by Bond's ("Bond's o' Euston Road"), London. Established in 1887, Bond's both manufactured and sold railroad and other models. This spread from the 162-page catalog—originally priced at 0s 6d (2½p, 4c)—shows electric locomotives by the famous German maker Marklin and by a British maker. Elsewhere, the toys of such other notable makers as Bing, Germany, and Bassett-Lowke, Bowman, and Hornby, Britain, are listed, along with a range of tools and parts.

2 "Meccano Magazine" (front cover shown) for January 1933. Although produced by the toy-making firm of Meccano Limited (including the Hornby and Dinky ranges), Liverpool, Great Britain, this was far from being simply a publicity exercise. The monthly magazine included authoritative articles on subjects ranging from philately and natural history—see (3)—to civil and military engineering. Its major interest for the collector today lies in its many illustrations of Meccano, Hornby, and (from 1934 onward) Dinky toys; its regular features on running toy railroads; and its illustrated advertisements for toys by a wide variety of makers.

3 Cover of "Meccano Magazine" for September 1931: the wide range of interests catered for is shown by the cover illustration.

4 Cover of "Meccano Magazine" for August 1937, with an illustration of a massive 800-ton press.

5 Cover of "Meccano Magazine" for December 1932: an excursion into science-fiction, with the fanciful illustration of a "magnetic" rail-car capable of a speed of 600mph (965km/h). December issues of "Meccano Magazine" are of especial interest today, since they carry particularly large sections of Christmas advertising.

6 This color advertisement for "Hornby Speed Boats" appeared

Cover of "Meccano Magazine" for January 1941. The wartime cover illustrations of the British monthly publication for hobbyists frequently featured modern weaponry; here, a British medium tank "In Action!"

Meccano Magazine covers and catalogs (items 12–19): Vol. XVII, No. 12 (December 1932); item 12, Meccano Magazine December 1943; item 13, spread "Railway News"; item 14, Meccano Magazine October 1942; item 15, Aeroplane Constructor Outfits; item 16, *Toys of Quality*, Hamleys, 200-202 Regent Street, London, W.1; item 17, *Hornby Trains Meccano — Known all round the World 1937 — ACORN MODELS, Swansea, G.B.*; item 18, *Toy Trains and Model Building for Pleasure*, Bulls Ltd., North Street, Chichester; item 19, *Hornby Book of Trains 1930-31*.

on the back cover of "Meccano Magazine" for July 1936. (Note that some of the boats in the advertisement are shown in actuality on *pages 132-133*.) Purchasers are urged to "Join the Hornby Speed Boat Club" and are offered tinplate pennants and a range of other accessories.

7 A facsimile reprint of the 1940 Catalog (the last compiled before World War II) issued by Britains Ltd, the internationally-known leader in the production of hollow-cast military figures. Since original Britains catalogs—see (8)—are scarce, reprints like this one, by Almark Publishing of Great Britain, issued in 1972, are welcomed by collectors.

8 Britains Catalog for February 1938: originally issued with a cover

of thin card, but in this case re-bound for preservation. This is particularly interesting in being a "shop catalog", intended for retailers rather than the general public, and including trade terms and conditions and retail prices, as well as a comprehensive listing of Britains products. Limited.

9 Leaflets like this example of *c*1905-06, listing the figures currently available in "Standard" (2·125in, 54mm) and "B" sizes, were often included in the boxes in which Britains figures were sold.

10 A similar item to (9), but in this case dating from *c*1955, listing items available from Britains.

11 A double-sided leaflet issued by Britains in *c*1955 to publicize its "Lilliput" series, designed for use with Gauge "OO" and "HO"

toy railroads.

12 Cover of "Meccano Magazine" for December 1943: wartime economy measures had dictated a reduction in size.

13 Spread for "Meccano Magazine" for April 1943; note how much information, in this case "Railway Notes", was packed onto the reduced-size page. The cover of this issue showed "The Mosquito Bomber", a famous aircraft of the Royal Air Force; see also the "wartime" cover shown at *Inset*.

14 Cover of "Meccano Magazine" for October 1942, showing a fire-crew in protective asbestos suiting at a British air base.

15 Meccano Catalog for 1938-39— see (16) for cover—this spread illustrating "Aeroplane Constructor Outfits" of the kind shown fully

assembled in the photograph on *pages 134-135*.

16 Cover of Meccano Catalog for 1938-39. This was produced by Meccano, but the yellow panel at its lower edge was left blank, for the insertion of the name of the retailer who would distribute it—in this case, the famous toyshop of Hamleys, Regent Street, London.

17 Facsimile reprint of a Meccano Catalog for 1937, issued by Acorn Models, Swansea, Great Britain— whose name appears in the panel meant for the retailer's name—in the late 1960s.

18 Meccano Catalog for 1935-36.

19 Back cover of "Meccano Magazine" for October 1930, bearing a two-color advertisement for the "Hornby Book of Trains"— itself now a collector's item.

Color Catalogs from British and French Toy Makers, 1950s–1970s

Like the earlier printed material shown on *pages 190-191* and *192-193*, these full-color modern catalogs are now collectable in their own right.

1 Corgi Toys Catalog, 1970. A 48-page listing of titles, specifications, and prices of the diecast models available from this British maker (Mettoy Co. Limited).

2 Corgi Toys Catalog, 1972; like (1), illustrated in color throughout.

3 Corgi Toys Catalog, 1967-68; a 48-page publication issued at a price of 0s 6d (2½p, 4c).

4 Corgi Toys Catalog, 1969. The cover shows "Chitty Chitty Bang Bang", a "novelty" item issued to coincide with the British release of the movie of the same name. The 48-page catalog lists a number of

similar novelties, notably "The Beatles' Yellow Submarine" and the "Monkeemobile".

5 Corgi Toys Catalog, 1962. A 32-page publication, priced at 0s 3d (1½p, 2c).

6 Lesney "Matchbox" Catalog, 1964; a 30-page publication, at 0s 3d (1½p, 2c). The appeal of the "Yesteryear" series (see *page 98-99*) to collectors in general, as well as to children, was recognized by Lesney, whose publications shown here and at (7) and (8) bear the words "Collector's Catalogue" on the cover. It also includes on each page a "check list", for the purchaser to check off each model as it was acquired.

7 Lesney "Matchbox" Catalog, 1969. A 48-page publication, priced at 0s 3d (1½p, 2c).

8 Lesney "Matchbox" Catalog, 1965; a 32-page publication.

9 Lesney "Matchbox International Pocket Catalogue", 1963. The cover of this 24-page publication, at 0s 2d (1p, 1c), emphasizes the toys' "pocket money" (child's allowance) prices.

10 Corgi Toys Catalog, 1965; a 40-page publication, priced at 0s 3d (1½p, 2c).

11 Dinky Toys Catalog, 1962; 32 pages, at 0s 2d (1p, 1c). A full price listing, with illustrations in color.

12 Dinky Toys Catalog, 1966. This 106-page publication in a new format, at 0s 6d (2½p, 4c), used larger illustrations, sometimes one to a page, as shown, and had an eight-page price list at the rear.

13 Dinky Toys Catalog, 1968 (No 4); in similar format to (12), including

information on the "real" vehicles as well as their miniature replicas.

14 Dinky Toys Catalog, 1967 (No 3); 106 pages in large format.

15 Dinky Toys Catalog, 1971 (No 7). A larger format still, but now only 24 pages, at 2p (3c).

16 Dinky Toys Catalog, 1972 (No 8); a page listing spares and tires currently available, from a 28-page publication.

17 Dinky Toys Catalog, 1970 (No 6); 24 pages, at 0s 3d (1½p, 2c).

18 Dinky Toys Catalog, 1969 (No 5); in large format, at 0s 3d (1½p, 2c).

19 Dinky Toys Catalog, 1979 (No 14). This was the last Dinky Toys catalog, with 44 pages, at 5p (7c).

20 Dinky Toys Catalog, September 1954; note retailer's name printed on the cover of this 24-page publication, priced at 0s 2d (1p, 1c).

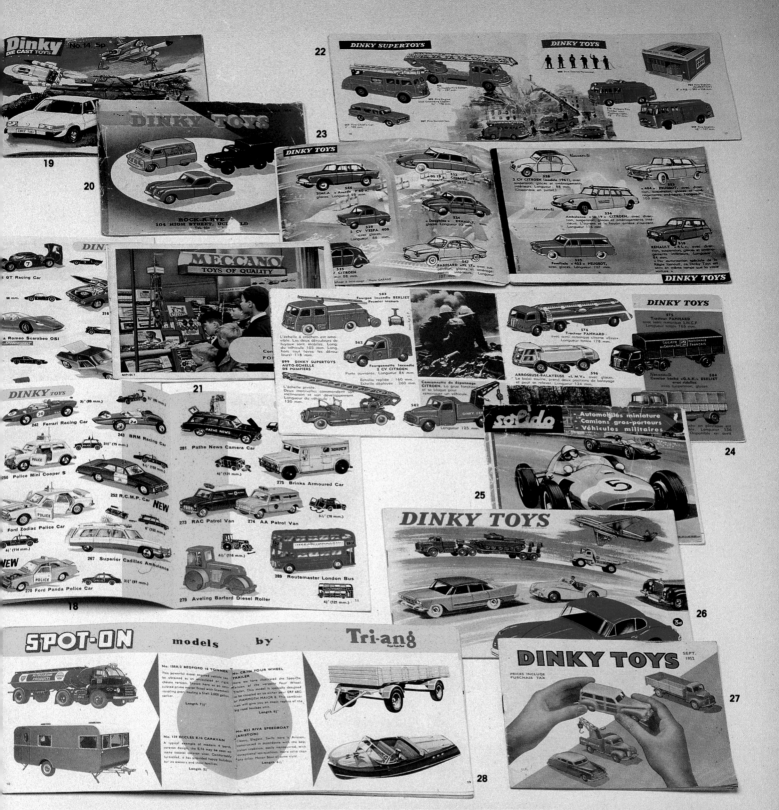

21 Meccano Catalog, 1955-56. This 28-page publication has a color cover but, internally, black-and-white illustrations of Meccano, Hornby, and Dinky products.

22 Dinky Toys Catalog, 1963. The center-spread of the 32-page publication is devoted to the ever-popular fire-fighting models.

23 French Dinky Toys Catalog, 1961. Much like the British parent company's catalogs in format, this spread from the 22-page catalog illustrates diecast models of French-built automobiles.

24 French Dinky Toys Catalog, c1963. An actuality photograph in monochrome is used to enhance the realism of the fire engines.

25 Catalog issued c1969 by Solido, France; a 12-page publication by a noted maker of diecast vehicles.

26 Dinky Toys Catalog, 1959. This 28-page publication, at 0s 3d (1½p, 2c), includes on its cover (foreground) a picture of a Jaguar XK 150 sports sedan—in fact, no model of this vehicle was ever issued by Dinky Toys.

27 Dinky Toys Catalog, September 1952. The small-format, 16-page catalog of this period is illustrated with monochrome photographs.

28 Catalog issued by Lines Brothers Limited, Great Britain, in c1963, for the "Spot-On" series of diecast models made under the "Tri-ang" trademark.

Brochure for "Minic" tinplate automobiles and accessories by Triang, Great Britain, c1952. These leaflets were packed into the boxes in which the toys were retailed.

Although coverage is not comprehensive, an attempt is made here and on the following spread to illustrate the trademarks of the world's leading toy manufacturers. They are arranged in alphabetical order of the name of the manufacturing company: a name different than that of the manufacturer sometimes featured on the trademark.

1 Alps Shoji Ltd, Tokyo, Japan: trademark: "ALPS". Founded in 1948, the company manufactured toy vehicles and novelties, often battery-powered and of mixed tinplate and plastic construction.

2 American Flyer, USA. The company emerged as a notable maker of toy railroads in the 1920s-30s. In 1938 it was acquired by A.C. Gilbert Company, and since World War II has made "S" Gauge railroad models for sale in the US market.

3 Arnold Company, Germany. Founded in 1906, Arnold was initially successful with aquatic toys, followed by novelty toys and stationary steam engine accessories. In the 1960s the company introduced the "Rapido" range of Gauge "N" railroads.

4 Bassett-Lowke Limited, Northampton, England: trademark "LOWKO". Founded in 1899, the company specialized in railroad models, initially marketing the products of leading German manufacturers and gradually building up its own production of high-quality Gauge "0" locos.

5-8 Gebrüder Bing, Nuremburg, Germany: trademarks "GBN" and "BW". The firm was founded as a retail business in 1863, beginning production of tinplate toys in the 1880s. In the years before and after World War I, it was internationally known for railroad and other transport toys, and also produced stationary steam engines and optical toys. A sharp decline in the later 1920s culminated in a takeover by Karl Bub, Nuremburg, in 1934. The trademarks shown are those appearing: (5) c1902-06; (6) c1906-19; (7) c1912-23; (8) the period c1923-34.

9 Blomer & Schüler, Nuremburg, Germany. "Jumbo" the elephant was the mark used by this company on its tinplate novelty toys from c1930 onward.

10 Brimtoy, Great Britain. Nelson's Column (Trafalgar Square, London) was incorporated into the trademark of this maker of tinplate, clockwork-powered vehicles from 1914 until the company's amalgamation with Wells, as Wells Brimtoy (qv), in 1932.

11-14 Britains Ltd, London. Founded in 1860, and at first a maker of mechanical toys, Britains pioneered the manufacture of "hollow-cast" metal soldiers from 1893 and became the acknowledged world leader. Production of lead figures continued until the 1960s, but following the change to injection molding in plastic, the company declined in the face of increasing competition. The marks shown are: (11) box label trademark; (12) paper label, as found on the bases of early figures; (13) embossed trademark on base of figure, c1900-1912; (14) later embossed base mark, 1930s-1940s.

15 Bowman, Norwich, Great Britain. Founded in the 1920s and active until c1935, the company manufactured simple, efficient, steam-driven locomotives and railroad rolling stock.

16 W. Butcher and Sons Limited, London: trademark "PRIMUS". This company produced vehicle and other construction kits in the 1920s and early 1930s.

17-18 Karl Bub, Nuremburg, Germany: trademark "KBN". Founded in 1851, the company was noted in the early 20th century for the production of model railroads and automobiles, and was associated in the manufacture of some toys with Carette (qv). In 1934, Bub took over the ailing Bing (qv) company: some railroad models from this period bear both Bub and Bing trademarks. Production ended in the 1960s.

19 Georges Carette & Cie, Nuremburg, Germany: the trademark illustrated is that used in c1898-1904. Founded in 1886, the company was internationally known before World War I, primarily as a manufacturer of tinplate automobiles, boats, and railroad models. As a French citizen, Georges Carette left Germany during World War I and his company's production came to an end in 1917.

20 Chad Valley, London. Founded at the end of the 19th century, the company established a reputation for games, jigsaw puzzles, and soft toys. Production of tinplate toys began with the "Ubilda" vehicle construction kits in the 1930s.

21 Compagnie Industrielle du Jouet, Paris, France: trademark "CIJ"; maker of the Alfa Romeo P2 Racing Car (see pages 76-77).

22 Crescent Toys Co. Ltd., Great Britain. Founded in the early 1920s, the company manufactured hollow-cast soldiers and other figures, later adding military models and diecast vehicles.

23 Johann Distler, Nuremburg, Germany: trademark (a later type, with globe background, is illustrated) "JDN". Founded c1900.

24 Doll et Cie, Nuremburg, Germany: trademark "DC". Founded in 1898, the company at first specialized in stationary steam engines and steam accessories, later adding clockwork novelty toys and railroad items to its range.

25 Gebrüder Einfalt, Nuremburg, Germany: trademark "Technofix". Founded in 1922—but not adopting the trademark shown until after 1935—the company produced a wide range of tinplate, clockwork-powered vehicles and novelty toys before World War II, returning to production in post-War years.

26 J. Falk, Nuremburg, Germany: trademark "JF". Founded in the late 1890s, this company produced a range of stationary steam engines, steam-driven boats, and "magic lanterns" (optical projectors) before World War II.

27 Georg Fischer, Nuremburg, Germany: trademark "GF". This company, active in the early 20th century and best known for the production of tinplate "penny toys", should not be confused with the more famous H. Fischer & Co, Nuremburg, maker of tinplate novelty toys and vehicles.

28 J. Fleischmann, Nuremburg, Germany; a post-1945 trademark is shown. Founded in 1887, the company was known in the 1920s for the production of good-quality toy boats. After its takeover of Doll et Cie (qv) around 1939, emphasis shifted to model railroads.

29 S. Günthermann, Nuremburg, Germany: trademark "SG" (the mark shown is that used in the 1920s-30s). Günthermann is notable as a major producer of tinplate novelties, vehicles and airplanes, both before and after World War II.

30 Gutmann, Paris, France: trademark "MEMO". Established after World War II, the company is known for its vehicles in lightweight tinplate.

31 Hausser, Ludwigsburg (later Neustadt), Germany: trademark "ELASTOLIN". Founded in 1904 and active as a maker of metal toys until the 1950s, Hausser was particularly noted before World War II for its fine military toys in tinplate—and for its military and other "composition" figures.

32 J.L. Hess, Nuremburg, Germany: trademark "JLH". Founded in 1826, the company was an early maker of tinplate, pull-along trains and other "carpet toys", later producing a good range of tinplate automobiles (marked "HESSMOBIL"). The company closed in the mid-1930s.

33 Heyde, Dresden, Germany: trademark "H". Founded in 1840, Heyde was among the most successful German makers of solid and semi-solid metal soldiers.

34 John Hill & Co, London: trademark "JOHILLCO". Founded c1900, the company was noted for its hollow-cast metal soldiers and diecast toys. It turned to production in plastic around 1960 and ceased operations in 1967.

35 Industria Nazionale Giocattoli Automatica Padova, Padua, Italy: trademark "INGAP". Founded in 1920, the company produced tinplate trains, vehicles, airplanes, and mechanical novelties.

36 Jouets en Paris, France: trademark "JEP". Founded in 1899 as Societé Industrielle de Ferblanterie (SIF), the company was renamed Jouets de Paris ("J de P": these initials featuring on trademarks of the period) in 1928, and bore its "Jep" name from 1932 until production ended in 1965.

37 G.G. Kellermann and Company, Nuremburg, Germany: trademark "CKO". Founded c1910, Kellermann remained active after World War II and is particularly noted for its clockwork-powered, tinplate motorcycles and toys.

38 Kingsbury, New Hampshire, USA. Founded by Harry T. Kingsbury on his acquisition of the Wilkins Toy Company in 1895 (and trading as Wilkins until 1919), Kingsbury is famous for its clockwork-powered automobiles, in particular its range of "record cars" of the 1920s-30s.

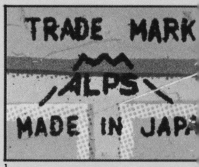
1

6

7

13

18

24

29

34

AMERICAN FLYER LINES

3 Arnold

4 LOWKO

5 GBN

BW Germany

9

10 "BRIMTOY" BRAND BRITISH MAKE

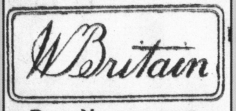

11 W.Britain

12 COPYRIGHT 1ST JUNE 1900 Wm BRITAIN JUNR

COPYRIGHT Wm BRITAIN JR 17.12.1903

15 BOWMAN MODELS

16 PRIMUS

17 K.B.N. GERMANY

C&C

20 MADE IN CHAD VALLEY ENGLAND

21 ETOILE FILANTE CIJ MADE IN FRANCE

22 MADE IN ENGLAND THE CRESCENT TOY Co Ltd MERCEDES-BENZ 2·5 LITRE G/PRIX

23 JDN

MARKE Technofix

26 J.J.

27 G

28 Fleischmann

MEMO

31 PLASTICUS GERMANY

32 HJL

33 &H Co

INGAP MARCA DI FABBRICA

36 JEP

37 CKo

38 KINGSBURY MOTOR DRIVEN

197

39 Kohnstam, Fürth, Germany: trademark "MOKO". The firm was founded in c1875 by Moses Kohnstam and was active as a European distributor of German-made toys, when many of the toys it handled were given Kohnstam's "MOKO" trademark. J. Kohnstam Limited, established in London after World War I, assisted in the establishment of the Lesney (qv) toy company in Britain after World War II, and itself became a part of Lesney Products in 1959 — the trademark illustrated here is taken from an early Lesney Products box.

40 Leeds Model Company, Great Britain: trademark "LMC". Active before World War II as a manufacturer of Gauge "0" locomotives and railroad coaches.

41 Lehmann, Brandenburg, Germany: note that the stylized "EPL" mark sometimes appears alone on the company's products. Founded by Ernst Paul Lehmann in 1881, the company established a high reputation. After World War II, production continued in the Brandenburg factory, now in East Germany, while Lehmann's heirs, the Richter family, established a manufactory under the Lehmann name at Nuremburg.

42 Lesney, London. Founded in 1947, and originally a manufacturer of diecast toys distributed by Kohnstam (qv) and others, Lesney began to produce its very successful range of small diecast models under the "Matchbox" label, followed by "Models of Yesteryear", in 1953.

43 Georg Levy, Nuremburg, Germany. Associated until 1910 with the toy company of H. Kienberger ("KiCo"), Nuremburg, Georg Levy began manufacture under his own name in c1920, producing tinplate novelties and automotive toys. Levy sold the company and left Germany in the 1930s, but the factory remained in production, as Nürnberger Blechspielwarenfabrik, until 1971.

44-46 Lines Brothers Limited, London. Founded in 1919, the company established its reputation with a wide range of toys. The "Minic" range of small, clockwork-powered, tinplate vehicles was initiated in the 1930s, and the "Spot-On" series of diecast models in 1959. Lines went into liquidation in 1971. The trademarks shown here are: (44) "TRIANGTOIS", as used on wooden toys, from c1927; (45) "MINIC", used from c1935; (46) "SPOT-ON", used from 1959.

47 Lionel, Irvington, New Jersey, USA. Founded in 1906 by Joshua Lionel Cowen, the Lionel company became one of the major American makers of toy railroads, and was especially successful when, after acquiring the major part of the famous Ives company in c1928-30, it concentrated on the production of Gauge "0" items.

48 Marklin, Goppingen, Germany. Founded in 1859, and trading as Gebrüder Marklin and Company from 1892, this maker had established a high reputation before World War I and today remains internationally famous.

49 Louis Marx & Co, New York, USA. Founded c1921, the company is internationally known for its tinplate novelties, railroads, and (after World War II) plastic military figures. During the 1930s, when it became one of the world's largest toy companies, Marx established a British subsidiary.

50 Masutoku Toys, Tokyo, Japan: trademark "MT". A maker of tinplate novelties, established after World War II.

51-56 Meccano Limited, Liverpool, Great Britain. Stemming from a company established in 1901 by Frank Hornby, Meccano Limited dates from 1908, and originally concentrated on the metal construction sets chiefly associated with the "Meccano" name. Clockwork and electric trains (Hornby) were produced from the 1920s, and automobiles and airplanes (Meccano), boats (Hornby), and diecast models (Dinky Toys) from the 1930s — the famous "Hornby Dublo" railroads appearing late in that decade. Subsidiaries operated at Bobigny, France, and (until 1928) in New Jersey, USA. Although the company's products remained generally successful after World War II, Meccano was taken over by Lines Brothers Limited (qv) in 1964, and a troubled history thereafter led to a halt in production in the early 1980s. The trademarks illustrated are: (51) "M Ld L", used on clockwork locomotive, c1922; (52) "MECCANO LTD/HORNBY SERIES", on locomotive, c1930; (53) "HORNBY", on tinplate boat, c1933; (54) "DINKY TOYS", post-1945 diecast model; (55) "DINKY TOYS", post-1945 diecast model made in France; (56) "HORNBY DUBLO", Gauge "00" railroad items.

57 J. Ph. Meier, Nuremburg, Germany. The "Dog Cart" trademark of this maker was registered in 1894.

58-59 Mettoy Company Limited, Great Britain. Founded in 1934 by the dispossessed owner of the Germany maker Tipp and Company (qv), the firm manufactured tinplate automotive and novelty toys and, after World War II, plastic items, under the "METTOY" trademark (58). In 1957, it introduced a successful range of diecast models under the "CORGI TOYS" trademark (59), before going into liquidation in 1984.

60 Mignot, Paris, France: trademark "CBG". Founded c1890, the company established a successful export market, particularly in the USA, for its solid metal soldiers and other figures during the early 20th century.

61 Paya, Alicante, Spain: the trademark "PAYA" is more common than the example illustrated. The company has produced tinplate novelties and Gauge "0" railroads.

62 Ernst Plank, Nuremburg, Germany. Founded in 1866, the company produced tinplate trains, automotive toys, boats, and airplanes from the early 20th century into the 1930s.

63 Rico, Alicante, Spain: trademark "RSA". The company manufactured tinplate novelties, automotive toys, and airplanes, both before and after World War II.

64 Karl Rohrseitz, Zindorf, Germany. Founded in the late 19th century, this company was known as a maker of tinplate novelties.

65 C. Rossignol, Paris, France: trademark "CR". Founded c1868, the company at first produced pull-along locomotives, later becoming known for Gauge "1" and "0" trains and for automotive toys.

66 Schreyer and Company: trademark "Schuco". Founded in 1912, the company gained particular success in the 1930s with its comparatively sophisticated mechanical novelties and "realistic" toy automobiles — a range that it still maintains.

67 Adolf Schuhmann, Germany: trademark "AS". In production in the 1920s-30s, the company is known for its fairly simple train sets and railroad accessories.

68 Stock, Solingen, Germany. Founded c1905 and active until the 1930s, this company is known for its clockwork-powered, tinplate novelty toys.

69 F.G. Taylor & Sons, London: trademark "FGT & SONS". Originally part of the Taylor & Barrett (qv) partnership, this company began to manufacture diecast (plastic, after World War II) figures and farm animals, and a small range of diecast vehicles, during the 1930s.

70 Taylor & Barrett, London: trademark "T&B". Founded c1930, the company made hollow-cast military and other figures and diecast vehicles.

71-72 Tipp and Company, Nuremburg, Germany. Founded in 1912, the company established its reputation with tinplate automotive toys, airplanes, and, especially in the 1930s, military toys, Production of tinplate toys was resumed after World War II and ceased in 1971. The marks shown are: (71) trademark: "TCo" monogram; (72) license-plate from a Tipp automobile.

73 Tootsietoy, USA. Founded c1910, Tootsietoy was one of the pioneer manufacturers of small diecast automobiles in the USA. It was particularly successful in the late 1920s-1930s.

74 Trix, Nuremburg, Germany: trademark "TTR". The company became established as an extremely successful maker of Gauge "00" locomotives and railroad accessories in the 1930s, setting up a British subsidiary with Bassett-Lowke (qv) as its agent.

75-77 Wells, London; Wells Brimtoy, Holyhead, Wales. The punning trademark of Wells, London, is shown at (75). Founded c1920, this maker of tinplate automotive toys acquired the Brimtoy (qv) company in 1932. A typical license-plate from a vehicle is shown at (76): it combines the company's initial with the date of design or issue. As Wells Brimtoy, manufacturing both tinplate and diecast vehicles, the company is best known for its tinplate buses made after World War II.

39

43

49

54

68

LMC

MARKE

LEHMANN

41

"MATCHBOX" SERIES
No 7   No 7
A MOKO LESNEY
PRODUCT
REG?

42

RICO TRADE MARK
TRIANGTOI
The Worlds
Best Toys

TRI-ANG
MINIC
TOYS
MADE IN . ENG . ...

45

SPOT-ON
MODELS by Triang
46

LIONEL LINES

47

Cie

48

TRADE MARK
TM
MODERN TOYS
MADE IN JAPAP

M .. E
L
1917

51

MADE IN ENGLAND
BY
MECCANO LTD.
HORNBY SERIES

52

MANUFACTURED IN ENGLAND
HORNBY
MECCANO LTD. LIVERPOOL

53

"DINKY TOYS"
S PARISIEN "SOMUA PANH
FABRIQUE EN FRANCE
PAS MECCANO

57

HORNBY
DUBLO

METTOY

58

CORGI
TOYS

59

C . B .
G

60

GERMANY
E. P.

.S.A.

63

K
Z

64

C . R

65

Schuco

66

AS

57

F.G.T.&SONS
LONDON

TC

71

T.C.9401

72

TRIX TWIN RAILWAY
TTR
TRADE MARK

74

MADE
T&B IN T&B
ENGLAND

TOOTSIETOY
MADE IN
USA

73

WELLS
O'
LONDON

75

WL 1933

76

BRITISH TOYS
ARE BEST

77

199

Bibliography

There are many books in print that will be of interest to the toy collector. The following list has no claim to be comprehensive, but an effort has been made to include those titles most likely to be of use to the novice collector.

Massimo Alberini
Model Soldiers (London, 1972)
Edwin P. Alexander
The Collectors Book of the Locomotive (USA, 1966)
Carlernst Baecker & Dieter Hass
Die Anderen Nürnberger (5 vols, Frankfurt-am-Main, 1973-1976)
Marcel Baldet
Figurines et Soldats de Plomb (Paris, 1961)
Bob Bard
Making and Collecting Military Miniatures (New York, 1957)
Bernard Barenholtz & Inez McClintock
American Antique Toys (London, 1980)
Bassett-Lowke Limited
Bassett-Lowke Railways; Commemorative Edition (London, 1969)
Udo Becher
Early Tinplate Model Railways (Germany, 1979)
Peter Blum
Military Models (New York, 1964)
Michael Buhler
Tin Toys 1945-1975 (London, 1978)
William Y. Carman
Model Soldiers (London, 1973)
Robert Culff
The World of Toys, (London, 1969)
Roy Dilley & Philip Stearns
Model Soldiers in Colour (Poole, UK, 1979)
Chris Ellis (editor)
Model Soldier Manual (King's Langley, UK, 1976)
Kenneth & Marguerite Fawdry
Pollock's History of English Dolls & Toys (London, 1979)
Donald Featherstone
Handbook for Model Soldier Collectors (London, 1969)
Pauline Flick
Discovering Toys and Toy Museums (Aylesbury, UK, 1971)
Michael Foster
Hornby Dublo Trains (London, 1980)
Antonia Fraser
A History of Toys (London, 1966)
Karl Fritzsch & Manfred Bachmann
An Illustrated History of Toys (London, 1965)
Roland Fuller
The Bassett-Lowke Story (London, 1984)

Gordon Gardiner & Alistair Morris
The Price Guide to Metal Toys (Suffolk, UK, 1980)
The Price Guide and Identification of Automobilia (Suffolk, UK, 1982)
John G. Garratt
Model Soldiers, a Collector's Guide (London, 1965)
Collecting Model Soldiers (Newton Abbot, UK, 1975)
The World Encyclopedia of Model Soldiers, (London, 1981)
Cecil Gibson
History of the British Dinky Toys 1934-1964 (Hertfordshire, UK, 1966)
F.R. Gorham (compiler)
Hornby Book of Trains (Reprint of Catalogue for 1927-1932) (Oxford, UK, 1973)
Jacques Greilsamer & Bertrand Azema
Catalogue of Model Cars of the World (Lausanne, Switzerland, 1967)
Theodor Hampe
Der Zinnsoldat (Berlin, 1924)
Henry Harris
How to go Collecting Model Soldiers (London, 1969)
Mary Hillier
Automata and Mechanical Toys (London, 1976)
A Pageant of Toys (London, 1976)
Erwin Hintze
Die Deutschen Zinngiesser und ihre Marken (Leipzig, Germany, 1921)
Bernard Huntingdon
Along Hornby Lines (Oxford, UK, 1976)
Claude Jeanmarie
Bing—Grandad's Model Railway (Switzerland, 1973)
Toys of Nuremburg: Schoenner's Toy Railways & Ships (Switzerland, 1977)
Peter Johnson
Toy Armies (London, 1981)
Constance Eileen King
Toys and Dolls for Collectors (London, 1973)
The Encyclopedia of Toys (Australia, 1978)
Allen Levy
A Century of Model Trains (London, 1974)
The Great Toys of George Carette (London, 1975)
Paul Martin & M. Vaillant
Le Monde merveilleux des soldats de plomb (Paris, 1959)

Ian McKenzie
Collecting Old Toy Soldiers (London, 1975)
Edoardo Massucci
Cars for Kids (New York, 1983)
Jacques Milet
Les Bateaux Jouets (Paris, 1967)
Patrick Murray
Toys (London, 1968)
O.S. Nock
Tri-ang Hornby Book of Trains (Middlesex, no date)
James Opie
Toy Soldiers (Aylesbury, UK, 1983)
Britains Toy Soldiers 1893-1932 (London, forthcoming)
Erwin Ortmann
Model Tin Figures (London, 1974)
Charlotte Parry-Crooke (editor)
Marklin 1895-1914 (London, 1983)
Reggie Polaine
The War Toys kriegsspielzeuge: No 1. The Story of Haussser-Elastolin (London, 1979)
David Pressland
The Art of the Tin Toy (London, 1976)
M-M. Rabecq-Maillard
Histoire du Jouet (Paris, 1962)
Gustav Reder
Clockwork, Steam & Electric: The History of Model Railways up to 1939 (Germany, 1969)
Jac Remise & Jean Fondin
The Golden Age of Toys (Lausanne, Switzerland, 1967)
Leonard W. Richards
Old British Model Soldiers 1893-1918 (London, 1970)
Mike & Sue Richardson
Dinky Toys & Modelled Miniatures (London, 1981)
Jean-Michel Roulet
History of French Dinky Toys 1933-1978 (Paris, 1978)
John Ruddle
Collectors' Guide to Britains Model Soldiers (Watford, UK, 1980)
S.W. Stevens-Stratten (editor)
The Hornby Book of Trains: 25 Year Edition (Kent, UK, 1979)
Patrick Trench
Model Cars and Road Vehicles (London, 1983)
Arno Weltens
Mechanical Tin Toys in Colour (Dorset, UK, 1977)
Guy R. Williams
The World of Model Cars (London, 1976)

Picture Credits

The publishers wish to thank the organizations listed below for supplying photographs for the introductory sections of this book. Copyright acknowledgments are made as follows:

Page 8: (left) Keystone Press Agency; **9:** (below right) Keystone Press Agency; **11:** (below right) Keystone Press Agency; **27:** (above right) BBC Hulton Picture Library; **29:** (below right) Keystone Press Agency; **63:** (below left) BBC Hulton Picture Library; **64:** (below left) Keystone Press Agency; **122:** (right) Keystone Press Agency; **134:** (right) Keystone Press Agency; **144:** (right) Topham; **185:** (right) Keystone Press Agency.

Index

This index is divided into two parts: the first section deals with the Toys themselves, listing both the name and the type of toy; the second covers Manufacturers. Entries to illustrations on text introduction pages are denoted by a **bold** page number.

MANUFACTURERS

A

B

206

PRINTED IN BELGIUM BY

proost
INTERNATIONAL BOOK PRODUCTION